NEW
MOZART
DOCUMENTS

NEW
MOZART
DOCUMENTS

A SUPPLEMENT
TO O.E. DEUTSCH'S
DOCUMENTARY
BIOGRAPHY

CLIFF EISEN

Stanford University Press
Stanford, California
1991

Stanford University Press
Stanford, California
© 1991 Cliff Eisen
Originating publisher: Macmillan Press Ltd.,
    London
First published in the U.S.A. by
    Stanford University Press, 1991
Printed in Hong Kong
ISBN 0-8047-1955-1
LC 91-65554
This book is printed on acid-free paper

Contents

Illustration acknowledgments

The publishers would like to thank the following institutions who have kindly provided photographic material for use in this book.

James M. and Marie-Louise Osborn Collections, Beinecke Rare Book and Manuscript Library, Yale University (Plates 1 and 2); Landesarchiv Salzburg (Plate 3); Universitätsbibliothek Munich (Plate 4); The Newberry Library, Chicago (Plate 5); Wiener Stadt- und Landesbibliothek, Vienna (Plate 6); The Huntington Library, San Marino (Plate 7); Bayerische Staatsbibliothek, Munich (fig.1).

General Abbreviations

Anh.	Anhang [appendix]
b	born
c	circa [about]
col(s).	column(s)
d	died
diss.	dissertation
ed.	editor, edited (by)
edn	edition
Eng.	English
esp.	especially
f.	folio
ff	following pages
facs.	facsimile
fl	floruit [he/she flourished]
ibid	ibidem [in the same place]
Jb	Jahrbuch [yearbook]
Jg.	Jahrgang [year of publication/volume]
Mass.	Massachusetts (USA)
n.	(foot)note
n.d.	no date of publication
no.	number
n.p.	no place of publication
op.	opus
p., pp.	page, pages
r	recto
rev.	revised (by)
ser.	series
suppl.	supplement
trans.	translation, translated (by)
U.	University
vol.	volume

Bibliographical Abbreviations

Briefe   Wilhelm A. Bauer, Otto Erich Deutsch and Joseph Heinz Eibl, eds., *Mozart: Briefe und Aufzeichnungen: Gesamtausgabe* (Kassel, 1962–75)

Chronik   Joseph Heinz Eibl, *Wolfgang Amadeus Mozart: Chronik eines Lebens* (Kassel, 1977)

Documentary Biography   Otto Erich Deutsch, *Mozart: a Documentary Biography*, trans. Eric Blom, Peter Branscombe and Jeremy Noble (London, 2/1966)

Dokumente   Otto Erich Deutsch, *Mozart: die Dokumente seines Lebens, gesammelt und erläutert* (Kassel, 1961) [= *NMA* X:34]

Eibl   Joseph Heinz Eibl, *Mozart: die Dokumente seines Lebens: Addenda und Corrigenda* (Kassel, 1978) [= *NMA* X:31/1]

Letters   *The Letters of Mozart and his Family*, ed. Emily Anderson (London, rev. 3/1985, ed. S. Sadie and F. Smart)

MJb   *Mozart-Jahrbuch des Zentralinstituts für Mozartforschung der Internationalen Stiftung Mozarteum*, ed. G. Rech (Salzburg, 1950–)

NMA [*Neue Mozart-Ausgabe*]   *Wolfgang Amadeus Mozart: Neue Ausgabe sämtlicher Werke* (Kassel, 1955–91)

H   A. van Hoboken, *Joseph Haydn: Thematisch-bibliographisches Werkverzeichnis* (Mainz, 1957–71)

K   L. von Köchel, *Chronologisch-thematisches Verzeichnis sämtlicher Tonwerke Wolfgang Amade Mozarts* (Leipzig, 1862; 2/1905 ed. P. Graf von Waldersee; 3/1937 ed. A Einstein, repr. 4/1958, 5/1963, with suppl. 3/1947; 6/1964 ed. F. Giegling, A. Weinmann and G. Sievers, repr. 7/1965, repr. 8/1983)

P   L. Perger, *M. Haydn: Instrumentalwerke*, Denkmäler der Tonkunst in Österreich, xxix, Jg.xiv/2 (1907)

Library Sigla

A: AUSTRIA

Sca	Salzburg, Salzburger Museum Carolino Augusteum, Bibliothek
Smi	—— Musikwissenschaftliches Institut der Universität Salzburg
Ssp	—— St Peter Benediktiner-Erzabtei
Su	—— Universitätsbibliothek
Wgm	Vienna, Gesellschaft der Musikfreunde in Wien
Whhst	—— Haus-, Hof- und Staatsarchiv
Wn	—— Österreichische Nationalbibliothek, Musiksammlung
Wsa	—— Stadtarchiv
Wsl	—— Stadt- und Landesbibliothek
Wu	—— Universitätsbibliothek

B: BELGIUM

Br	Brussels, Bibliothèque Royale Albert 1er/Koninklijke Bibliothek Albert I

C: CANADA

Tul	Toronto, University of Toronto Library

CH: SWITZERLAND

BEsu	Bern, Stadt- und Universitätsbibliothek
Zz	Zürich, Zentralbibliothek, Kantons-, Stadt- und Universitätsbibliothek

D: GERMANY

AN	Ansbach, Regierungsbibliothek
As	Augsburg, Staats- und Stadtbibliothek
Asa	—— Stadtarchiv

Library Sigla

_B_	Berlin, Staatsbibliothek (Stiftung Preuischer Kulturbesitz)
_Gs_	Göttingen, Niedersächsische Staats- und Unversitätsbibliothek
_HR_	Harburg über Donauwörth, Fürstlich Oettingen-Wallerstein'sche Bibliothek (now Augsburg Universitätsbibliothek)
_KA_	Karlsruhe, Badische Landesbibliothek, Musikabteilung
KBa	Koblenz, Staatsarchiv
Mbs	Munich, Bayerische Staatsbibliothek
Msa	_____ Staatsarchiv München
Mth	_____ Bibliothek des Theatermuseums (Clara-Ziegler-Stiftung)
Rtt	Regensburg, Fürst Thurn und Taxis Hofbibliothek
_SI_	Sigmaringen, Fürstlich Hohenzollernsche Hofbibliothek

_DK_: DENMARK

_Ou_	Odense, Odense Universitetsbibliotek

_F_: FRANCE

_Pa_	Paris, Bibliothèque de l'Arsenal
_Pc_	_____ Bibliothèque nationale (formerly Fonds du Conservatoire national de musique)
_Pn_	_____ Bibliothèque nationale

_GB_: GREAT BRITAIN

Kpro	Kew, Public Record Office
Lbl	London, British Library
Lblc	_____ British Library, Colindale
Lpro	_____ Public Record Office

_H_: HUNGARY

_Bn_	Budapest, Országos Széchényi Könyvtár

_I_: ITALY

Bas	Bologna, Archivio di Stato, Biblioteca
_Mb_	Milan, Biblioteca nazionale Braidense
Mcom	_____ Biblioteca comunale

_S_: SWEDEN

Skma	Stockholm, Kungliga Musikaliska Akademiens Bibliotek

Uu	Uppsala, Universitetsbiblioteket

SF: FINLAND

Hy	Helsingin Yliopiston Kirjasto (Helsinki University Library)

US: UNITED STATES OF AMERICA

AA	Ann Arbor, University of Michigan, Music Library
ATS	Athens, University of Georgia Libraries
BEb	Berkeley, University of California, Bancroft Library
CA	Cambridge, Harvard University, Music Libraries
CAw	_____ Harvard University, Widener Library
Cn	Chicago, Newberry Library
Io	Ithaca (NY), Cornell University, John M. Olin Library
NYp	New York, New York Public Library at Lincoln Center
NYpl	_____ New York Public Library, 42nd Street
NYpm	_____ Pierpont Morgan Library
PRu	Princeton, Princeton University Library
SM	San Marino (Calif.), Henry E. Huntington Library and Art Gallery
Wc	Washington (DC), Library of Congress, Music Division

YU: JUGOSLAVIA

Lu	Ljubljana, Narodna in univerzitetska knjižnica
Zha	Zagreb, Hrvatski glazbeni zavod

Preface

Otto Erich Deutsch's *Mozart: die Dokumente seines Lebens* (Kassel, 1961) is not only a monument to his pioneering scholarship but also, together with the first complete edition of the Mozart family letters (Kassel, 1962–75) and the *Neue Mozart-Ausgabe* (*NMA*; Kassel, 1955–91), a cornerstone of modern Mozart studies. Yet it is also fundamentally different: unlike the collected works and letters, the majority of important sources for which were already known before the editions were undertaken, the documentary biography drew on a range of material the scope, location and importance of which could not even be imagined at the outset. What is more, while critical editions of the letters and works had a long and distinguished history, 'documentary biography' was, to all intents and purposes, Deutsch's invention.

As a new 'genre', the documentary biography set high standards for future Mozart studies. It also encouraged research along various more or less clearly defined lines, based on assumptions concerning the relative worth and importance of its material – in these respects it was a reflection of its times, a mid-century view of Mozart and the sources for his biography and works. Consequently, this book is both a supplement to Deutsch, including documents published in the secondary literature since 1960 as well as a substantial number of previously unknown documents, and a revision. Its organization has been dictated, on the one hand, by the uses to which Deutsch has been put, and, on the other, by different views of the nature and value of the material.

Documents relating directly to Mozart's life and works, mainly from Salzburg, Vienna and other places visited by the Mozarts, are given separately from those concerned essentially with the publication and performance of his works elsewhere. In this way, the thread of Mozart's life – insofar as a collection of contemporary writings about Mozart actually documents what Leopold Mozart, in describing good composition, called *il filo* – is unencumbered by references to editions, performances and opinions that do not derive directly from Mozart or his immediate circle. By and large, this division reflects the ways in which Mozart documents have been used: as direct evidence for Mozart's life and works, or as the basis for 'reception' studies organized on national, regional or local lines. The distinction, however, is not a hard and fast one and the line between the two kinds of documents is often blurred. It is not out of the question that further discoveries will show that some apparently 'local' documents have a more direct bearing on Mozart. Certainly this has already proved to be the case with advertisements by north German music dealers for Mozart's works.[1] As when using the Deutsch *Documentary Biography*, it is necessary here to consult all possible documents, regardless of their provenance and apparent importance.

The documents are also given in chronological order according to the events they describe, not, as in Deutsch, according to their dates of publication or writing. This, too, contributes to the uninterrupted thread of the biography. Although the events described in many later documents cannot be verified, they nevertheless purport to be first-hand evidence concerning Mozart and his activities. Consequently, they do not deserve to be relegated to the end of the book unless shown to be otherwise, though they must be read with caution. Deutsch's arrangement was based on the tacit assumption that contemporaneous documents are more reliable than posthumous writings about Mozart. As we now know from the family letters, however, both Mozart and his father were given to distortion, hyperbole and, at times, outright lying.[2] And it is clear that Leopold Mozart had a hand in writing some earlier documents. What is more, like other important public figures, the Mozarts had both supporters and detractors. These opposing points of view inform the contemporaneous documents, many of which are themselves interpretations of the events they report, as much as they do the posthumous writings.

Exact locations are given for documents not published in the secondary literature, except for material taken from well-known 18th- and early 19th-century music periodicals – among them Carl Friedrich Cramer's *Magazin der Musik*, Heinrich Philipp Bossler's *Musikalische Realzeitung* and *Musikalische Korrespondenz der teutschen Filarmonischen Gesellschaft*, and Friedrich Rochlitz's *Allgemeine musikalische Zeitung* – which are readily available in numerous libraries and have been published in facsimile editions. A list of sources consulted, including those that did not yield new documents, is given on pp.161–72 below. Many of these manuscripts, journals, newspapers and books include valuable and previously unknown information concerning the lives and works of other 18th-century composers; the list of sources con-

---

[1] See, for example, Neal Zaslaw and Cliff Eisen, 'Signor Mozart's Symphony in A Minor, K.Anhang 220 = 16a', *The Journal of Musicology*, iv (1985–6), 191–206, esp. 194–9; and Cliff Eisen, 'Contributions to a New Mozart Documentary Biography', *Journal of the American Musicological Society*, xxxix (1986), 615–32, esp. 628–30.

[2] See Neal Zaslaw, 'Mozart's Paris Symphonies', *The Musical Times*, cxix (1978), 753–7; and Alan Tyson, 'Mozart's Truthfulness', ibid, 938–9.

sulted will facilitate future research by preventing unnecessary duplicate searches. Literature relevant to the documents, but not including them, is given at the end of the commentaries.

This book is not a 'completion' of Deutsch – indeed, a 'complete' documentary biography is probably something to which scholarship can only aspire.[3] Rather, it is an attempt to explore systematically a number of previously overlooked sources, principally newspapers and other periodicals of the 18th century, as well as some selected archives. With few exceptions, posthumous writings about Mozart are not given here. This rich treasure trove of Mozartiana includes Friedrich Schlichtegroll's article on Mozart for the *Nekrolog auf das Jahr 1791* (Gotha, 1793), Franz Xaver Niemetschek's *Leben des k. k. Kapellmeisters Wolfgang Gottlieb Mozart nach Originalquellen beschrieben* (Prague, 1798), Ignaz Ferdinand Cajetan Arnold's *Mozarts Geist: seine kurze Biographie und ästhetische Darstellung* (Erfurt, 1803), Georg Nikolaus Nissen's *Biographie W. A. Mozarts nach Originalbriefen* (Leipzig, 1828), Vincent and Mary Novello's Salzburg travel diaries (1829), Edward Holmes's *The Life of Mozart* (London, 1845) and Franz Gräffer's *Kleine wiener Memoiren und wiener Dosenstücke* (Vienna, 1845), as well as entries in countless biographical dictionaries. Although these works continue to inform and shape our interpretations of Mozart's life, the lines of transmission, revision and distortion among them have yet to be disentangled; consequently they require a thorough and comprehensive study of their own. Additionally, there is a conspicuous need for editions of the most important early 19th-century catalogues of Mozart's works, in particular the various catalogues by Johann Anton André, who in 1799 purchased the bulk of Mozart's estate from the composer's widow,[4] and Breitkopf & Härtel's *Thematisches Verzeichniss der sämmtlichen Werke von W. A. Mozart*, probably the first comprehensive attempt to catalogue all of Mozart's works, and a continuing source of problematic attributions.[5]

---

[3] For a more general description of the various types of Mozart documents and their importance in Mozart research, see Cliff Eisen, 'Sources for Mozart's Life and Works: Documents' in *The Mozart Compendium: a Guide to Mozart's Life and Music*, ed. H. C. Robbins Landon (London, 1990), 164–71.

[4] André's various catalogues are described in Wolfgang Plath, 'Mozartiana in Fulda und Frankfurt (Neues zu Heinrich Henkel und seinem Nachlass)', *MJb 1968–70*, 356–8. See also, Plath, 'Chronologie als Problem der Mozartforschung', in *Bericht über den Internationalen Musikwissenschaftlichen Kongress Bayreuth 1981*, ed. Christoph-Hellmut Mahling and Sigrid Wiesmann (Kassel, 1984), 371–8.

[5] Some aspects of Breitkopf & Härtel's *Thematisches Verzeichniss der sämmtlichen Werke von W. A. Mozart* are discussed in Cliff Eisen, 'Problems of Authenticity among Mozart's Early Symphonies: the Examples of K.Anh.220 (16a) and 76 (42a)', *Music and Letters*, lxx (1989), 505–16; and Neal Zaslaw, *Mozart's Symphonies: Context, Performance Practice, Reception* (Oxford, 1989), 130–33 and 558–9.

All documents are presented in English; translations are my own unless otherwise acknowledged. English-language documents are reproduced in their original orthography and capitalization.

*

This book could not have been completed without the generous help of colleagues. A number of documents, as well as some corrections to Deutsch, were brought to my attention by Dexter Edge, Warren Kirkendale, H. C. Robbins Landon, Wolfgang Plath, Pamela L. Poulin and John Rice. Sven Hansson (Stockholm) kindly gave me permission to publish Elizabeth Rothman's receipt signed by Mozart. I am also grateful to Peter Branscombe, Nelly Furman and Kathleen M. Vernon for correcting some of my translations. Any infelicities that remain are my own.

I am particularly indebted to Neal Zaslaw and Maynard Solomon, who not only brought material to my attention but also read earlier drafts of this book and offered many useful suggestions for its improvement. A grant from *Music and Letters* generously supported research in London.

I wish to thank the following libraries and individuals who gave me access to their collections, allowed me to examine old and generally inaccessible catalogues and reference works (in the attempt to track down rare periodicals and newspapers as well as manuscript collections), or provided me with copies and transcriptions of the documents: University of Michigan, Music Library, Ann Arbor; Regierungsbibliothek, Ansbach; Stadsarchief, Antwerp; University of Georgia Library, Athens, Georgia; Staats- und Stadtbibliothek, Augsburg; Stadtarchiv, Augsburg (Dr J. Mančal); University of California, Bancroft Library, Berkeley; Boston Public Library; Bibliothèque Royale Albert 1er, Brussels (Dr B. Huys); Algemeen Rijksarchief, Brussels (F. Daelemans); Országos Széchényi Könyvtár, Budapest; Harvard University Libraries, Cambridge, Massachusetts; Newberry Library, Chicago; Rigsarkivet, Copenhagen (H. S. Clausen); Archivio di Stato, Cremona; Amy Daken; Scottish Record Office, Edinburgh; Bibliothèque publique et universitaire, Geneva (P. Monnier); Algemeen Rijksarchief, The Hague (Dr B. J. Slot); Yliopiston Kirjasto (University Library), Helsinki; County Record Office, Hertfordshire (A. Pegrum); John M. Olin Library, Cornell University, Ithaca, New York; Public Record Office, Kew (H. Forde); Badische Landesbibliothek, Karlsruhe (K. Häfner); Landeshauptarchiv Koblenz; Archives de la Ville de Lausanne (G. Coutaz); Alan Tyson, London; Museum and Historical Research Section, Bank of England, London (P. Smith); Royal Commission on Historical Manuscripts, London; British Library, London; Sir John Soane's Museum, London (S. Palmer); Narodna in Univerzitetna

Knjižnica, Ljubljana (T. Martelance); Biblioteca Ambrosiana, Milan; Biblioteca nazionale Braidense, Milan; Bayerische Staatsbibliothek, Munich; Staatsarchiv, Munich; Deutsches Theatermuseum, Munich; Yale University Library, New Haven, Connecticut (S. Parks); James J. Fuld, New York; New York Public Library; Pierpont Morgan Library, New York (J. Rigbie Turner); Bibliothèque Nationale, Paris; Bibliothèque de l'Arsenal, Paris; Národní Muzeum, Prague (M. Rutova); Princeton University Library, Princeton, New Jersey; Fürst Thurn und Taxis Zentralarchiv und Hofbibliothek, Regensburg (H. Angerer); Bibliothek und Archiv, Erzabtei St. Peter, Salzburg (A. Hahnl); Amt der Salzburger Landesregierung, Salzburg; Salzburger Museum Carolino Augusteum, Bibliothek; Musikwissenschaftliches Institut der Universität, Salzburg (G. Walterskirchen, E. Hintermaier); Universitätsbibliothek, Salzburg; Henry E. Huntington Library, San Marino, California (S. Hodson); Archivio di Stato, Turin (I. Massabo' Ricci); Universitetsbibliotek, Uppsala; Stadt- und Landesbibliothek, Vienna; Österreichische Nationalbibliothek, Vienna; Haus-, Hof- und Staatsarchiv, Vienna; Gesellschaft der Musikfreunde, Vienna (O. Biba); Universitätsbibliothek, Vienna; Zentralbibliothek, Kantons-, Stadt- und Universitätsbibliothek, Zürich.

Wolfgang Amadeus Mozart
*c*1760–92

1 Benedikt Pillwein, *Biographische Schilderungen oder Lexikon salzbur-gischer, theils verstorbener, theils lebender Künstler, auch solcher, welche Kunstwerke für Salzburg lieferten* (Salzburg, 1821) [refers to *c*1760]

Spitzeder (Franz Anton), chamber singer to the Prince of Salzburg. Born at Traunstein in 1732, he died in 1796, not far from Aigen, of a stroke. He was among the first music teachers of the great Mozart.

Source *A-Smi* 701 A1 Pil 80, p.226.

Commentary Franz Anton Spitzeder (*b* 1735 [not 1732]; *d* 1796) was active in Salzburg as a choirboy from about 1748. He served as court tenor from 1 January 1760 to June 1796, as figural music instructor at the Kapellhaus from 8 January 1770 to June 1796 and keyboard instructor at the Kapellhaus from 22 December 1777 to 17 January 1779. In a letter of 3 December 1764, Leopold Mozart wrote to his Salzburg landlord Lorenz Hagenauer that Wolfgang wished Spitzeder and the violinist Wenzel Hebelt to perform the recently-published sonatas K8–9 for Archbishop Schrattenbach (*Briefe* i.178, *Letters* 53); according to the Salzburg court diaries, 'a small *Cammer-Musique*, composed by the young son of Mozart, the resident Vice-Kapellmeister here, who is at present in London together with his son', was given on 3 January 1765 (*Dokumente* 39, *Documentary Biography* 38). Later Spitzeder sang the roles of the Christgeist in *Die Schuldigkeit des ersten Gebots* K35 (1767) and Polidoro in *La finta semplice* K51 (1769). In 1778, he taught Mozart's Piano Concerto K246 to a certain Mademoiselle Villersi (*Briefe* ii.369, *Letters* 545). There is no other evidence that Mozart had lessons with Spitzeder.

Literature Werner Rainer, 'F. A. Spitzeder als Klavierlehrer am Kapellhaus', *MJb 1964*, 138–41; Ernst Hintermaier, *Die Salzburger Hofkapelle von 1700 bis 1806: Organisation und Personal* (diss. U. of Salzburg, 1972), 413; Heinz Schuler, 'Der Hoftenorist Franz Anton Spitzeder, Freund der Familie Mozart: Zu seiner Biographie und Familiengeschichte', *Jb der Heraldisch-Genealogischen Gesellschaft Adler*, 3rd ser., ix (Vienna, 1978), 27–35.

2 Records of the Royal Household, Koblenz 14 October 1763

14 October. Chamber Director Mainone reimbursed for the ten Carolines at 11 fl = 73 Reichsthaler 18 alb given at his Highness's command to the musician Mozart from Salzburg.

Source Gustav Bereths, *Die Musikpflege am kurtrierischen Hofe zu Koblenz-Ehrenbreitstein* (Mainz, 1964), 250.

Commentary The Mozarts were in Koblenz from 17 to 27 September 1763. They played for Elector Johann Philipp von Walderdorf on 18 September and, according to a letter of 26 September, Leopold received 10 louis d'or for the performance (*Briefe* i.92, *Letters* 28–9).

3 Leopold Mozart's letter of recommendation for Sebastian Winter, Paris 2 March 1764

We, Leopold Mozart, music director to his Serene Highness the Prince Archbishop of Salzburg, certify that Bastien Winter, hairdresser, has served us very faithfully for one year. He merits our recommendation because of his good qualities. Madame the Princess of Fürstemberg-Möskirch, whom he would be honoured to serve, may rest assured that she is acquiring an excellent subject.

Paris the 2nd of March 1764.
Mozart

Source   Hans-Rudolf Wiedemann, 'Ein "Figaro" als Förderer Mozartscher Schöpfungen', in *Festschrift Albi Rosenthal*, ed. Rudolf Elvers (Tutzing, 1984), 291 (including facs.).
Commentary   Sebastian Winter (1743–1815) had worked for the Mozarts as a general servant and hairdresser. In 1764 he took a position as chamber servant to the Fürstenberg court at Donaueschingen. Later, in 1786, he acted as an intermediary when Mozart sold several compositions to the Fürstenberg court.
Literature   Friedrich Schnapp, 'Neue Mozart-Funde in Donaueschingen', *Neues Mozart-Jb*, ii (1942), 211–23.

4   From Charles Burney's musical notebook, London 1771 or early 1772 [refers to 1764 and 1765]

Mozart. See Mr. D. Barrington's acc[t]. of him. Phil. Trans. Vol.60. p.54. & MS. Journal. wth original Certificate of his Birth, & Letter from Baron Haslang to L[d] Barrington. relate what I saw & heard myself at his Lodgings on his first Arrival in England & at M[r] Frank's – Extemporary & sight Playing, Composing a Treble to a given Base & a Base to a Treble, as well as both on a given Subject, & finishing a Composition began by another. his fondness for Manzoli – his imitations of the several Styles of Singing of each of the then Opera Singers, as well as of their Songs in an Extemporary opera to nonsense words – to which were [added] an overture of 3 Movem[ts] Recitative – Graziosa, Bravura & Pathetic Airs together with Several accomp[d] Recitatives, all full of Taste imagination, with good Harmony, Melody & Modulation. after w[ch] he played at Marbles, in the true Childish Way of one who knows Nothing.

[added later] He's engaged to compose a 2[d] opera for Milan next Carnaval (Vienna intelligence Sept? 1772.)

Source   *Memoirs of Dr Charles Burney 1726–1769*, ed. Slava Klima, Garry Bowers and Kerry S. Grant (Lincoln, Nebraska, and London, 1987), 164.
Commentary   With the exception of the last sentence, Burney's account was probably written in 1771 or early 1772. It postdates Daines Barrington's

'Account of a very remarkable young musician' (*Dokumente* 86–92, *Documentary Biography* 95–100) but predates a letter of Louis De Visme, written to Burney from Munich, not Vienna, on 30 November 1772, which provides the information that Mozart was to compose *Lucio Silla* for Milan (*see* Document 38). It is not necessarily the case that the meeting described here took place after the London début of the Italian castrato Giovanni Manzuoli (*c*1720–82) on 24 November 1764, as the editors of the *Memoirs* suggest. In his article on Mozart for Abraham Rees's *Dictionary* (London, 1819), Burney stated that 'During his residence in London we had frequent opportunities of witnessing his extraordinary talents and profound knowledge in every branch of music'. Consequently, Burney's comments may refer to different times during the Mozarts' 15-month stay in London from April 1764 to July 1765. 'Mr Frank' is presumably the 'Mr. Frenck' listed in Leopold Mozart's undated travel notes. Possibly he was the jeweller Aaron Franks (1685–1775), a well-known philanthropist (*Briefe* v.139); Napthali Franks (1715–96) of Mortlake, Surrey, later a leading member of the Great Synagogue in London (*Memoirs*, 76 n.4); or another member of the prominent Franks family. In Burney's account, the passage 'overture of 3 Movem^{ts}' originally read 'overture of 2 movem^{ts}'.

Literature   Cecil B. Oldman, 'Dr Burney and Mozart', *MJb 1962–3*, 75–81; idem, 'Dr Burney and Mozart: Addenda and Corrigenda', *MJb 1964*, 109–10. [*See plate 1*]

5   Charles Burney to his daughter Fanny, London 13 December 1790 [refers to 1764 and 1765]

I had just stuck the little boy [Hummel] down to my large Piano forte wch in the morning I had tuned very nicely; when behold the Pac came. I made him begin the Piece again, wch was one of his master Mozart's, as I found – a Fr. Air with very difficult & ingenious variations, wch were executed with the utmost precision. . . . I then brought him some Music I have just rec^d from Germany – ill printed, but good composition. He first played a song by Mozart, wch he entered into the Spirit of very well. (It is in a periodical work to wch I have subscribed, printed at *Speier*, called *Bibliothek der Grazien*, Library of the Graces. The title is affected, but the music often excellent.) I next set the little man to work at a very fine Symphony of Haydn's, but extremely *recherchée* and difficult. . . . It is odd that 30 years after his Master Mozart had been recommended to me, & played on my knee, on subjects I gave him, that this little Man sh^d also claim and merit my kindness.

Source   Kerry S. Grant, *Dr Burney as Critic and Historian of Music* (Ann Arbor, 1983), 202.

Commentary   The child prodigy Johann Nepomuk Hummel (1778–1837) was Mozart's pupil in Vienna in 1787 and 1788; it is sometimes said that his first public performance was at a concert in 1787 directed by Mozart. In 1789 he undertook a concert tour, performing at Prague, Dresden and Berlin, where Mozart may have heard him play on 23 May (*see* Document 92), arriving in London in autumn 1790. 'Pac' is the Italian soprano castrato Gasparo

Pacchiarotti (1740–1821), a friend of Burney's. Pacchiarotti's final visit to London is generally assumed to have been in 1791. According to this document, however, he must have arrived in autumn 1790. The aria by Mozart was either 'Vedrai carino' or 'Mi tradì quell'alma ingrata', both from *Don Giovanni*, published in the first year (1789) of Bossler's *Bibliothek der Grazien*; no arias by Mozart were published in the second year (1790). All of Mozart's variations on French airs, including к264/315*d* ('Lison dormait'), 265/300*e* ('Ah, vous dirai-je'), 352/374*c* ('Dieu d'amour'), 353/300*f* ('La belle Françoise') and 354/299*a* ('Je suis Lindor'), had been published by this time. The symphony by Haydn may have been н I:83 or I:84, keyboard arrangements of which were also published in the *Bibliothek der Grazien* in 1789.

Literature Hans Schneider, *Der Musikverleger Heinrich Philipp Bossler, 1744–1812* (Tutzing, 1985), 309–14.

6 *Lloyd's Evening Post*, London 22 February 1765

One Wolfgang Mozart, a German boy, of about eight years old, is arrived here, who can play upon various sorts of instruments of music, in consort or solo, and can compose music surprizingly; so that he may be reckoned a wonder at his age.

Source *GB-Lblc* without shelfmark (1765), p.183. Reprinted in *The London Evening Post* for Thursday 21 February to Saturday 23 February 1765 [unpaginated].

Commentary The immediate stimulus for this notice was the Mozarts' public concert at the Little Theatre, Haymarket, on 21 February (*Dokumente* 42, *Documentary Biography* 41–2). Curiously, it suggests that Mozart was newly-arrived in London; in fact, the family had arrived there almost a year earlier, on 23 April 1764. An exactly contemporary article in the *Oprechte Saturdagse Haerlemse Courant* for 16 February 1765 begins in a similar vein: '(London, 8 February) Also arrived here is a composer and master of music of about eight years of age, who is truly a wonder, such as was never known before' (*Dokumente* 41, *Documentary Biography* 41–2).

7 *The European Magazine and London Review*, London June 1784 [refers to 1765]

Impartial and Critical Review of Musical Publications. The favourite Overture to La Buone Figliuola, adapted for two performers on one Harpsichord or Piano Forte. Price 2s. Skillern.

This sprightly well-known overture is composed by Sig. Piccini, and is extremely well formed into a Duetto by D. Holloway. . . . The first instance of two persons performing on one instrument in this kingdom, was exhibited in the year 1765, by little Mozart and his sister; and the first musick of this nature printed as duettos, was composed by the ingenious Dr. Burney.

Source *GB-Lbl* P.P.5459.z (1784), p.452.

Commentary This review represents the earliest independent reference to Mozart as the first performer, and possibly composer, of keyboard duets. According to a partial manuscript of Georg Nikolaus Nissen's *Biographie W. A. Mozarts*, now in the library of the Mozarteum, Leopold wrote to his Salzburg landlord Lorenz Hagenauer on 9 July 1765: 'In London Wolfgangerl composed his first work for 4 hands. Until then, a 4-hand sonata had never been composed'. However, the passage does not appear in the published version (Leipzig, 1828), and its genuineness has been questioned (A. Hyatt King, *Mozart in Retrospect*, 1955, 100–1); possibly the passage derives from a different, now-lost letter (*Briefe* v.130). It is generally assumed that K19*d* is the four-hand sonata composed by Mozart in London although no authentic source supports this hypothesis. The document usually cited as evidence for Mozart's composition of K19*d* is an announcement in *The Public Advertiser* for 13 May 1765: 'Concerto on the Harpsichord by the little Composer and his Sister, each single and both together, &c.' (*Dokumente* 44, *Documentary Biography* 44–5). Uncharacteristically for the Mozarts, however, who were careful to publicize Wolfgang's own compositions, no composer is named and it may be that the concerto was not Mozart's. According to the family letters, Leopold Mozart had acquired several concertos by Wagenseil in Vienna in 1762 (*Briefe* i.61, not in *Letters*); almost certainly these included concertos for four hands at two keyboards (*Briefe* v.179, *Letters* 77). In any event, the 13 May 1765 announcement does not refer to a sonata (*pace* Wolfgang Rehm, *NMA* IX:24/2, p.vii). Burney, in the preface to his *Four Sonatas or Duets for two Performers on One Piano Forte or Harpsichord* (London, 1777), makes no mention of Mozart's early performances or composition of duets. Nicola Piccinni's *La buona figliuola* was first performed in London in November or December 1766 and revived there almost every season until 1785. Holloway was organist at Grafton Chapel.

Literature Georges de Saint-Foix, 'Une sonate inconnue de Mozart: cette sonate, pour le piano à quatre mains serait-elle le premier duo des enfants prodiges?', *La revue musicale* (1921) no.2, pp.99–110, and no.11, pp.286–8; Alan Tyson, 'Mozart's Piano Duet K19*d*: the First English Edition?', *The Music Review*, xxii (1961), 222; idem, 'The Earliest Editions of Mozart's Duet-Sonata K19*d*', *The Music Review*, xxx (1969), 98–105.

8   *The World*, London 1 March 1790 [refers to 1765]

The Storace, with a new Buffo, Mussini, and in some new Music of Bianchi and Mozart, La Villanela Rapita, altogether filled the House, and with much fashion. . . . The Music is pretty and express-ive – the Trio and the Duo of Storace and Borselli, are the best. The last was properly encored.

Bianchi, last year at Venice, is now at Verona – Mozart, is he who was some 25 years ago, the Infantine Wonder of London, who at six years old played at Hickford's, then the Grand Gala Room of London! Whom the Duke of York accompanied – and Liotard painted, after he had heard.

Source   *GB-Lblc* without shelfmark (1790) [unpaginated].

Commentary   No portrait of Mozart by Jean-Etienne Liotard is known; prob-ably the reference is an error. The fashionable Liotard (1702–c1776) worked in

London from September 1753 to late 1755 and from 1772 to 1774, but not during the time of the Mozarts' visit there in 1764–5. The pasticcio *La villanella rapita* was given at the King's Theatre, Haymarket, on 27 February 1790. The performance included Mozart's 'Dite almeno, in che mancai' K479, and 'Mandina amabile' K480. Anna Storace also sang 'Deh vieni non tardar' from *Le nozze di Figaro* and 'Batti, batti' from *Don Giovanni*. Hickford's Rooms in Brewer Street was one of the leading concert halls in London during the first half of the 18th century. Mozart (who was then eight years old, not six) was supposed to perform there on 22 May 1764 but was unable to because of illness. William Henry (1743–1805), Duke of York and brother to King George III, first met the Mozarts in London; they met again in Milan in October 1771. The singer Nicolò Mussini (birth and death dates unknown) was engaged at the King's Theatre, Haymarket, from 27 February to 10 July; he sang the role of the Count in *La villanella rapita*.

Literature N. S. Trivas, 'London Society Portrayed by Liotard', *The Connoisseur*, xcix (1937), 30–34; Hans Vollmer, *Allgemeines Lexikon der bildenden Künstler von der Antike bis zur Gegenwart*, xxxii (Leipzig, 1929), 263–4; Joseph Heinz Eibl, 'Der "Duc de York"', *Mitteilungen der Internationale Stiftung Mozarteum*, xxiii (1975), 47–50.

9 Minutes of the Standing Committee of the Trustees of the British Museum, London 19 July 1765

Lord Cardross having presented a portrait of Queen Elizabeth, Mr. Mozart a copy of the printed music of his son, and Dr. de Or a copy of his Theological Inaugural Dissertation printed at Leyden 1765
Ordered
that thanks be returned for the same.

Source A. Hyatt King, 'The Mozarts at the British Museum', in *Festschrift Albi Rosenthal*, ed. Rudolf Elvers (Tutzing, 1984), 158.

Commentary The *Book of Presents of the Trustees* noted for 19 July: 'A copy of the Printed Music of his son: from Mr. Mozart. Omitted in the Donation Book'. The gift apparently included the sonatas K6–9, probably given to the British Museum in June, the sonatas K10–15, probably donated in mid-July, and the motet 'God is our Refuge' K20.

10 *The Kentish Post or Canterbury News-Letter*, Canterbury 20 July 1765

On Thursday July 25, at Eleven in the Forenoon, Will Be A Musical Performance, At the Town-Hall, in Canterbury, for the Benefit of Master Mozart, the celebrated German Boy, Aged eight years, and his Sister, Who have exhibited with universal Applause to the Nobility and Gentry in London. The Compositions and extempore Performances of this little Boy are the Astonishment of all Judges of Music. Admission 2s. 6d.

Source Christopher Roscoe, 'Two 18th-century non-events', *The Musical Times*, cxii (1971), 18.

Commentary   There is no evidence as to whether this concert took place. The Mozarts were in Canterbury from 24 to 31 July.

11   *Gazette d'Utrecht*, Utrecht 20 September 1765

From Utrecht, *the* 19th of *September*. . . . According to news from The *Hague*, yesterday a child of 8 years, a native of *Saltzbourg* named J. G. Wolfgang *Mozart*, had the honour of performing admirably in the presence of his Serene Highness the Prince, Stadholder, several difficult pieces of instrumental music, all by the greatest masters, as well as some nearly-as-excellent works of his own composition. His *Serene Highness*, as well as the lords and ladies of the court, greatly applauded this marvellous child.

Source   *F-Pa* 4° H.8931 (1765) [unpaginated].
Commentary   The exact date of Mozart's performance for Prince William V of Orange, 18 September 1765, was previously unknown; according to Leopold Mozart's letter of 19 September, Wolfgang played once for the Prince, and twice for his sister, Princess Caroline of Nassau-Weilburg, during their first eight days at The Hague (*Briefe* i.203, *Letters* 59). The family had arrived there about 10 September.

12   *Augspurgische Ordinari Postzeitung*, Augsburg 5 October 1765

The Hague, the 27th of September.
  To everyone's delight, the health of his Highness, Holder of the Hereditary Lands, grows increasingly stronger. His Serene Highness occupies himself untiringly with affairs of state and often attends the assembly of the Estates-General. Among the entertainments which occupy him at other times, music seems to be his principal interest. In particular, he has expressed his satisfaction with the great talent of the musician and composer J. G. Wolfgang Mozart, born at Salzburg and barely 8 years of age, who has performed several times in his Highness's presence.

Source   *D-Mbs* 4.Eph.Pol.53 (1765) [unpaginated].
Commentary   Performances by Mozart for Prince William V of Orange were previously unknown for the period 19 to 27 September. For Mozart's performances before 19 September, *see* Document 11.

13   Joseph Yorke to his brother Philip Yorke, 2nd Earl of Hardwicke, The Hague 1 October 1765

. . . We have got the little German Boy here who plays upon the Harpsichord like Handel, & composes with the same facility, he is really a most extraordinary effort of Nature, but our Professors in

Physick don't think he will be long lived. He is to be at a Concert at my House this Evening.

Source   *GB-Lbl* Add.35367, f.347r.
Commentary   Joseph Yorke, Baron Dover (1724–92), was the British Minister, later Ambassador, at The Hague from 1751 to 1780. His brother, Philip Yorke (1720–90), was the second Earl of Hardwicke. Joseph Yorke is mentioned twice in Leopold Mozart's travel diary for the period 11 September 1765 to 10 May 1766, first as '*à la Haye* . . . l'Ambassadeur d'Angleterre Mr: York' and later, possibly referring to the spring of 1766, as 'Der Engl: Gesandte Ritter de York' (*Briefe* i.215–16, not in *Letters*). Philip Yorke is not mentioned in the correspondence. Daines Barrington, in his 'Account of a very remarkable young musician', also compared Mozart to Handel (*Dokumente* 91, *Documentary Biography* 100).

14   *Amsterdam*, Amsterdam 28 January 1766

On Wednesday, the 29th of this month, Sieur Mozart, Kapellmeister to the Prince Archbishop of Salzburg, will have the honour of giving a grand Concert at the Salle du Manege in this city, at which his son and daughter, the first aged eight years and 11 months, the other 14 years, will perform concertos at two harpsichords, as well as at one harpsichord, four-hands. All of the overtures will be by this little composer, who, never having found his like, was the admiration of the courts of Vienna, Versailles and London. Music lovers may present him pieces of music, as they please, which he will perform at sight. The price is two florins per person. Tickets may be obtained from Sieur Mozart, lodging at the Lyon d'Or in the Warmoestraat, and from Sieur J. J. Hummel, music dealer on the Vygendam. Money will not be accepted at the door.

Source   *F-Pa* 4°8929 (1766) [unpaginated].
Commentary   An earlier version of this announcement (*Amsterdam*, 21 January) is almost identical to a notice published in the *Amsterdamsche Dingsdagsche Courant* for 21 January 1766 (*Dokumente* 50, *Documentary Biography* 51). In the earlier version, the phrase 'at two harpsichords, as well as at one harpsichord, four-hands' reads only 'at the harpsichord'; and the sentence beginning 'Tickets may be obtained . . .' reads 'Tickets may be obtained from Sieur J. J. Hummel . . .', without mentioning Leopold Mozart or his residence.

15   *Amsterdam*, Amsterdam 25 February 1766

By request, the children of Sieur Mozart will have the honour of giving a second concert on Wednesday 26 February, at 6 o'clock in the evening, at the Salle du Manege in Amsterdam, at which these children will not only perform together concertos on different harpsichords; but also with four hands on one of these instruments. To conclude, the son will play on the organ caprices, fugues of his own invention, and other pieces of profound music. The price is two florins per person, and as money will not be accepted at the door, tickets may be obtained from the said Sieur Mozart, at the Lion d'Or in the Warmoestraat, and from Sieur J. J. Hummel on the Vygendam, where the *Opera* 1, 2 & 3 of sonatas for harpsichord with violin accompaniment, composed by this young composer, are available.

Source *F-Pa* 4°8929 (1766) [unpaginated].
Commentary An almost identical announcement, also in French, but omitting the time of the performance, appeared in the *Amsterdamsche Dingsdagsche Courant* for 25 February (*Dokumente* 51, *Documentary Biography* 52).

16 *Amsterdam*, Amsterdam 15 April 1766

By request, next Wednesday, the 16th of this month, the children of Sieur Mozart will have the honour of giving a third concert at the Salle du Manege in this city, at which they will perform together not only concertos on different harpsichords, but also with four hands on one of these instruments. The price is two florins per person. Tickets are available from J. J. Hummel on the Vygendam, where the three opuses of sonatas for harpsichord composed by the young Mozart are available, as well as his fourth opus, published today together with a catalogue of new pieces of music.

Source *F-Pa* 4°8929 (1766) [unpaginated].
Commentary A similar announcement in French, but lacking the advertisement of the sonatas op.4 (κ26–31), was published in the *Amsterdamsche Dingsdagsche Courant* for 15 April (*Dokumente* 52, *Documentary Biography* 53). Hummel also announced the sonatas in the *'s-Gravenhaegse Woensdagse Courant* for 16 April (*Dokumente* 52, *Documentary Biography* 53).

17 Mozart's dedication of the Sonatas κ26–31, [The Hague March] 1766

To Her Serene Highness, Madame the Princess of Nassau-Weilburg etc.

Madame!
About to leave Holland, I cannot think of this moment without sorrow. The virtues of Your Most Serene Highness, Your generosity, Your kindnesses which recalled me to life, the sweetness of Your voice, the pleasure of accompanying it and rendering it honour by my small talents, all this has accustomed me to Your amiable court, to which my tender heart will be forever bound. Deign, Madame, to receive a token of it. Deign to accept this fruit of my hard work and

deign to regard it as a mark of my genuine gratitude and the profound respect with which I am,

> Madame
>> Your Serene Highness's
>>> very humble, very obedient
>>> and very small Servant.

> J. G. Wolfgang Mozart
>> of Salzburg.

Source *S-Skma* VP-R. Facsimile in Gertraut Haberkamp, 'Eine unbekannte
Widmung W. A. Mozarts zu den Klavier-Violinsonaten KV 26–31', *Acta
Mozartiana* xxvii (1980), 38; idem, *Die Erstdrucke der Werke von Wolfgang Amadeus
Mozart* (Tutzing, 1986), ii.17.
Commentary Possibly the phrase 'Your kindnesses which recalled me to life'
is an oblique reference to Mozart's serious illness during November 1765. The
sonatas κ26–31, published at Amsterdam by J. J. Hummel and at The Hague
by B. Hummel, were first advertised on 15 April, not 16 April as stated by
Deutsch (*Dokumente* 52, *Documentary Biography* 53–4). It was common to repeat
the phrase 'published today' in later advertisements. (*See* Document 16.)

18   *Gazette d'Utrecht*, Utrecht 18 April 1766

As requested, the children of Sieur Mozart will have the honour of
giving a concert at the Concert Room in Utrecht next Monday, 21
April; not only will they perform together pieces on two different
harpsichords, but also together at the same time, with four hands, on
only one of these instruments. The price is 2 florins for a single
person and only 3 florins for a gentleman with a lady. Tickets are to
be had of Sieur Winter, Musician.

Source *F-Pa* 4° H.8931 (1766) [unpaginated].
Commentary A similar announcement in Dutch, published in the *Utrechtsche
Courant* of the same date, makes no mention of the four-hand performance on a
single harpsichord, which by then was a standard feature of many of Mozart's
concerts (*Dokumente* 53, *Documentary Biography* 54). In the Dutch announcement,
tickets were stated to be available from Leopold Mozart, lodging with Sieur
Mos in the Plaets-Royal, Utrecht. Oswald Winter, a local shopkeeper, played
the horn in the Collegium Musicum Utrajectinum; he is listed in Leopold
Mozart's travel notes for the period 11 September 1765 to 10 May 1766 as 'Mr.
Winter Music[us]' (*Briefe* i.217, not in *Letters*). Presumably the appearance of
the advertisements in the *Gazette d'Utrecht* and the *Utrechtsche Courant* was
arranged while the Mozarts were still in Amsterdam. They did not arrive at
Utrecht until 18 April.

19   *Augspurgische Extra-Zeitung*, Augsburg 10 June 1766

Paris, 27 May. Because extraordinary talent is highly prized here
these days, the arrival of the Salzburg Kapellmeister Leopold Mozart

with his remarkable children has aroused all the more pleasure since the distressing news became known that both children were dangerously ill in Holland; now, however, one has the pleasure of seeing them restored to good health and to admire the remarkable development of their very special talents. Some weeks before their arrival, the fourth opus of keyboard sonatas appeared that this small but great composer wrote at The Hague for the Princess of Nassau-Weilburg. It has also been confirmed that he played on the famous organ at Haarlem while he was there. Yesterday this gifted family was favoured by a visit from the hereditary Prince of Brunswick, and we understand that the reigning Duke of Zweibrücken and other persons of rank will do him similar honour.

Source *D-Mbs* 4.Eph.Pol.53 [unpaginated].
Commentary The Mozarts' meeting on 26 May with Karl Wilhelm Ferdinand, Hereditary Prince of Brunswick, was previously supposed to have taken place about the middle of June (*Chronik* 28). The sonatas 'Opus four' (K26–31) were published by Hummel at The Hague in April 1766. Mozart performed on the organ at Haarlem in early April. The publication of this notice in Augsburg may have been arranged by Leopold Mozart, who was a native of the city.
Literature Cliff Eisen, 'Contributions to a New Mozart Documentary Biography', *Journal of the American Musicological Society*, xxxix (1986), 617–19.

20 Gabriel Cramer to Baron Friedrich Melchior von Grimm, [Geneva summer] 1766

I will go to the city presently to inform myself about your children, and to do for them what can be done; there is the Comédie and I imagine the impresario would be able to turn your fine musician to account by putting his harpsichord on the stage.

Source *Voltaire's Correspondence*, ed. Theodore Besterman (Geneva, 1953–66), lxi, letter 12502, p.175.
Commentary Presumably Grimm had written a letter (now lost) to Cramer in anticipation of the Mozarts' arrival at Geneva, where they stayed from 20 August to about 10 September 1766. For the Mozarts' public concerts there, *see* Document 23. Gabriel Cramer (1723–93) was Voltaire's publisher in Geneva. Presumably he meant that Mozart could perform as an entr'acte.

21 Minutes, Dijon July 1766

Having been informed that His Serene Highness, Mylord the Prince of Condé wished to hear a harpsichord concert by the two young children of the Archduke of Salzburg's Kapellmeister, the music of which was composed by one of the said children aged eight, Messrs the Viscount Mayor and the aldermen made ready for this gathering the Great Assembly Hall, which was decorated with cut-glass chandeliers and ornate candelabras lit with wax candles, a president's chair of crimson velvet placed on a platform in the middle of the hall for His Said Highness, and risers on all sides for seating the distinguished persons of His retinue. Having arrived at eight o'clock in the evening at the Town Hall, accompanied by Mr de La Tour du Pain, commandant of this province, by the administrative officer, and by several other lords, His Said Highness was received by Messrs the Viscount Mayor, the aldermen, the syndic, the secretary, and the substitutes for the syndic's commissioner of police, all dressed in cloaks and cravats in the manner of Ponchartrin; and He was led into the said hall where, being within, His Highness ordered removed the president's chair and platform that had been prepared for him, and seated himself on the benches among the ladies. Then refreshments were offered to His Highness, along with assurances [of fealty] inspired by this prince's goodness, which he accepted, and refreshments were likewise offered to the ladies and lords who accompanied his Highness. And after the concert finished and the Prince arose, he was followed by the entire magistracy and accompanied to his carriage, and when he had climbed into it, everyone retired.

Source Eugène Fyot, 'Mozart à Dijon', *Mémoires de l'Académie des Sciences, Arts et Belles-lettres de Dijon: année 1937* (Dijon, 1938), 26; translation in Neal Zaslaw, *Mozart's Symphonies: Context, Performance Practice, Reception* (Oxford, 1989), 66–7.
Commentary The Mozarts' concert in Dijon took place on 18 July (*Dokumente* 55–6, *Documentary Biography* 57–8). They had been invited there by Louis-Joseph de Bourbon, Prince de Condé.
Literature R. Thiblot, 'Le Séjour de Mozart à Dijon en 1766', *Mémoires de l'Académie des Sciences, Arts et Belles-lettres de Dijon: année 1937* (Dijon, 1938), 139–43.

22 *Merkwürdigkeiten der neuesten Welt-Geschichten*, Schaffhausen 13 September 1766

Geneva, 6 September.
The children of Herr Mozart, Kapellmeister at Salzburg, have been in our city for some days. They are two genuine wonders with regard to musical talent and known everywhere as such. The boy, who is not older than 9 years of age, was the admiration of the courts at Versailles, Vienna and London. He performs, at the keyboard, all sorts of pieces that are put before him. He also improvises and plays caprices. In short, he excels in the art and can be compared with – and is a match for – the greatest masters. His sister, a girl of 14 years, plays the most difficult pieces by the greatest masters with unequalled neatness and accuracy. In addition to their talents, these

two children also have quite lovely and engaging dispositions, which endears them to everyone. They will depart from here in a few days, and make their way via Lausanne, Berne and Zürich back to Germany.

Source Lucas E. Staehelin, *Die Reise der Familie Mozart durch die Schweiz* (Berne, 1968), 24.

Commentary The tone of this report, including phrases nearly identical to those used to advertise the children elsewhere, suggests that Leopold Mozart may be its author, or perhaps had a hand in its composition. André-Ernest-Modeste Grétry apparently heard Mozart play in Geneva in 1766, recording the event in the first volume of his *Mémoires, ou Essais sur la musique* (Paris, 1789, not 1795 as recorded in *Dokumente*): 'Once in Geneva I met a child who could play everything at sight. His father said to me before the assembled company: So that no doubt shall remain as to my son's talent, write for him, for tomorrow, a very difficult sonata movement. I wrote him an Allegro in E flat; difficult, but unpretentious; he played it, and everyone, except myself, believed that it was a miracle. The boy had not stopped; but following the modulations, he had substituted a number of passages for those which I had written' (*Dokumente* 415, *Documentary Biography* 477).

23 Draft of a letter, Pierre-Michel Hennin to Friedrich Melchior Grimm, Geneva 20 September 1766

M. Grimm

I was honoured to receive from M. Mozart the letter of recommendation you wrote for him. His children's reputation was already so well-known here that they had no need of recommendations. They were well-received and fêted. The government permitted them to give two concerts at the Town Hall, and were it not the season when the number of inhabitants in Geneva is much diminished, they would have had to have been as pleased with this town as with those capitals where they were best received.

The little Mozart's talents remind me of those of a young Frenchman whom I saw draw with all possible force and truth. If things continue in this way, soon one will become a painter or musician before reaching maturity, and what we have admired as incredible will be so common that our praise will appear absurd. Yet there is also a distressing side to prodigies in the arts, and that is that we do not see that they have spread out everywhere, so that one might compare these child prodigies to an impatient traveller who, setting out in advance of the public conveyance, arrives early at the inn, and sadly waits, seated on a milestone, for his travelling companions whom he might just as well have never left behind. . . .

Source Lucas E. Staehelin, *Die Reise der Familie Mozart durch die Schweiz* (Berne, 1968), 93–4.

Commentary Pierre-Michel Hennin (1728–1807) had been the French resident ambassador in Geneva since 1765. The Mozarts' public performances in Geneva, where they stayed from 20 August to about 10 September, were previously unknown; programmes for the concerts do not survive.

24 From the manuscript journal of Jean-Henri Polier, Lausanne 15 September 1766

Monday, 15 September 1766
The said Mosard, son of the Kapellmeister of Salzburg, aged 9 or 10 years, gave a concert at the Town Hall, at 40 sous per head; he performed with great skill and composed to everyone's great astonishment; 70 people attended.

Source Lucas E. Staehelin, *Die Reise der Familie Mozart durch die Schweiz* (Berne, 1968), 95.
Commentary Deutsch asserts that the Mozarts were in Lausanne for five days, arriving on 11 September (*Dokumente* 57; *Documentary Biography* 59, however, reports a visit of seven days and concerts on 15 and 18 September), while Eibl states first that they were there from 11 to about 16 September, but later that the visit was from 11 to 18 September (*Chronik* 28 and 123). A letter of 10 November 1766 confirms a stay of five days. Probably, however, these were 14 or 15 to 18 or 19 September: the Mozarts gave concerts at Lausanne on 15 and 18 September (*see also* Document 25, *Briefe* i.230 and v.165, *Letters* 67). In a letter of 1792 written to Friedrich Schlichtegroll, Nannerl Mozart incorrectly stated that the visit in Lausanne was eight days (*Briefe* iv.190, *Documentary Biography* 457). Jean-Henri Polier (1715–91) was the representative at Lausanne of the provincial governor of Berne.

25 Salomon de Sévery, *Livre des comptes pour la dépense commencé le 17 mars 1766*, Lausanne September 1766

September [1766] carried forward	–	–	–	304.. 4..
15 For the little Mozart's concert	–	–	–	4..
18 For Mozart's second concert	–	–	–	4..

Source Jacques Burdet, 'Mozart à Lausanne en 1766', *Revue Historique Vaudoise*, lxi (1953), 107 (with facs. facing p.107); idem, *La musique dans le pays de Vaud sous le Régime Bernois (1536–1798)* (Lausanne, 1963), 433 (facs.); Lucas E. Staehelin, *Die Reise der Familie Mozart durch die Schweiz* (Berne, 1968), 31.
Commentary Salomon de Charrière de Sévery (1724–93) was *gouverneur* to the Princes of Hesse-Cassel. *See also* Document 24.

26 *Post- und Ordinari Schaffhauser Samstags Zeitung*, Schaffhausen 11 October 1766

Extract from a letter from Zürich to a friend here, of 7 October. Herr Kapellmeister Mozart and his family will arrive in your city next

Saturday, the 11th of this month. Surely you know from the public papers and elsewhere of the universal admiration they excited during their journey through England, Holland and France. Imagine as you may how exceptional this wonder is, when you hear young Herr Mozart, the virtuoso of 9 years, and Mademoiselle Mozart, his sister of 13 years, you will find, as did our connoisseurs of music here, that they far exceed all possible expectations. They are on their way back to Salzburg.

Source Lucas E. Staehelin, *Die Reise der Familie Mozart durch die Schweiz* (Berne, 1968), 75–6.

Commentary Assuming that the Mozarts left Lausanne on 19 September (*see* Document 24), and making allowance for travel time, it is more likely that they arrived at Schaffhausen about 14 October, as Eibl and Deutsch suggest (*Chronik* 29, *Dokumente* 62), than on 11 October as reported in *Documentary Biography* (p.66). 11 October, the date mentioned in the *Post- und Ordinari Schaffhauser Samstags Zeitung*, presumably represents their original plan.

27 *Aristide ou le Citoyen*, Lausanne 18 October 1766

Not everyone has seen what the young Mozart has in common with the goal that we propose; that is because not everyone has a moral perspective. This phenomenon seems to me to hold to the most interesting truths. If only I could express them as I feel them. Perhaps the flowers with which our artist was crowned will also bear fruit for us. . . .

Without talent, I dare to defend the cause of talent against the man of genius who abandons it. The great artists in all genres, these prodigies so uncommon to mankind, fill me with admiration for the all-powerful hand which formed them. I do not see the painter, the musician, the sculptor. I see only the inimitable workings of nature. My spirit prostrates itself with religious respect before this creative spirit, which makes itself present in some way to my senses by means of the powerful emotions that it produces. It is not at all a feeling of terror that I experience, similar to that excited by a flash of lightning or a storm; it is an impulse of tenderness and gratitude that consoles me, elevates me, and fills me with joy. The thunderbolt announces to me a redoubtable master, and Mozart's harpsichord, or Le Brun's brush, shows me a father who is close to his children and who does not disdain to play – so to speak – with them. . . .

When I see the young Mozart so light-heartedly create these tender and sublime symphonies, which one could take for the language of the immortals, all the fibres of my being resonate, so to speak, immortality – just as all the force of my spirit desires it. Carried away by a delightful illusion, beyond this narrow sphere which confines my senses, I could almost take this child, so blessed by heaven, for one of those pure geniuses who inhabits the happy realm destined for me.

Source Jacques Burdet, 'Mozart à Lausanne en 1766', *Revue Historique Vaudoise*, lxi (1953), 114–15; Lucas E. Staehelin, *Die Reise der Familie Mozart durch die Schweiz* (Berne, 1968), 101–2; *Dokumente* 520 and *Documentary Biography* 66 (incomplete).

Commentary Le Brun may be Charles Le Brun (1619–90), whose career as an artist began in his teens; in 1648, at the age of 27, Le Brun took a decisive role in the founding of the Académie Royale de Peinture et de Sculpture. For Mozart's concerts in Lausanne, *see* Documents 24 and 25. About 8 December, Friedrich Melchior Grimm wrote to Caroline of Hessen-Darmstadt (1721–74), a well-known patroness of the arts, concerning *Aristide ou le Citoyen*: 'I was not familiar with the periodical published under the auspices of Prince Louis of Wurtemberg which spoke at great length concerning little Mozart and which a friend, who knows how interested I am in this child, sent to me. To judge by this sample, clearly there is some of the vague and slender metaphysics which the French refugees have established in Germany after Wolf's philosophy, but it is not entirely badly written and I was not surprised that it was from time to time interesting. It is, I believe, more a work of morals than literature.' (Jochen Schlobach, *Correspondance inédite de Frédéric Melchior Grimm*, Munich, 1972, 67).

28 *Aristide ou Le Citoyen*, Lausanne 6 December 1766

A young whipper-snapper of a doctor here had the insolence to assure us most definitely that with pages of Mozart's music alone, he cured a case of insomnia that had resisted all other remedies.

Source Lucas E. Staehelin, *Die Reise der Familie Mozart durch die Schweiz* (Berne, 1968), 102.

29 *Notizie del Mondo*, Florence 20 March 1770

Milan 14 March

Monday evening at the palace of His Excellency Count Firmian there was a magnificent academy, with vocal and instrumental music, attended by Her Most Serene Highness the Princess of Este and many of the nobility. At this academy, the young German who has been here for some time gave proof of his skill.

Source *US-NYpl* BAA, p.182.

Commentary Count Karl Joseph Firmian (1716–82) was Governor-General of Lombardy; Mozart performed at Firmian's on 12 March. According to a letter of 13 March, the concert included '3 Arien und 1 Recit: mit Violinen'. Deutsch asserts these were the soprano arias K77/73e, 78/73b and 79/73d and 88/73c (*Dokumente* 100, *Documentary Biography* 110). Probably, however, they included 'Misero tu non sei' K73A (lost, but mentioned by Leopold Mozart in a letter of 26 January 1770); 'Misero me . . . Misero pargoletto' K77/73e; and 'Fra cento affanni' K88/73c. K78/73b and 79/73d are apparently earlier works; the scores are on Dutch paper commonly found in Mozart autographs of 1765–6. The 'Recit: mit Violinen' remains unidentified although *Briefe* suggests it may be the accompanied recitative to K77/73e, not a fourth work (*Briefe* v.234). Other details of the performance are unknown.

Literature   Alan Tyson, *Mozart: Studies of the Autograph Scores* (Cambridge, Mass., and London, 1987), 13.

30   P. Giovanni Biringucci, *Diario de' PP. Biringucci e Romano*, Rome 2 May 1770

At 10:15 p.m. a small boy from Salzburg, 12 or 13 years old, came to the College with the permission of the Father Rector. He played the harpsichord astonishingly, and extemporized at length on a theme given to him without notice by our Maestro di Cappella before the entire community assembled in the room. In similar fashion he then improvised on other themes presented to him, accompanied two arias, and then everyone gathered in the church where he playe̊d the organ. He appeared gratis, thanks to his fellow countryman Sig. Mölck, to whose family he professed obligations. For the rest, he is travelling throughout Europe with his father, Maestro di Cappella at Salzburg, and it is said that he is to compose an opera for the next Carnival at Milan. He is truly a prodigy, and frequently invited to gatherings in Rome; it is said that he receives 20 [scudi] for each appearance.

Source   Heinz Sonnemans, 'Wolfgang Amadeus Mozarts Besuch im Collegium Germanicum in Rom am 2. Mai 1770', *Wiener Figaro*, xli (1974), 9; *Briefe* v.253 (incomplete).
Commentary   Giovanni Xavier Biringucci was Minister at the Collegium Germanicum from 1765 to 1776, probably vice-director. Mölck may be Albert Andreas Mölck, a Salzburg student at the Collegium, 1768–71, who later served as Canon at Maria Schnee, Salzburg. According to Leopold's letter of 2 May, the Salzburg court bassist Joseph Meissner (?1725–95) also performed with Mozart at the Collegium Germanicum (*Briefe* i.345, not in *Letters*). *Briefe* states that the time of the performance may have been 11:30 a.m.

31   *Staats- und gelehrte Zeitung des hamburgischen unpartheyischen Correspondenten*, Hamburg 22 May 1770

Rome, 2 May. The son of the Kapellmeister of Salzburg has been here for some time and is admired by all for his extraordinary and precocious musical talent.

Source   *US-PRu* 0902.873 (1770) [unpaginated].
Commentary   The Mozarts had arrived in Rome on 11 April.

32   *Notizie del Mondo*, Florence 1 January 1771

Milan. 26 December. This evening the drama il Mitridate will be staged in the Ducal theatre.

Source   *US-NYpl* BAA, p.7.
Commentary   *Mitridate, rè di Ponto* was first given at the Teatro Regio Ducal in Milan on 26 December.

33   *Staats- und gelehrte Zeitung des hamburgischen unpartheyischen Correspondenten*, Hamburg 27 March 1771

From Italy, 7 March. Young Mozart, a famous keyboard player, fifteen years old, excited the attention and admiration of all music lovers when he gave a public performance in Venice recently. An experienced musician gave him a fugue theme, which he worked out for more than an hour with such science, dexterity, harmony, and proper attention to rhythm, that even the greatest connoisseurs were astounded. He composed an entire opera for Milan, which was given at the last Carnival. His good-natured modesty, which enhances still more his precocious knowledge, wins him the greatest praise, and this must give his worthy father, who is travelling with him, extraordinary pleasure.

Source   *US-PRu* 0902.873 (1771) [unpaginated].
Commentary   Mozart's public academy in Venice took place on 5 March. Other details of the performance are unknown.
Literature   Cliff Eisen, 'Contributions to a New Mozart Documentary Biography', *Journal of the American Musicological Society*, xxxix (1986), 624–5.

34   *Augspurgische Ordinari Postzeitung*, Augsburg 28 September 1771

Milan, 15 September. Everything is lively here on account of the grand and expensive preparations for the forthcoming wedding of his Royal Highness Archduke Ferdinand to the Princess of Modena. An opera by the famous Metastasio, *Il Ruggero*, or **Heroic Gratitude**, will be presented. The most famous singers in Italy are being called here to perform this opera, the music of which is composed by the famous Hasse, a Saxon, and Kapellmeister to the Elector of Saxony. All of the sets will be designed and arranged with the greatest magnificence. The ballets, choreographed by Messrs. Pich and Favre, and Mesdames Binetti and Blasge, will be exceptionally fine, and the performance will include 40 dancers. Similarly, other theatrical spectacles will be very elegant and various in their presentation. The Fachini company will be seen in a magnificent masquerade, with decorative emblems appropriate to the occasion. Each day three hundred persons will dine at court, where there will be masked balls, and at the theatres masked balls will also take place. Moreover, the theatres will be magnificently lighted, as will the whole city, three nights in a row, and for three evenings tickets to the theatrical performances will be distributed gratis. There will be races with horses and also races with light carriages. A part of the race course will be converted into a gallery, covered with the interlaced boughs of verdant trees, and beautifully lighted, and underneath 150 poor maidens, to be married the same day to 150 similar young men, and given dowries by the royal bridal couple, will dine and celebrate their weddings. Two fountains will flow with wine instead of water, various orchestras with musicians will perform, and, finally, a Serenade, entitled *Ascanio in Alba*, composed by Abbate Parini and set to music by Herr Mozzart, will be performed. Numerous other entertainments, impossible to describe, will also be given, and it is expected that an astonishing number of visitors will arrive here to see them.

Source *D-Mbs* 4.Eph.Pol.53 (1771) [unpaginated].

Commentary The serenata *Ascanio in alba* K111 was first given at the Teatro Regio Ducal in Milan on 17 October to celebrate the marriage of Archduke Ferdinand of Austria to Princess Maria Beatrice Ricciarda d'Este of Modena. Its success far surpassed that of Johann Adolf Hasse's opera *Il Ruggiero ovvero L'eroica gratitudine*, also composed for the wedding festivities (*see* Document 35).

35 *Notizie del Mondo*, Florence 26 October 1771

Milan 19 October. . . . The opera has not met with success, and was not performed except for a single ballet. The serenata, however, has met with great applause, both for the text and for the music.

Source *US-NYpl* BAA, p.662. Reprinted with minor changes in the *Diario Ordinario*, Rome 2 November 1771, p.11, and in German in the *Staats- und gelehrte Zeitung des hamburgischen unpartheyischen Correspondenten*, 13 November 1771 [unpaginated].

Commentary This notice confirms Leopold Mozart's report in a letter of 19 October on the success of *Ascanio in alba* and the failure of Hasse's opera: 'We are constantly addressed in the street by cavaliers and other people who wish to congratulate Wolfgang. In a word, *it grieves me*, but Wolfgang's Serenata has so overshadowed Hasse's opera that I cannot describe it' (*Briefe* i.444, *Letters* 202).

36 *Wienerisches Diarium*, Vienna 6 November 1771

Milan 12 October. Yesterday the Royal bridal couple did not appear at the usual promenade; instead there was an audience at court in the evening. Today, finally, was the masquerade of the so-called Fachini, the magnificence of which evoked general admiration, just as the Serenata received universal applause for its composition and very excellent music.

Source *A-Wst*.

Commentary Because the wedding took place on 15 October, the date of this report, 12 October, must be a mistake. Perhaps it is to be dated 21 October.

37 From an anonymous account of the election and installation of Hieronymous Colloredo as Archbishop of Salzburg, Salzburg 1772

29 April. . . . At 7 o'clock there was a large gathering of ladies and knights in gala at court, at 9 o'clock a grand dinner in 2 rooms, namely the princely table for the ladies, capitularies and ministers in the so-called Kaiser-Saal, and for the chamberlains and knights in the Marcus Sitticus-Saal, altogether one hundred and 60 persons, with elegant table music and a cantata.

Source *A-Sca* Hs.2341 germ., pp.161–2 (*Salzburgische Nachrichten von dem Frommen Lebenslauf, und Traur Vollen Hinscheiden . . . Sigismundi Christophori . . . von Schrattenbach, bis Nach dem Feyerlichen Einzug und Regierungs-Antritt . . . Hyeronimi . . . von Kolloredo den 13. März ao 1772*). The same passage occurs in a contemporary copy of this manuscript (*A-Sca* Hs.1944 germ., p.135).

Commentary Possibly this document refers to *Il sogno di Scipione*, which was previously thought to have been given during the festivities celebrating the election of Hieronymus Colloredo as Archbishop of Salzburg (*Dokumente* 127, *Documentary Biography* 141) but which more recent opinion suggests may have remained unperformed (*NMA* II:5/vi, ed. Josef-Horst Lederer). Originally composed for Archbishop Schrattenbach, apparently to celebrate the 50th anniversary on 10 January 1772 of his ordination, *Il sogno di Scipione* could not be given because of Schrattenbach's death on 16 December 1771. Revisions to the work in March or April 1772, however, and in particular the composition of an additional *licenza* as well as the alteration throughout the score of the name Sigismondo (= Schrattenbach) to Girolamo (= Colloredo), suggest that the work was to be revived. Nevertheless, concrete documentary evidence for a performance is lacking, and no festive theatrical presentation is known for the installation celebrations, possibly as a result of Colloredo's efforts to economize.

At least part of the argument against a production of *Il sogno di Scipione* rests on the tacit assumption that the work was staged. Generically, however, the composition is a serenata, as Lederer demonstrates elsewhere; and as Pierluigi Petrobelli later showed, such works were unstaged (see below, Literature). In contemporary writings, large-scale unstaged serenatas were sometimes referred to as cantatas. The travel journal of Archduke Maximilian, for example, gives the following description of a performance on 23 April 1775 of Mozart's serenata *Il rè pastore*: '. . . the evening was again concluded, as on the day before, with a *musique-concert* and supper at the palace, and as regards the concert, the difference was made for a change that, as the music for the past day had been written by the well-known Kapellmeister *Fischietti*, so the *musique* for the cantata sung this evening was by the no less famous *Mozart*' (*Dokumente* 137, *Documentary Biography* 152). Consequently the description of a 'cantata' performance during the installation festivities for Colloredo on 29 April 1772 may well refer to a work similar, if not identical, to *Il sogno di Scipione*.

Literature Josef-Horst Lederer, 'Zu Form, Terminologie und Inhalt von Mozarts theatralischen Serenaden', *MJb 1978–9*, 94–101; Pierluigi Petrobelli, '*Il rè pastore*: una serenata', *MJb 1984–5*, 109–14.

38   Louis De Visme to Charles Burney, Munich 30 November 1772

I passed lately some days at Salsburg and had a great deal of Musick at the Archbishop's, as he is a Dilettante & plays well on the Fiddle. He takes pains to reform his Band, which, like others, is too harsh. He has put Fischietti at the head of it, Composer of il Mercato di Malmantile & il Dottore &c. There is among them an excellent Composer for the Bassoon & other wind Musick. Secchi & Raineri (for so Reiner is to be called for the future by my direction) are to go there on purpose to play before him, that he may learn their stile & write for them. Young Mozhart is too of the band, you remember this prodigy in England. He composed an Opera at Milan for the marriage of the Archduke & he is now to do the same this Carnaval tho' but sixteen years of age. He is [a] great master of his Instrument; for I went to his Father's house to hear him. He and his Sister can play together on the same Harpsicord, but she is at her summit which is not marvellous, and if I may judge by the Musick I heard of his composition in the Orchestra, he is one further instance of early Fruit, which is more extraordinary than excellent.

Source   C. B. Oldman, 'Charles Burney and Louis De Visme', *The Music Review*, xxvii (1966), 95–6.
Commentary   Burney included much of this passage, with minor changes, in his *The Present State of Music in Germany, the Netherlands, and the United Provinces, or, the Journal of a Tour through these Countries, undertaken to collect Materials for a General History of Music* (London, 1773) (*Dokumente* 132, *Documentary Biography* 147). [*See plate 2*]

39   Folchino Schizzi, *Elogio Storico di Wolfgango Amadeo Mozart* (Cremona, 1817) [refers to December 1772]

Having just arrived at Milan in the autumn of 1770, Mozart composed the opera seria *Mitridate* for the Teatro Regio Ducal, which was performed twenty nights in succession, to universal applause. He was then engaged to compose another opera, *Lucio Silla*, which was performed at the Carnival in 1773, winning even greater success than the first, being performed twenty-six nights in succession, each time with the same enthusiastic approval. At that time, the famous Buonsolazzi was the prima donna at the Teatro Ducal. She did not know Mozart, and was surprised when she was told that he had been chosen to compose the opera in which she was to show her rare talent for singing; she considered him too young and incapable of accommodating her voice. So she took Mozart gently by the hand and asked him to tell her what his ideas were concerning the arias and scenes in which she was to sing, adding that she would take care of the composition herself. Mozart laughed to himself at her pride and answered that he would do as she wished. A few days later Mozart presented himself at the rehearsal and apologized to Buonsolazzi for having completely written the first aria. The singer took this composition in her hands, gave it a quick look, and, taken aback by its many beauties and the mastery with which it was composed, could not stop praising the boy, and reproaching herself. Mozart told her with a smile that if she did not like the aria, he could present her with a completely different one, composed especially for her; and that if the second was also not pleasing to her, he could submit a third. All of these arias, examined by Buonsolazzi and the experts, were masterpieces such as could hardly be imagined by even the most experienced composers. This was a great triumph for Mozart, but a private one: it was the public that crowned his success. A famous Maestro and harpsichord player could not be persuaded that Mozart was as celebrated for improvisation as was said. He challenged him to a public contest and the two professors went to the Chiesa della Passione where there were two organs. Wolfgango Amedeo took the themes which the other professor played on the first organ and improvised on the second in a way that can only be described as divine.

Source   *US-NYp* *MEC (Mozart), pp.25–8.
Commentary   Buonsolazzi was the singer Anna de Amicis, who sang the role of Giunia in *Lucio Silla*, which was first given at the Teatro Regio Ducal in Milan on 26 December 1772. Giunia's arias include 'Dalla sponda tenebrosa', 'Vanne t'affreta . . . Ah, se il crudel periglio', 'In un istante oh come . . . Parto, m'affretto', and 'Sposo . . . mia vita . . . Frà i pensier più funesti'. Mozart's participation at this time in an organ improvisation contest is not recorded in the family letters or other documents.

40   *Notizie del Mondo*, Florence 5 January 1773

Milan 30 December. On Saturday evening the *dramma in musica*, *Lucio Silla*, was given at the Regio Ducal Teatro here, in which Rauzzini and De Amicis distinguished themselves, just as the ballets won the greatest applause for Signor Picq.

Source   *US-NYpl* BAA, p.15.
Commentary   *Lucio Silla* was given for the first time on 26 December at the Teatro Regio Ducal in Milan. The soprano Venanzio Rauzzini (1746–1810) sang the role of Cecilio; Mozart later composed the motet *Exsultate, jubilate* K165/158*a* for him. Anna de Amicis sang the role of Giunia. Carlo de Picq (1749–1806) danced in the ballet; Picq had known the Mozarts at least since 1771 in Milan, when he performed at the wedding festivities of Archduke Ferdinand of Austria and Princess Maria Beatrice Ricciarda d'Este of Modena, for which Mozart composed the serenata *Ascanio in Alba*.

41 Beda Hübner, *Umständliche Geschichte, des allerersten feyerlichst gehaltenen Jahrhunderts, zu Maria Plain nächst Salzburg . . . Welche dabey vom 13ten. bis auf dem 21sten. August 1774. gehalten worden,* Salzburg 1774

The conclusion of the very profitable eulogy was followed immediately by the customary High Mass, celebrated with the obliging permission of our most gracious Prince and Archbishop by His Reverence and Grace, the gracious, retired Herr Prelate of Ettall, Benediktus. His Grace, the retired Herr Prelate, has been at the ancient monastery of St Peter in Salzburg for more than fourteen years, where, after his resignation, he decided to live out his remaining years. Today there was particularly beautiful and agreeable music at the High Mass at Maria Plain; primarily because it was produced almost exclusively by the princely court musicians, and especially by the older and younger, both famous, Motzarts. The young Herr Motzart played an organ and a violin concerto, to everyone's amazement and astonishment. And in general there was exceedingly exquisite music at today's High Mass.

Source Ernst Hintermaier, 'Die Familie Mozart und Maria Plain', *Österreichische Musikzeitschrift,* xxix (1974), 354.
Commentary Hübner's manuscript was published in an abbreviated version, without reference to the Mozarts, in 1775. The wording of the original ('der iunge Herr Motzart ein Orgel, und ein Violinkonzert . . . gemacht') leaves open the possibility that Mozart composed the works performed on this occasion. However, no organ concerto by him is known – although the reference here may be to a church sonata – and among the violin concertos, only K207 had been composed by this time; a number of earlier cassations and serenades, however, including K63, 185/167a, and especially K203/189b, composed in August 1774, also include concerto movements for violin. According to Hintermaier, Mozart's Mass K194/186h is also likely to have been performed on this occasion.

42 *Specification was zu der Churfürst. Hof Capellen von Ersten Jenner biß letzten Mart ao 775 copiert worden,* Munich 1775

Offertory by Sig. Mozart new   35 [sheets] 4 fl. 22xr. 2Pf.

Source Robert Münster, 'Mozarts Kirchenmusik in München im 18. und beginnenden 19. Jahrhundert: Stiftskirche zu Unserer Lieben Frau—Augustinerkloster—Kurfürstliche und Königliche Hofkapelle', in *Festschrift Erich Valentin zum 70. Geburtstag,* ed. Günther Weiß (Regensburg, 1976), 148.
Commentary Probably the reference is to K222/205a, written for Elector Max III Joseph, about February or March 1775.

43 *Journal de Paris,* Paris 21 April 1778

Today, Concert Spirituel at the Château des Tuileries. It will begin with a new symphony by Signor Sterkel. – Madame Hizelberg will sing an Italian air. – M. Schick will perform, for the first time, a violin concerto. – M. Raaff will sing an Italian air by Bach. – A new oratorio by M. Cambini will be performed, sung by Mlle. Duchateau and MM. Guichard and le Gros. – M. Ramm will perform an oboe concerto. – M. Savoy will sing an Italian air by Signor Mezart. – The concert will conclude with a concerto for hunting horn performed by M. Punto.

Source Rudolph Angermüller, *W. A. Mozarts musikalische Umwelt in Paris (1778): ein Dokumentation* (Munich and Salzburg, 1983), 53.

Commentary 'Mezart' may be a corruption of Mozart or another similar name. The tenor Gaspero Savoi (*fl* 1758–92) was active in London from 1766. Between 15 August 1777 and 24 April 1778 he made 14 appearances at the Concert Spirituel, singing works by Sacchini, J. C. Bach, Majo, Alessandri and Pergolesi. According to Angermüller (p.lxvii), the aria may have been 'Se al labbro mio non credi/Il cor dolente' K295.

Literature Constant Pierre, *Histoire du Concert Spirituel 1725–1790* (Paris, 1975), 307–9.

44 *Courier de l'Europe*, London 23 June 1778

Paris, from 15 to 18 June. Last Thursday the Bouffons Italiens opened at the Opéra with *La Finte Gemelle* or *Les Jumelles supposées*, a work in two acts, with music by M. Piccini. . . . This piece was followed by a ballet by M. Noverre entitled *Les petits riens*, made up of several anacreontic scenes, which could not have been more agreeable. We expect to have an opportunity to return to all these subjects.

Source Rudolph Angermüller, *W. A. Mozarts musikalische Umwelt in Paris (1778): ein Dokumentation* (Munich and Salzburg, 1983), 131.

Commentary The *Courier de l'Europe* (earlier, *Courier Politique et Littéraire or, French Evening Post*) was published in London on Tuesdays and Fridays. Noverre's ballet *Les petits riens*, with music by Mozart, was first performed on 11 June.

45 Leopold Mozart's petition to Archbishop Colloredo, Salzburg [mid-August 1778]

I humbly prostrate myself at Your Serene Highness's feet. Because the Kapellmeister has died, and this Lolli received only the salary of a deputy Kapellmeister, [and because] Your Serene Highness knows that I have already served the Archdiocese for 38 years, since 1763 as deputy Kapellmeister, and that during the last 15 years I have uncomplainingly carried out, and continue to carry out, virtually all my duties, I therefore recommend myself to Your Serene Highness, my gracious Prince and Lord's most humble and obedient servant, Leopold Mozart.

[Decree of the Archbishop, 30 August 1778] We have accordingly granted the supplicant one hundred gulden annually in addition to his current salary with the stipulation that, until the arrival of my new Kapellmeister, he appear diligently at the court and cathedral music, and additionally instruct others with regard to their obligations, and industriously supervise the instructors and students at the Kapellhaus.

Source *Briefe* ii.462 and v.554; Ernst Hintermaier, *Die Salzburger Hofkapelle von 1700 bis 1806: Organisation und Personal* (diss. U. of Salzburg, 1972), 293.

Commentary Leopold Mozart's petition to succeed the Kapellmeister Giuseppe Lolli, who was buried on 11 August, was refused. Lolli's successor, Luigi Gatti (1740–1817), did not arrive in Salzburg until 1782. The Mozarts had known Gatti at least since their visit to Mantua in 1770, as a letter of 11 June 1778 from Leopold to Mozart, then in Paris, shows: 'The Archbishop has been sending off letters to all the towns in Italy but he cannot find a Kapellmeister. He has written to Vienna and Prague and Königgrätz, and cannot get a decent organist and keyboard player. An agreement with Bertoni about the post of Kapellmeister cannot be made – and – you will laugh! *Luigi Gatti of Mantua* (you will remember him, for he copied out your mass there), whom the Archbishop of Olmütz had recommended as an eminent keyboard player, will not leave Mantua for more than two or three months' (*Briefe* ii.373, *Letters* 547–8). [*See plate 3*]

46 Leopold Mozart to an unidentified Salzburg Privy Councillor, 7 September 1778

[7 September 1778]
[extract] The unexpected, very sad death of my late wife in Paris carries with it the customary high official taxes. Since, however, my late wife, when we were married, had not the least property and because of modest means did not expect to acquire any in the future, and because she took her clothes and her few other things with her, and accordingly has no estate: I humbly ask your Most Worthy, High-born Count and Grace graciously to set aside the tax and, further, because there is not the least estate, to exempt me from the otherwise attendant expenses.

Source Present location unknown. Auctioned at Sotheby's (London) on 22 November 1989, lot 139.

Commentary Anna Maria Mozart had died in Paris on 3 July 1778.

47 Mozart's dedication of the sonatas K301–6, 1778

To Her Serene Electoral Highness
Madame the Electoress Palatinate

Madame

The kindness with which your Serene Electoral Highness has deigned to receive my small talents justifies the liberty I dare to take in publishing a work under Your august protection. The exalted reputation which the chapel and school of Mannheim deservedly enjoys throughout Europe, both for the celebrity of its theatre and its large number of excellent professors [of music], would make timid any music master who would lay his productions at the feet of your Most Serene Electoral Highness. But if the brilliance of so many of the masterpieces to come out of this famous school is daunting, the kindness which characterizes its august founders reassures and inspires a boundless trust in the indulgence of your Most Serene Highness of which I have, at this moment, such great need.

I am with the most profound respect
Madame,
Your Serene Electoral Highness's

very humble and
very obedient servant
Wolfgang Amado Mozart

Source Gertraut Haberkamp, 'Ein bisher unbekannte Widmung Mozarts an die Kurfürstin Maria Elisabeth von Bayern zur Erstausgabe der Sonaten für Klavier und Violine KV 301–306', *Musik in Bayern*, xviii–xix (1979), 7 and 11; idem, *Die Erstdrucke der Werke von Wolfgang Amadeus Mozart* (Tutzing, 1986), ii.78.

Commentary Mozart's sonatas were published by Sieber and first advertised in the *Journal de Paris* on 26 November 1778, after he had already left Paris. According to a letter of 26 October, written at Strasbourg, Mozart had also not corrected proofs for the sonatas: 'I hope that you received my last letter of 15 October from Strassburg. I do not want to run down M. Grimm any more; but I must say that it is entirely due to his stupidity in hurrying up my departure that my sonatas have not yet been engraved, or have not appeared – or, at any rate, that I have not yet received them. And when I do get them, I shall probably find them full of mistakes. If I had only stayed three more days in Paris I could have corrected them myself and brought them with me!' (*Briefe* ii.503, *Letters* 628). The dedication to Elisabeth Maria Aloysia Auguste (1721–94), wife of Carl Theodor, Elector of the Pfalz and Bavaria, may have been composed by Baron Friedrich Melchior von Grimm, who wrote the dedication of Mozart's sonatas K8 and 9 and, presumably, K6 and 7 as well (*Dokumente* 30 and 33, *Documentary Biography* 29 and 31–2).

48 From the brotherhood book of the Holy Cross Confraternity, Salzburg 1780

1780 *Leopold Mozart* mpia   Deputy Kapellmeister. *Father*
Wolfgang Amade Mozart. – *Son.*

Source *A-Sca* Hs.2468 lat. et germ., f.57r. Facsimile in Walter Hummel, 'Das Bruderschaftsbüchl der hl. Kreuz-Bruderschaft an der Bürgerspitalskirche in Salzburg', *Jahresschrift des Salzburger Museum Carolino-Augusteum*, v. (1960), 206.

Commentary The Holy Cross Confraternity was founded in 1683, possibly in connection with the construction of a new rood altar in the Bürgerspitalskirche, now the Stadtpfarrkirche zum hl. Blasius, Salzburg. Many of Salzburg's most important 18th-century musicians were members.

49 From Michael Haydn's appointment as court and cathedral organist and keyboard instructor at the Kapellhaus, Salzburg 30 May 1782

Because, on the one hand, the health of our Konzertmeister Johann Michael Heyden no longer permits him to render service as a violinist, and because, on the other, he would no longer have anything to do, we accordingly appoint him as our Court and Cathedral organist, in the same fashion as young Mozart was obligated, with the additional stipulation that he show more diligence, instruct the chapel boys, and compose more often for our Cathedral and chamber music, and, in such cases, himself direct in the Cathedral on every occasion.

Source Gerhard Croll and Kurt Vössing, *Johann Michael Haydn: sein Leben— sein Schafen—seine Zeit* (Vienna, 1987), 66–7 (with facs.); Gerhard Croll, 'Symposion I. Johann Michael Haydn: Vorbemerkung', *MJb 1987–8*, 29; Heinz Schuler, 'Salzburger Kapellhauslehrer zur Mozartzeit', *Acta Mozartiana*, xxxv (1988), 31.
Commentary Because Michael Haydn had not previously held an appointment as instructor at the Kapellhaus, the stipulations to his appointment may represent an indirect criticism of Mozart's performance at the Salzburg court.

50 *Staats- und gelehrte Zeitung des hamburgischen unpartheyischen Correspondenten*, Hamburg 19 July 1782

Vienna, 10 July. . . . The opera *Die Entführung aus dem Serail* will be performed soon at the Imperial Royal National Theatre; the new music by the famous Kapellmeister Mozart is said to be a masterpiece of its art.

Source *US-PRu* 0902.873 (1782) [unpaginated].
Commentary *Die Entführung aus dem Serail* was first given on 16 July. *See* Document 51.

51 *Staats- und gelehrte Zeitung des hamburgischen unpartheyischen Correspondenten*, Hamburg 26 July 1782

Letter from Vienna, 17 July. . . . Yesterday the new German opera, *Die Entführung aus dem Serail*, was performed to universal applause. The music by the famous composer Mozart is extraordinarily agreeable and artful.

Source *US-PRu* 0902.873 (1782) [unpaginated].

52 *Biographische Skizze von Michael Haydn: von des verklärten Tonkünstlers Freunden entworfen, und zum Beten seiner Wittwe herausgegeben* (Salzburg, 1808) [refers to 1783]

Michael Haydn was supposed, on high orders, to write duets for violin and viola. However, he could not supply them by the appointed time because he had become seriously ill, and was incapacitated for longer than was anticipated. The patron was not prepared to offer a *quid pro quo*: perhaps he was too little, or even falsely, informed of Haydn's circumstances. Mozart, who visited him daily, heard of this, sat down, and wrote for his afflicted friend with such indefatigable industry that the duets were finished in a few days, and given out under Michael Haydn's name. In later times we have often delighted ourselves with these marvellous works of charity, the original of which our master preserved as a sacred relic . . .

Source *US-AA* Rare ML 410 H43 S34, pp.38–9. Editions: Georg Nikolaus Nissen, *Biographie W. A. Mozarts nach Originalbriefen* (Leipzig, 1828), 476–7 (abridged and altered); *NMA* VIII:21, p.vii (following Nissen); Gerhard Croll and Kurt Vössing, *Johann Michael Haydn: sein Leben—sein Schafen—seine Zeit* (Vienna, 1987), 83 (following Nissen); H. C. Robbins Landon, *Mozart: the Golden Years* (London and New York, 1989), 90 (translation). Another version of this anecdote appeared in the *Intelligenzblatt von Salzburg* for 13 May 1809; see Rudolph Angermüller, 'M. Haydiniana und Mozartiana: ein erster Bericht', *Mitteilungen der Internationalen Stiftung Mozarteum*, xxix (1981), 63.

Commentary The *Biographische Skizze von Michael Haydn* is usually attributed to the flautist Georg Schinn (1768–1833) and the violinist Joseph Otter (*c*1760–1836), both students of Michael Haydn. However, it may also have been based, at least in part, on material provided by Haydn's friend P. Werigand Rettensteiner (1751–1822), whose manuscript of the biography survives in the library of the Mozarteum, Salzburg. The two duets composed by Mozart are said to be K423 and 424, and if the anecdote is correct they must have been written in Salzburg during Mozart's visit there in the summer and early autumn of 1783. The *NMA* notes that the keys of Mozart's duets, G major and B♭ major, do not duplicate those of four similar compositions attributed to Michael Haydn (consequently fitting well in a cycle of six such works), and that Mozart's autographs are neither signed nor dated, suggesting that he attempted to conceal his authorship of them, as well as their time and place of composition. That they were completed in 1783, possibly in Salzburg, is apparently confirmed by letters of 6 and 24 December 1783 in which Mozart, then in Vienna, asked his father to send his 'Violin Duetten' (letter of 6 December; 'Duetten' in the letter of 24 December). Wolfgang Plath argues that the anecdote would be more plausible if the duets had circulated under Michael Haydn's name, which appears not to be the case ('Zur Echtheitsfrage bei Mozart', *MJb 1971–2*, 34). In this regard, a review in the *Augsburger musikalischer Merkur auf das Jahr 1795* (pp.24–6), of an edition of *six* sonatas for violin and viola attributed to Michael Haydn, is, of interest:

> **Michael Haydn's six sonatas for violin and viola**. . . . Every movement of the third **Sonata** is entirely filled with **Mozart's** spirit. Ah, the beautiful melodies, the rich harmony, the succession of the most exquisite ideas, the

naive simplicity, and their rich nobility, how they delight the calmly hovering heart with Elysian bliss! Mozart himself, our **Haydn's** intimate friend and sincere admirer, never conceived of a more beautiful work. . . . This third sonata has the character of the beautiful, brave spirit of a cheerful, budding youth, who gradually feels the power of the spirit preparing for manhood. But everything is coloured with mezzotints, for the greater part of active nature still sleeps in him, and the tenderness of the gentle child still has the upper hand over the frugal, spluttering spirits. The efforts of this insurgence are blended with the elegant sheaves of this fragile mood, and keep the listener in a pleasant uncertainty concerning the success of this adolescent struggle, which begins with an **Allegro**, continues with a touching **Adagio**, and ends with the daintiest **Rondo** imaginable. Who would not guess that the entire action of this scene, written entirely in **Mozart's** spirit, would resolve itself to the advantage of tenderness? Ah, the heavenly Rondo, where the transition back to the first sentiment has a true superabundance of beauty; where the boundlessly delighted spirit swims in the most sensuous rapture, and continues to feel the full beauty of harmony long after this has ceased to whisper its incomparable tones sighing to the ear!

We will save the review of **Mich. Haydn's** last three sonatas to a later issue, where, at the same time, we will advertise their subscription price. . . . Post-paid letters subscribing to these three sonatas, which will appear very soon, are being accepted by the **Gombart** music shop in Augsburg.

The sonata described here corresponds in its number and order of movements, as well as its tempo indications, to both Michael Haydn's duet P127 and Mozart's K423. In the absence of a copy of the print, however, the identity of the work remains uncertain. Possibly the edition never appeared. No copy survives, and it is not listed in Gombart's *Catalogue des Ouvrages de Musique mises au Jour par Gombart & Compe., Editeurs & Graveurs de Musique à Augsburg*, which includes an edition of Beethoven's sonatas op.49 and therefore dates from 1805 or later (copy in *D-Asa* Conzessionsakt Gitter Andreas P I G 350). According to a manuscript copy of Haydn's duos (in *YU-Zha* Udina-Algarotti Hs. XXVII.H) the dedicatee was Archbishop Colloredo. There is no evidence that Michael Haydn once owned Mozart's autographs.

Literature Ernst Hintermaier, 'Materialien zur Musik und Musikpflege im Benediktinerstift Michaelbeuern im 17., 18. und 19. Jh.', in *Benediktinerabtei Michaelbeuern: eine Dokumentation anläßlich der Eröffnung und Weihe der neu adaptierten Räume für Internat, Schule und Bildungsarbeit* (Salzburg, 1985), 243.

53 *Das Wienerblättchen*, Vienna 30 September 1783

Concertos by Mozart.
Available from Johann Traeg at the Essigmacher House, Nr. 654, first floor: the 3 latest keyboard concertos by A. W. Mozart, 10 florins. Also new quartets, trios, symphonies and Italian arias by the most famous masters.

Source *A-Wsl* 9316 (1783), p.32. Discovered by Dexter Edge.
Commentary The concertos are probably K413/387a, 414/385p and 415/387b, which Mozart had attempted to sell by subscription in January 1783 (*Dokumente* 187–8, *Documentary Biography* 212). Traeg advertised the same works in the

Wiener Zeitung for 27 September (*Dokumente* 194, *Documentary Biography* 218–19). Whether Mozart was Traeg's source for the concertos is uncertain; when the advertisement first appeared, Mozart was in Salzburg.

54   *Das Wienerblättchen*, Vienna 4 November 1783

Music. The following arias, arranged for keyboard, are available from Lorenz Lausch, music dealer in the Kärntnerstrasse:

Dorina mia Carina, quartetto; Che vi pare Dorina bella, terzetto
Un Giardinier par mio; Compatite miei signori   ·
Come un Agnello; all from the opera: Fra due litiganti il terzo gode, by Herr Sarti.
Dee [*sic*] per piacere la Donna, from la Scuola de' Gelosi, by the same master.
Saper bramante bella; Lode al Cie; both from the Barbier v. Seviglien by Herr Paisello.
E Felice chi in Amore, terzetto from le Gelosie villane by Herr Sarti.
Also to be had of the same are the three new keyboard concertos by Mozart.

Source   *A-Wsl* 9316 (1783), p.106. Discovered by Dexter Edge.
Commentary   The concertos K413/387*a*, 414/385*p* and 415/387*b* were first advertised by Johann Traeg in the *Wiener Zeitung* for 27 September 1783 (*see* Document 53). Possibly Lausch's manuscripts were based on exemplars obtained from Traeg: Mozart had still not returned from Salzburg to Vienna; at the end of October and the beginning of November he was in Linz. Lausch ran a similar advertisement in the *Wienerblättchen* for 5 December 1783, including many of the same numbers by Paisiello and Sarti, as well as selections from Salieri's *La scuola de' gelosi* and Sarti's *Le gelosie villane*. The advertisement of the Mozart concertos, however, was not repeated.

55   From Johann Thomas von Trattner's *Haus-Zins-Buch des ehehinnigen Freysinger- nun aber von Trattnerschen Freyhofes in Wien am Graben von Georgii 1777 bis [1861]*, Vienna 1784

Mozart Wolfgang Amadeus, Kapellmeister to the prince of Salzburg, from Salzburg. He has to pay for the half-year from St. George's to Michaelmass 784 . . . . 75 fl.
Lighting . . . . 1 fl.
1784 Remainder for the following half year . . . . 10 fl.
   24 February *Drangeld* . . . . 2 fl.
   18 June Balance of the half-yearly rent from
      St. George's to Michaelmass 784 . . . . 63 fl.
   Lighting . . . . 1 fl.

Note: On 23 June 1784 this party gave legal notice of removal at Michaelmass 784.

In future he will lodge at Nr.816, at the Camesina House in the city, in the Grosse Schulerstrasse.

Source Hermine Cloeter, *Johann Thomas Trattner: ein Großunternehmer im Theresianischen Wien* (Graz and Cologne, 1952), 99. Cited but not reproduced in *Dokumente* 197, *Documentary Biography* 222.
Commentary On 29 September, Mozart moved to no.846 (not 816) in the Grosse Schulerstrasse.

56 *Wiener Zeitung*, Vienna 27 October 1784

The following new music . . . is available from Johann Traeg at the Pilate House, 1st floor: . . . 1 double concerto by Mozart. Keyboard concertos by Haydn, Mozart, Bach, Zimmermann, etc. . . . Symphonies by Mozart, Zimmermann, Haydn. . . . Keyboard variations by Mozart, Bach, Sarti, Haydn, Richter.

Source Alexander Weinmann, *Die Anzeigen des Kopiaturbetriebes Johann Traeg in der Wiener Zeitung zwischen 1782 und 1805* (Vienna, 1981), 18; *Dokumente* 203, *Documentary Biography* 229 (incomplete).
Commentary Traeg's advertisement of symphonies and keyboard variations is lacking in *Dokumente*. The works cannot be identified with certainty.

57 *Wiener Kronik*, Vienna [November 1784]

On the 5th of this month at the Kärntnertor Theatre, Herr Schikaneder and Kumpf surprised lovers of German operetta in a pleasant way with *Die Entführung aus dem Serail*. . . . Herr Mozart, who composed the music, wrote a concert aria in the second act for Konstanze, to let the virtuosi in the orchestra of the National Theatre show off; however, because these artists are now with the orchestra in Pressburg, Herr Franz Täuber composed another [aria] in its place which, although it does not display the mastery of our Mozart, is nevertheless praiseworthy. In the first scene, Mademoiselle Kaiser seemed to be nervous, which befalls almost every player appearing for the first time on a new stage. However, she soon recovered, compensating us doubly. Herr Schikaneder and Kumpf perform every Friday and Saturday.

Source *A-Wsl* A 11066, pp. 188–9.
Commentary Konstanze's aria was 'Martern aller Arten'. The composer of the unidentified substitute aria was Franz Teyber (1758–1810), who was highly thought of by Leopold Mozart (*Briefe* iii.358, not in *Letters*). Teyber's association with Schikaneder was previously thought to date from 1785 or 1786. Margarethe Kaiser (birth and death dates unknown) had previously been active at Munich from 1776 to 1784 (1783 according to Ernst Ludwig Gerber, *Historisch-biographisches Lexicon der Tonkünstler*, Leipzig, 1790–2, i, col.706). The

success of Schikaneder's venture was reported in the *Wiener Zeitung* for 22 December (reprinted in the *Staats- und gelehrte Zeitung des hamburgischen unpartheyischen Correspondenten* for 31 December 1784 [unpaginated]): 'The company of German players directed by Herr Schikaneder and Kumpf, which has entertained us at the Kärntnertor Theatre with German operas and plays since the beginning of last month, distinguishes itself more every day. Among private undertakings, it is the best that we have seen for several years at the Kärntnertor Theatre. . . . On Saturday this company gave Herr Haydn's great opera *La fedeltà premiata*. The house was so full at 6 o'clock that, the large capacity of the theatre notwithstanding, more than 600 people had to be turned away. – The most incontrovertible evidence of the excellence and rank with which this company distinguishes itself is that His Majesty, the Emperor himself, who has already often graced the performances with his presence, on this occasion, too, was present with the entire court.'

Literature Cliff Eisen, 'Contributions to a New Mozart Documentary Biography', *Journal of the American Musicological Society*, xxxix (1986), 626–8; H. C. Robbins Landon, *Haydn: Chronicle and Works*, ii: *Haydn at Esterháza 1766–1790* (Bloomington, Indiana, and London, 1978), 499.

58 Minutes of the meeting of the Vienna Tonkünstlersozietät, 11 February 1785

[5.] *Referenda*. . . . On 3 January it was resolved to take up again the *arrangements for the* Lent *academy*.

Conclusa. . . . The concert shall begin with a new symphony in D minor by Joseph Haydn, followed by the same composer's two new choruses with a preceding aria [sung] by Mademoiselle Cavalieri. After this, an aria [sung] by Signore Mandini, then another symphony by Joseph Haydn. Then a concerto, which Messrs. Borra and Schenker are invited [to perform]. Then the Psalm by Herr Mozart and to conclude a[nother] symphony by Joseph Haydn.

First rehearsal on 10 March in the *Redoutenzimmer* at 9 o'clock in the morning.

Final rehearsal on 12 March in the theatre at 9 o'clock in the morning.

Performances on 13 and 15 March.

Admission prices as usual. Free boxes as necessary.

[7.] *Wolfgang Amadeus Mozart* requests admission to the Society; at the time, however, he cannot produce his birth certificate, which he has promised to do later. The matter is suspended, in part for lack of the birth certificate, and, further, until the Society's [internal] disputes are resolved.

Source *NMA* I:4/iii, ed. Monika Holl (Kassel, 1987), p.xi (incomplete). Corrected text provided by Dexter Edge.

Commentary Mozart did not complete the commissioned Psalm; in its stead he offered the Tonkünstlersozietät his *Davidde penitente* K469 (*see* Document 60). Also, he never produced his birth certificate; consequently he never became a member of the society. Stefano Mandini was the first Count Almaviva in *Le* *nozze di Figaro.* According to Holl, the violinist Johann Borra, from Turin, gave an academy in Vienna on 14 February 1785; the otherwise unidentified Schenker may have been a harpist in the service of Prince Conti at Paris.

59 *Wiener Zeitung*, Vienna 16 February 1785

Music. Johann Traeg, at the Pilate House, first floor, has the honour to announce to music lovers the following new, handwritten music: . . . 3 symphonies by W. A. Mozart. . . . Keyboard variations by W. A. Mozart.

Source Alexander Weinmann, *Die Anzeigen des Kopiaturbetriebes Johann Traeg in der Wiener Zeitung zwischen 1782 und 1805* (Vienna, 1981), 19; *Dokumente* 210, *Documentary Biography* 237 (incomplete).
Commentary Traeg's advertisement of the keyboard variations is lacking in *Dokumente*. The three symphonies probably included arrangements of the serenades K203/189*b* and 320, and a further symphony in D major; see Neal Zaslaw and Cliff Eisen, 'Signor Mozart's Symphony in A-Minor, K.Anhang 220 = 16a', *The Journal of Musicology*, iv (1985–6), 196–8. The variations cannot be identified with certainty.

60 Minutes of the meeting of the Vienna Tonkünstlersozietät, 21 February 1785

Referenda. . . . Because Herr Mozart has not been able to complete the promised Psalm, he offers instead another Psalm, completely new to Vienna, which, however, is only half as long. Accordingly, another *plan of the Academy* should be established.
Conclusa. . . . The opening will be Herr Joseph Haydn's symphony in D minor, then Sacchini's chorus in E.
1ˢᵗ day: Aria sung by Signor Mandini.
2ⁿᵈ day: Aria sung by Madame Le Brun.
Symphony by Herr Jos: Haydn. Aria and chorus by the same, sung by Mademoiselle Cavalieri.

Concertos
1ˢᵗ day: Monsieur le Brun.
2ⁿᵈ day: Monsieur Schenker.
Then the Psalm by Herr Mozart. . . .

Director ['Salieri' erased and replaced by] Herr Mozart.
Violin director Herr Anton Hofmann
Keyboard Herr Umlauf

Source *NMA* I:4/iii, ed. Monika Holl (Kassel, 1987), p.xi.
Commentary *Davidde penitente* was put together from the unfinished C minor mass K427/417*a*, with two new arias. The soloists included Catarina Cavalieri, the first Constanze in *Die Entführung aus dem Serail*; Elisabeth Distler, at whose

academy on 5 February 1785 Mozart performed the D minor Piano Concerto K466; and the tenor Josef Valentin Adamberger, the first Belmonte. Other works on the programme included Haydn's D minor symphony H I:80 and probably an aria and chorus from his *Il ritorno di Tobia*. The oboist Ludwig August Lebrun and his wife, the singer Franziska Dorothea, gave academies at the Burgtheater on 23 and 28 February 1785; Mozart performed at one, if not both, of these concerts. Ignaz Umlauf (1746–96) was active at the German Nationaltheater in Vienna from 1778 and, after its dissolution in February 1783, at the Italian theatre, where he worked as Salieri's assistant; Anton Hofmann, violinist at the Schottenkirche and at St Peter's, was later a violinist in the Hofkapelle.

Literature   H. C. Robbins Landon, *Mozart: the Golden Years* (London and New York, 1989), 127–8.

61   *Brünner Zeitung*, 2 July 1785

Plan for a grand music collection from Vienna available on subscription. . . . I have now decided to lay before lovers of music a plan, according to which they can purchase an entire library of original music over the course of several years. . . . To this end I have already made agreements with our best local composers, Haydn, Mozart, Wanhall, Albrechtsberger, Pleyel, Mitscha, v. Ordonnez &c, as well as foreign masters, together with my own works, to receive new products from month to month.

Franz Anton Hoffmeister

Music Kapellmeister and publisher, living on the old Wiede across from the Klagbaum in the Baron Fischer House nr.3

Source   *A-Wsl* A 92302 (nr.53, Beilage), pp.285–7.

Commentary   In Vienna, this advertisement first appeared on 6 August. Hoffmeister's subscription series included Mozart's sonatas for piano K330, 331 and 533; the rondos K485 and 511; the four-hand works K426, 501 and 521; the sonatas for violin and piano K481 and 526; the piano trio K496; the piano quartet K478; the string quartet K499; and the fugue K546. According to Nissen, Hoffmeister cancelled a contract for three piano quartets sometime after the publication of K478 in December 1785: 'Mozart's first piano quartet, *in G minor*, was thought so little of at first that the publisher Hoffmeister gave the master the advance portion of the honorarium on the condition that he not compose the two other agreed-upon quartets and that Hoffmeister should be released from his contract' (*Biographie W. A. Mozarts*, Leipzig, 1828, 633). Maynard Solomon doubts the truth of this anecdote, noting that Hoffmeister continued to publish works by Mozart. Other evidence, however, suggests Hoffmeister may have cancelled part of his contract with Mozart after the completion of the second piano quartet, K493, on 3 June 1786. Artaria's edition of the work, published in July 1787, includes viola, cello and piano parts already engraved by Hoffmeister.

Hoffmeister's subscription series, and consequently many of Mozart's works, were widely disseminated throughout Europe. A similar announcement published in the *Staats- und gelehrte Zeitung des hamburgischen unpartheyischen Correspondenten* for 22 July 1785 [unpaginated], lists his agents:

Augsburg, Kletts Wittwe und Frank. Anspach, Haueisen. Amsterdam, Hummel. Bern, Haller. Braunschweig, Maysenbaus Buchhandlung. Breslau, Korn der ältere. Brünn, Wild, Geigen und Lautenm. Brüssel, J. van den Berghen. Cassel, Cramer. Cölln, Metternich. Coburg, Abl. Copenhagen, Prost. Constanz, Wagner. Dessau, Buchhandlung der Gelehrten. Dresden, Walter Gebr. Edenburg, Thurnernistr. Gaßner. Erlang, Walther. Frankfurt, Eßlingenr. Freyburg, Wagner. Gera, Beckmann. Gotha, Ettinger. Göttingen, Dietrich. Graz, Müller bey Allerh. Halle, Hemerde. Hamburg, Bohn. Hannover, Hellwing Gebr. Heidelberg, Gebr. Pfähler. Herrmanstadt, Hochmeister, Buchdr. Kaschau, Weingand und Köpf. Klagenfurt, Walliser. Königraz, Knays, Buchbinder. Königsberg, Dengel. Laybach, Promberger, Buchhändler. Leiden, Luchtmanns. Leipzig, Kummer. Lemberg, C. G. Pfaff. Linz, Wappler. Lübeck, Donatius. Lüttich, Bassonpierre. Magdeburg, Scheidhauer. Maynz, Schott. Mastheim, Schwan. München, Strobel. Münster, Perrennon. Nürnberg, Felseckers Söhne. Passau, Rothwinkler. Pest und Osen, Weingand und Köpf. Petersburg, Logan. Prag, Gerle. Preßburg, Löwe. Regenspurg, Küster Schmid. Riga, Hartknoch. Salzburg, Meyer. Stuttgard, Metzler. Strasburg, akademische Handlung. Speyr, Boßler. Stockholm, Suederus, Troppau, Mayer, Buchhändler. Tübingen, Heerbrand. Ulm, Stettin. Warschau, Gröll. Weymar, Hoffmann. Wien, Rudolph Gräffer. Wienerisch Neustadt, Thurnermeister Trapp. Würzburg, Stahel. Winterthur, Steiner und Comp. Zürich, Caspar Füesli.

Literature Alexander Weinmann, *Die Wiener Verlagswerke von Franz Anton Hoffmeister* (Vienna, 1964), esp. 27, 31–2, 46, 48, 62, 68–9, 82, 84, 86–7 and 91; Maynard Solomon, review of Wolfgang Hildesheimer, *Mozart* (New York, 1982), in *The Musical Quarterly*, lxix (1983), 270; Gertraut Haberkamp, *Die Erstdrucke der Werke von Wolfgang Amadeus Mozart* (Tutzing, 1986), i, 241, 263 and 433.

62 From the papers of John Pettinger, Vienna summer 1785

It was a hot day but Mozart was quite formally dressed. He had been hard at work on some compositions for string quartet but seemed not at all put out at being interrupted. Indeed, he continued to put down occasional notes during our conversation. I was surprised, when he rose to find him of not more than about five feet and four inches in height and of very slight build. His hand was cold but his grip was firm. His face was not particularly striking, rather melancholy until he spoke, when his expression became animated and amused and his eyes, which constantly darted from Klein to myself, were full of kind concern in our doings about which he enquired with obvious interest. He had not been to London since a boy but seemed to remember it well and spoke of his old friend Bach, who had died some three years past, and was greatly interested in my dealings with him. I think he would have chatted of this and that for many hours but as we had later appointments that day, Klein turned our talk to the business in hand.

Source Peter Gammond, *One Man's Music* (London, 1971), 111.

Commentary John Pettinger (1759–1831), an employee of several London music publishers, made numerous trips to the continent between 1783 and 1826. The reference to 'string quartets' is unclear. The last of the six quartets dedicated to Haydn (K465) was completed in January, and it is unlikely that K499, finished in August 1786, was begun this early. Possibly Mozart was reading proofs of the 'Haydn' quartets, which were published by Artaria in September; or perhaps the reference is to the piano quartet K478, completed in October. Klein remains unidentified, although Gammond describes him as a 'Professor' and states that he was Pettinger's translator.

63 Texts of two Masonic songs by Mozart performed on 12 August 1785

For the opening of the Master Lodge.
Only a Mason can look calmly upon the work of Death, the dread of decay; he is not terrified by the putrefaction;
In the midst of decay he sees burning the flame of a better life, and hopes for the light of Truth.

*

Shrouded in dark shadows, filled with pain and purity of mind, we surround your holy grave;
O A . . . m! Great Master, send one of your wise Spirits into this Brotherhood.

*

So that they may fully recognize your Work, and not just call themselves your pupils, and be *Gabaon's* through deeds.
How blessed are those who compare to you in Spirit and Strength, and win the infinitely rich reward of your great works.

*

With this hope we return to our work, true Brothers! The work, in which the Master delights;
And so, with cheerful courage, elevate the Brother, consecrated to light, from Doom's turgid blood.

By a brother of the ☐
Set to music by Brother M . . t

At the conclusion of the Master Lodge.
The Masters' work is done, he who was dead is once again awakened;
we have brought a worthy offering to the Father of the Spirits.

*

In images deeply hidden, in signs and words concealed;
still, the morning, which awakens us in Life, does not redden.

*

Only when the trumpet calls us to see the light in the east,
when bodies arise from the dust and men from graves and scales

*

fall from the eyes of the blind, then is the affirmation true:
'Him whom I find in the adornment of a Master, to him will the
Masterword also be clear.'

*

Until that blessed hour, Brothers! let us renew daily our witness to
the eternal Bond, to which we consecrate ourselves thrice times
three.

*

And spread charity and love, and implore blessings from above.
Only he who is accompanied by such witnesses goes to the grave as a
Master.

By a Brother of the ☐
Set to music by Brother M . . t

Source Philippe A. Autexier, *Mozart & Liszt sub Rosa* (Poitiers, 1984), 36–7
(including facs.).
Commentary These two Masonic songs by Mozart are otherwise unknown.
Gabaon is derived from the name of the town of Gibeon (El Jeb) and denotes
'perfect friend'.

64 Thomas Attwood to an unidentified correspondent, ?London
[n.d., refers to 1785–7]

[extract] . . . Mozart at the time I was with him, appeared to be of
cheerful habit, his health not very strong. In consequence of being so
much over the table when composing, he was obliged to have an
upright Desk & stand when he wrote. . . . I attempted two Quartetts
for Two V., viola & violoncello – which Mozart corrected; & after
they were done, He said, 'you seem to like composition therefore we
will begin again'. . . . He was so fond of Sebastian Bach's Preludes &
Fugues that he had a separate Pianoforte with Pedals, fixed under
the Other – was very kind to all of Talent who came to Vienna &
generally played at their Benefit Concerts with the Pianofortes as
directed above – The last time I heard him, He play'd his concerto in
D Minor & 'Non temere' at Storace's Benefit for whom he composed
that Cantata with the Pianoforte solo. . . . The Emperor Joseph gave
Mozart 100 for the Opera of Figaro & gave Martini 200 for La cosa
rara!!! . . .

Source Privately owned. Auctioned at Sotheby's (London) on 12 May 1981,
lot 161.
Commentary Thomas Attwood (1765–1838) was Mozart's pupil in Vienna
from at least the middle of 1785 to the end of 1786. Ann (Nancy) Storace had
gone to Vienna in 1783 with her brother, the composer Stephen Storace.
Storace's benefit may have been her farewell concert of 23 February 1787 (*see*

Document 75). Although details of the concert are unknown, Deutsch's specu-
lation, that she and Mozart performed 'Ch'io mi scordi di te/Non temer, amato
bene' (K505), written expressly for Storace by Mozart, is apparently correct
(*Dokumente* 251, *Documentary Biography* 285). The performance of the concerto
K466, however, was unsuspected. Although Sotheby dates Attwood's letter to
about 1830, possibly it is earlier, for in a letter of 19 May 1828 Attwood wrote to
an unnamed correspondent that he could not remember some details of his
acquaintance with Mozart: 'My Dear Sir, I shall be most happy to give you all
the information in my power, but doubt much my ability to answer your
expectations on so interesting a Subject. It is now forty two Years since I took
my farewell of my much revered Master, and not having calculated upon
writing his life, I confess I cannot (at least immediately) recall to my mind the
particulars you require. When the hurry of the season is over I hope to have the
pleasure of meeting you, when probably more may be elicited than I can at
present anticipate . . .' (*US NYpm* Cary [Bennett], pp.65–6).

65 *Augsburgisches Intelligenz-Blatt*, 12 December 1785

Miscellaneous Advertisements. Available from the book-dealer
Stage, in **Augsburg** by the Obstmarkt. . . . *Die Entführung aus dem
Serail*, a comic Singspiel in 3 acts. The music is by the excellent Herr
von Mozart, the keyboard arrangement by Herr Abbé Starck,
engraved and published by B. Schott, Electoral Court Music
Engraver in Mainz. Oblong folio, 1785. 7 florins 12 kreuzer.

Source   *D-Mbs* 4.Eph.pol.53 (1785), p.199.
Commentary   This advertisement was referred to by Leopold Mozart in a
letter of 16 December 1785:

> What I predicted to my son has now happened. A keyboard arrangement of
> the Abduction has already been published by the Augsburg bookseller Stage
> for seven florins and [I]-don't know how many kreutzer. Canon Stark
> arranged it for keyboard – and [it was] engraved at *Mainz*, and trumpeted
> forth in the Augsburg papers with many laudatory remarks about the *famous
> Herr von Mozart*. If Torricella has already engraved a large part of it, then he
> will lose considerably – and your brother will have wasted his time arranging
> two acts (*Briefe* iii.471, *Letters* 805).

Apparently Torricella had attempted unsuccessfully to publish *Die Entführung*
by subscription in November 1784. An arrangement of the first act of the opera,
published by Artaria in December 1785 and possibly based on the Torricella-
Mozart version, is lost. For evidence that Mozart may have completed an
arrangement of at least part of the opera, *see* Document 67. [*See plate 4*]

66 *Lista Von denen, den 22ᵗᵉⁿ und 23ᵗᵉⁿ Xbris [1]785. abzuhaltenden musicalischen Societäts Accademien*, Vienna [possibly later but refers to] 23
December 1785

Concertisten . . . H Wolfg. Amad. Mozart.

Source   *A-Wsa* Haydn-Verein, A1–3b. Discovered by Dexter Edge.

Commentary On 23 December 1785, Mozart played at one of the semi-annual performances mounted by the Vienna Tonkünstlersozietät. According to the proceedings of the society and the (now lost) handbill for the concert, he performed 'a new concerto of his own Composition' as an entr'acte during a performance of Dittersdorf's oratorio *Esther* (Carl Ferdinand Pohl, *Denkschrift aus Anlass des hundertjährigen Bestehens der Tonkünstler-Societät*, Vienna, 1871, p.61; *Dokumente* 227, *Documentary Biography* 258–9). The Köchel catalogue (6/1964) and *Dokumente* suggest that the concerto was K482. The list of performers at the concert, however, shows that the orchestra did not include clarinets, which are called for in the work. On the other hand, as Monika Holl has shown, neither were they included in the orchestra for the performance of Mozart's *Davidde penitente*, which unquestionably includes those instruments (*NMA* I:4/iii, p.xii; *see also* Documents 58 and 60); presumably some of the oboists also played the clarinet.

67 *Oberdeutsche allgemeine Literaturzeitung*, Salzburg 2 November 1791 [refers to *c*1785?]

Die Liebe im Narrenhause. A comic opera in two acts. Composed by **Ditters von Dittersdorf**; arranged for keyboard by **Ignaz Walter**. Mainz, Schott, engraved on 204 oblong pages (price 10 Rhenish florins). . . . We may not close without giving Herr **Ignaz Walter** his due. He has managed what a conscientious man can manage. Making keyboard arrangements is not for everyone. One can have considerable musical knowledge without measuring up to the task. How many operas have not already been ruined because of this? Consider **Mozart's** masterpiece, **Die Entführung aus dem Serail**, and compare with it the keyboard arrangement, also published by **Schott**, made by **Abbé Stark**. Who would recognize **Mozart** in it? How dissimilar the **overture** seems when **Stark's** arrangement is compared with that published by Götz in Mannheim, which the arranger is supposed to have obtained from **Mozart** himself. No master of the keyboard could learn to play the former in proper tempo, nor would he compose it so – to what end? The harmony and melody drown out the drone bass. This is not the place, however, to speak of this further; it would be too easy to expose in any keyboard reduction a series of mistakes that, at least in part, go against the first rules of composition. We would much rather satisfy ourselves with the observation that there is a great difference in reducing the works of a **Mozart** and a **Dittersdorf**; but we are absolutely convinced that Herr **Walter** would very well understand how to manage the former, just as he has understood how to manage his **Dittersdorf**, even if the latter is much easier to arrange.

Source D-Mbs Eph.Lit.27a, cols.829–30.

Commentary The editor of the *Oberdeutsche allgemeine Literaturzeitung*, Lorenz Hübner, was well known to the Mozarts; consequently the source of his information that Götz's edition of *Die Entführung* included an arrangement of the overture by Mozart may have been authentic. Other direct evidence for Mozart's arrangement is lacking, although a keyboard version of the duet 'Vivat Bacchus' was published in the *Wiener Musik- und Theateralmanach* for 1786 and fragmentary autograph keyboard scores, possibly intended for Torricella, survive for 'Martern aller Arten' and 'Welche Wonne, welche Lust'. According to Ernst Laaff, Leopold Mozart sued both Schott and Götz for publishing without Mozart's knowledge or approval authentic keyboard arrangements of the opera. Unpublished documents supporting this assertion, however, are allegedly lost. 'Herr Walter' may be (Johann) Ignaz Walter (*b* Radonitz [Radonice], 1755; *d* Regensburg, 1822), whom Mozart had suggested as the first Pasha Selim in *Die Entführung*. Walter and his wife, Juliane Browne Roberts (1759–1835), were active at the combined theatres of Frankfurt and Mainz from 1786, and as court singers from 1789 to 1792.

Literature   *Dokumente* 203–4 and 225, *Documentary Biography* 229–30 and 256; Cliff Eisen, 'Contributions to a New Mozart Documentary Biography', *Journal of the American Musicological Society*, xxxix (1986), 630–32; Ernst Laaff, 'Prozess um Mozarts "Entführung"', in *Symbolae historiae musicae: Hellmut Federhofer zum 60. Geburtstag*, ed. Friedrich Wilhelm Riedel and Hubert Unverricht (Mainz, 1971), 190–93; Karl M. Pisarowitz, 'Mozarts Urbassa', *Mitteilungen der Internationalen Stiftung Mozarteum*, xiii/3–4 (1965), 15–20; Douglas D. Himes, 'Mozarts Eigenhändiger Klavierauszug zur "Entführung"', *Die Musikforschung*, xxxix (1986), 240–45.

68   Joseph Martin Kraus to his sister Marianne, Paris 26 December 1785

Kozeluch is a man after my own heart. Clementi is more for the intellect and fingers, Abbé Sterkel for lazy sight-readers. If you want to become acquainted with some other good composers, there are Mozart, Reichardt, Haydn, Häßler, Türk, Eckhardt, Adam, Küfner and my excellent friend Albrechtsberger in Vienna. How are things with your theatre in Frankfurt? What are the newest and best productions? Do you know Mozart's Entführung aus dem Serail? At present he is working on his Figaro, an operetta in 4 acts, which I very much look forward to.

Source   Irmgard Leux-Henschen, *Joseph Martin Kraus in seinen Briefen* (Stockholm, 1978), 310 (with further references).

Commentary   Joseph Martin Kraus (1756–92) was deputy Kapellmeister at the Swedish court from 1781 and Kapellmeister from 1788. From 1782 to 1787 he undertook a study tour in Europe, including visits to Vienna in 1783 and Paris in 1784 and 1785. Possibly he was personally acquainted with Mozart although there is no evidence to establish this; Kraus is not mentioned in Mozart's letters.

69   Mozart's Zoroastran riddles, Vienna February 1786

We are many sisters; it is painful for us to unite as well as to separate. We live in a palace, yet we could rather call it a prison, for we live securely locked up and must work for the sustenance of men. The most remarkable thing is that the doors are opened for us quite often, both day and night, and still we do not come out, except when one pulls us out by force.

I am an altogether patient thing, I let myself be used by everyone. Through me the truth, the lie, erudition and stupidity are proclaimed to the world. He who wants to know everything need only come and ask me, for I know everything. Since everybody needs me I am told everything. Money changers can well use me; I also serve barbers sometimes. I am inevitably necessary to the [illegible word] and [illegible word]. Through me the most important affairs of state are arranged, wars conducted, and lands conquered. Through my endurance the sick receive health, also frequently death. In brief, happiness, unhappiness, life, and death often depend upon me. One would imagine that so many superior qualities would make me happy; O no! My death is generally terrifying – painful, and when it happens gently, base and contemptible. Nevertheless, should I die in the last manner at the hand of a beautiful woman, so shall I take that consolation with me to the grave, that I have seen some things which not everyone gets to see.

I am an unusual thing; I have no soul and no body; one cannot see me but can hear me; I do not exist for myself: only a human being can give me life, as often as he wishes; and my life is only of short duration, for I die almost the moment in which I am born. And so, in accordance with men's caprice, I may live and die innumerable times a day. To those who give me life I do nothing – but those on whose account I am born I leave with painful sensations for the short duration of my life until I depart. Whatever passions a man finds in himself at the time when he grants me life I will surely bring those along into the world. For the most part, women produce me gently and amiably; many have modestly confessed their love in this way. Many have also saved their virtue through me; in these cases, however, my life can scarcely endure a quarter of an hour. I must come into the world by a singular stroke of fortune: otherwise there is no outlet – the man is deformed.

I serve many as an ornament, many as a mutilation. However, I am highly necessary to everyone. Sometimes it would be better if I were not there; sometimes, on the other hand, it is a blessing that I am there. Frequently even entire [illegible word] are uncovered through me. Frequently many men are even freed of [illegible word] insults through me. Men regard me as a good recommendation to women. I serve old people also, beyond my obligations; on that account [two illegible words] people who become old [illegible word] take care of me, so that I am not spoiled, let alone die before my time.

We are created for man's pleasures. How can we help it if an accident befalls by which we become the opposite of them? If he is lacking one of us, then he is – defective.

Source Joseph Heinz Eibl, 'Mozart verfasst Rätsel', *Österreichische Musikzeitschrift*, xxvi (1971), 65–71 (including facs.); *Briefe* vi.713–15; Maynard Solomon, 'Mozart's Zoroastran Riddles', *American Imago*, xlii (1985), 347–51 (English translation and facs.).

Commentary Mozart's 'Excerpts from the Fragments of Zoroaster', eight riddles and 14 proverbs printed on a broadsheet, were composed for the Viennese carnival of 1786 and subsequently sent to Leopold Mozart, who arranged to have one riddle and seven proverbs published in the *Oberdeutsche Staatszeitung* for 23 March (*Dokumente* 234–5, *Documentary Biography* 268). Until their recent discovery the other riddles, two of which are obliterated, were considered lost. Of the rediscovered riddles, Mozart's solution is known only to the third: 'The Box on the Ear' (*Briefe* iii.546, not in *Letters*).

Literature Joseph Heinz Eibl, 'Mozartiana aus der Sammlung Hermann Härtel', *Die Musikforschung*, xxiii (1970), 445.

70 Heinrich August Ottakar Reichard, *Taschenbuch für die Schaubühne auf das Jahr 1787*, Gotha [1786]

Vienna's Private Theatres. (**Extract from a letter**.) In the hope that emendations and corrections will not offend you, I risk telling you that someone grossly lied with the reports concerning Vienna's [theatrical] companies. How could anyone believe that taste here has become so spoiled, and that the distance between Vienna and Augsburg is so great. Accordingly, you should know that not more than 4 private theatres can be counted in all of Vienna, those of Prince Carl Auersperg, Count Altheim, Count Johann Esterhazy, and Herr Lackenbauer. Italian and German operas are given at the first, as well as German and French comedies. They are performed by the nobility, at times with the participation of one or two actors or actresses. Recently *Il Re Idomeneo*, *La Serva Patrona* and *L'Ami de la Maison* were given there. *Gabriele de Vergy*, *Le Mariage de Figaro* etc. were given at Count Altheim's and *Stille Wasser sind betrüglich* etc., directed by Herr Brockmann, at Count Esterhazy's. At Herr Lackenbauer's, 20 of the best German works were given in turns, and the players received unanimous applause. These are all of the private theatres in Vienna that are known to the public and the police, and that have existed for 6 years.

Source *GB-Lbl* P.P.4739.cd., pp.94–5.

Commentary. The performance of *Idomeneo* conducted by Mozart at Prince Johann Adam Auersperg's on 13 March 1786 included the additional numbers 'Spiegarti non poss' io' k489 and 'Non più, tutto ascoltai/Non temer, amato bene' k490. *Figaro* is undoubtedly Beaumarchais' *comédie*, not Mozart's opera.

71   *Wiener Zeitung*, Vienna 13 May 1786

Music. The following new music, cleanly and correctly written, and at inexpensive prices, is available from Johann Traeg, No.423 on the Hohe Market, at the *Glasser* House: . . . Various arias and duets from *Le Nozze di Figaro* by Mozart.

Source   Alexander Weinmann, *Die Anzeigen des Kopiaturbetriebes Johann Traeg in der Wiener Zeitung zwischen 1782 und 1805* (Vienna, 1981), 22–3.

Commentary   Traeg's advertisement for selections from *Figaro* considerably predates a similar advertisement by the other major Viennese dealer in manuscript music, Lorenz Lausch, in the *Wiener Zeitung* for 1 July (*Dokumente* 242–3, *Documentary Biography* 276–7). Traeg's advertisement of 13 May also included '1 Concerto in B â Clavicembalo, vom Mozart', possibly a reference to K456; the concerto had first been advertised on 21 December 1785, together with 'new symphonies' by Mozart (*Dokumente* 227, *Documentary Biography* 258).

72   *Uiber das deutsche Singspiel den Apotheker des Hrn. v. Dittersdorf* (Vienna, 1786)

It is almost unbelievable, and truly vexing, how the German Singspiel, and those who are interested in it, are treated in the German capital. Until now there remained but a glimmer of hope – in spite of a conspiracy by the aristocracy and some influential musical scholars – of some time seeing fulfilled the wishes of our monarch, himself the founder of it. For the basic principle of this sect has been to find nothing good that has not been wafted to us by a foreign breeze. And these scholars have gone to so much trouble to decry every honourable man as an idiot, that everyone . . . must agree with them in finding everything so magnificent and beautiful (and in fact must surely know that nothing the common man finds pleasurable can be good – or indeed that he is perhaps capable of judging), because they are – scholars.

For this reason it came to the point that – the poor German muse, hunted from the stage in order to tyrannize our taste with foreign nations (and there have been significant wagers with which the gloating foreign partisans jeered at so many native lovers of the art) – it was unlikely ever again to find a German opera at the National Theatre . . . [or] to hear good music for an Italian Singspiel by a German master. [But] they ¡have completely lost their bet, for Mozart's *Nozze di Figaro*, and the subsequently reintroduced German opera, have put to shame the ridiculous pride of this fashionable sect. . . .

And so be thanked, true, great musical poet. . . . Be thanked, in the name of all patriotic art lovers, for the triumph you have won from the German musical muse. . . . Be thanked for all those pleasurable moments you have given us – or will give us in the future

45

through your zeal – for the noble thoughts which you delightfully have inspired in us directly through your works – and with which you will rouse us in the future – that we can compare Salieri and Paisielli, those two famous men for whom we have so much respect, with a Ditters, a Mozart. Be thanked – but what thanks can I say to you that you have not already enjoyed in the ecstasy of the tumultuous public, and in the consciousness of your works of art?

Source *A-Wsl* A 12718, pp.5–6 and 15–16.
Commentary Dittersdorf's *Doktor und Apotheker* was first performed on 11 July 1786 at the Kärntnertortheater.

73 *Verzeichniss einiger neuen Werke welche in der musicalischen Niederlage bey Johann Christoph Westphal & Comp. in Hamburg angekommen sind,* Hamburg July 1786

Manuscript Music. . . . Symphonies.
Mozart, 1 ditto a 10. A minor. N[ew]
_____ 1 ditto a 14. C major. N[ew].
_____ 1 ditto a 13. with timpani and trumpets. D major. No.4
Mozart, 1 Divertimento a 6. 2 Viol. Viola, 2 Corni et Basso. F major
_____ , 6 Quatuor, 2 Viol. Alt et Violoncel. No.10
Mozart, 1 [Quatuor], Cemb. Viol. Alto e Basso. G minor
Mozart, 1 [Keyboard Trio]. E-flat major.

Source *A-Wgm* 205/3 (July 1786), pp.12–14.
Commentary The symphony in A minor is κAnh.220/16*a*; the symphony in C major probably κ200/189*k*, 338 or 425. The symphony in D major, identified by comparison with Breitkopf & Härtel's *Alter handschriftlicher Catalog von W. A. Mozart's Original Compositionen Abschrift* (*A-Wgm* 4057/38), is an expanded version, including trumpets and timpani, of κAnh.219/Anh.C11.06, a symphony by Leopold Mozart (*New Grove* D11, Eisen D11). Westphal's advertisement is the earliest known reference to κAnh.220/16*a*, a unique copy of which survives in *DK-Ou*. Neither the source nor the style of the work suggests that the symphony is by Mozart.
Literature Jens Peter Larsen and Kamma Wedin, ed. *Die Sinfonie KV 16a 'del Sigr. Mozart': Bericht über das Symposium in Odense anlässlich der Erstaufführung des wiedergefundenen Werkes Dezember 1984* (Odense, 1987); Cliff Eisen, 'Problems of Authenticity in the Early Symphonies attributed to Wolfgang Amadeus Mozart: the Examples of κ. Anh. 220 (16a) and 76 (42a)', *Music and Letters*, lxx (1989), 505–16; Neal Zaslaw and Cliff Eisen, 'Signor Mozart's Symphony in A-Minor, K.Anhang 220 = 16a', *The Journal of Musicology*, iv (1985–6), 196; Neal Zaslaw, *Mozart's Symphonies: Context, Performance Practice, Reception* (Oxford, 1989), 265–81; Scott Fruehwald, 'The Authenticity of the Symphony in A Minor (κ16a) Attributed to Mozart: a Stylistic Study', *College Music Symposium*, xxviii (1988), 24–39; Cliff Eisen, 'The Symphonies of Leopold Mozart: their Chronology, Style and Importance for the Study of Mozart's Early Symphonies', *MJb 1987–8*, 181–93.

74 Christoph Gottlob Breitkopf to Johann Gottlob Immanuel Breitkopf, ?Vienna 5 December 1786

[summary] In Vienna, Breitkopf met Mozart, Vanhal, Ditters and Gluck, who offered their works to the publisher.

Source Formerly in the archives of Breitkopf & Härtel, Leipzig, now lost. Summarized in Hermann von Hase, *Joseph Haydn und Breitkopf & Härtel* (Leipzig, 1909), 3.

Commentary There is no other evidence that Mozart met Breitkopf or that he provided the publisher with copies of his works. Throughout the 1770s Leopold Mozart repeatedly offered Mozart's works to Breitkopf, apparently without success, and during the 1780s the numerous works by Mozart handled by Breitkopf were readily available in printed editions.

Literature *The Breitkopf Thematic Catalogue: the Six Parts and Sixteen Supplements 1762–1787*, ed. Barry S. Brook (New York, 1966), cols.287, 327, 810, 815, 846, 849, 866–7 and 872–3.

75 *Staats- und gelehrte Zeitung des hamburgischen unpartheyischen Correspondenten*, Hamburg 15 December 1786

Letter from Vienna, 6 December. . . . The famous composer Herr Mozart is preparing to travel early in the coming New Year to London, where he has most favourable offers. He will go by way of Paris.

Source *US-PRu* 0902.873 (1786) [unpaginated]. Reprinted in the *Prager Oberpostamtszeitung* for 26 December 1786 (*Dokumente* 248, *Documentary Biography* 282).

Commentary Mozart apparently first mooted plans for a trip to London in the autumn of 1786; possibly he intended to accompany his English friends Ann and Stephen Storace, Michael Kelly, and Thomas Attwood, who returned there in the spring of 1787. Apparently the plan was not abandoned until the following year; according to a letter of 12 January, Leopold Mozart had heard that rumours of the proposed journey were circulating in Vienna, Prague and Munich (*Briefe* iv.7, *Letters* 902). *See also* Document 221.

76 Carl Friedrich Cramer, *Magazin der Musik*, Hamburg 26 July 1787

From Italy (in January 1787.) Among the various musicians who have been here for some time, both Herr **Krause**, from Stockholm, and **Pleyel**, from Vienna, have been very popular and favoured everywhere, both for their beautiful playing and compositions, and for their marvellously agreeable conduct. They have entry to the most respected houses, where they are always gladly seen. It is not easy to see such virtuosos as these two excellent men depart so reluctantly. It is said that Pleyel has been appointed Kapellmeister at Strasburg with a salary of 1000 Reichsthaler. He has composed some beautiful keyboard sonatas, which are impatiently asked after here. His agreeable melodies in them are not as difficult as Clementi's and Mozart's sorcery; he is more true to nature, without, however, violating the rules of composition.

It is certain that Clementi, during his stay in Vienna, studied with several German composers, principally **Haydn**, **Mozart** and **Kozeluch**. For from this time on, his newest compositions display German characteristics, and a better working out of the inner voices. This man has much genius; for its development, however, he does not have his compatriots, the Italians, who wish to place him above all modern players and composers, but the Germans to thank.

Source Facsimile edition, p.1378.
Commentary The alleged change in Clementi's style may refer to the period after December 1781; his only documented visit to Vienna, including his participation in a pianoforte contest with Mozart on 24 December 1781, dates from that time.

77 Programme of a concert at the Kärntnertortheater, Vienna 7 March 1787

Today, Wednesday, 7 March 1787, at the I[mperial] R[oyal] Theatre next the Kärntnertor, a benefit for three siblings, named Willmann, will be given.

1) A very grand symphony by Herr Winter.
2) Mademoiselle Willmann the younger will sing a scene with accompanied recitative by Herr Cherubini.
3) Frau von **, out of friendship, without any personal benefit and solely to oblige this family, will be heard in a grand concerto on an entirely new and improved harp [*Leyer*].
   As both her talent and instrument are so rare, it is hoped that the Academy will be all the more agreeable and entertaining.
4) Fraulein von **, for the same reasons, will sing the Polish rondo, which a few months ago Madame Buccarelli gave to such great applause in the same theatre.
5) Mademoiselle Willmann the elder will perform a grand fortepiano concerto by Herr Mozart.
6) Mademoiselle Willmann the younger will sing the very popular aria from the opera *La Cosa Rara*, 'Dolce mi parve un di', by Herr Martin.
7) Herr Willmann, the brother, will play a violoncello concerto with variations.
8) Mademoiselle Willmann and the above-named young lady will sing the beautiful duet from the opera *Giulio Sabino*, by Herr Sarti.

9) To conclude with a grand symphony by Herr Hayden.

Because these three siblings were so fortunate, two years ago, to receive the adulation of such a discriminating public, so they flatter themselves that the same will be even more the case now since from that time they have not lacked for effort and diligence. The singers, greatly moved by the very kind reception when they recently had the honour to appear in the new German opera *Zémire*, oblige themselves in particular to do their utmost to deserve this exceptional kindness.

The prices are those prevailing at the I. R. National Court Theatre.

To begin at 7 o'clock.

Source *A-Wn* Theatersammlung. Cited but not reproduced in *Dokumente* 252, *Documentary Biography* 286.

Commentary The musical Willmann family included the pianist Maximiliana Valentina Willmann (1769–1835), who on this occasion performed a concerto by Mozart; Johanna Willmann-Galvani (1771–1801), a soprano at the court theatres; and the cellist Maximilian Willmann (1767–1813). Deutsch gives the names of the sisters as Walburga and Magdalena, respectively, noting that Walburga is said to have been a pupil of Mozart. It is usually suggested that K503 was performed on this occasion although there is no convincing evidence for the assertion; at the time, several of Mozart's other concertos circulated in Vienna in manuscript copies or printed editions.

Literature Mary Sue Morrow, *Concert Life in Haydn's Vienna: Aspects of a Developing Musical and Social Institution* (Stuyvesant, NY, 1989), 265 and 459.

78 Programme of a concert at the Kärntnertortheater, Vienna 14 March 1787

Today, Wednesday 14 March 1787, at the Imperial Royal Court Theatre next the Kärntnertor, Herr Ramm, the famous oboist, will have the honour of giving a grand musical academy for his benefit. The pieces to be performed are the following:

1. A symphony by Herr Mozart
2. A new aria, composed last year in Naples by Herr Paisello, sung by Mlle. Giovanna Nanj.
3. An oboe concerto by Herr Ramm.
4. An aria by Herr Mozart, sung by Mad. Lang.
5. An oboe concerto by Herr Ramm.
6. A grand new scene, composed by Herr Wranizky, sung by Mlle. Giovanna Nanj.
7. A symphony.

The prices are those prevailing at the Imperial Royal National Court Theatre.

To begin at 7 o'clock.

Source *A-Wn* Theatersammlung. Cited but not reproduced in *Dokumente* 252, *Documentary Biography* 286.
Commentary Friedrich Ramm (*b* 1744; *d* after 1808), an oboist in the Hofkapelle at Mannheim, had known Mozart at least since 1777. He had performed the oboe concerto K271*k* (presumably identical to K314/285*d*) on 13 February 1778 at a private concert at Cannabich's (*Briefe* ii.282, *Letters* 482). Ramm was also intended to be one of the soloists in Mozart's Sinfonia concertante KAnh.9/297*B*. His 1787 concert at the Kärntnertortheater was noted by Count Karl Zinzendorf in his diary: 'In the evening to the Kärntnertor Theatre. Concert by Ramm. His oboe pleased me, in one piece he imitated the chalumeau. Neither Mademoiselle Nani's nor Madame Lang's voice pleased me much'.
Literature Mary Sue Morrow, *Concert Life in Haydn's Vienna: Aspects of a Developing Musical and Social Institution* (Stuyvesant, NY, 1989), 230, 266 and 517.

79 Programme of a concert at the Kärntnertortheater, Vienna 21 March 1787

Today, Wednesday 21 March 1787, at the Imperial Royal Court Theatre next the Kärntnertor, Herr Ludwig Fischer, chamber singer to his Highness the reigning Prince of Thurn and Taxis, will have the honour of giving a grand musical academy for his benefit. The pieces to be performed are the following:

1. A symphony by Herr Kapellmeister Mozart.
2. An aria by Herr Piccini, sung by Herr Fischer.
3. A bassoon concerto, played by Herr Rauzner.
4. An aria by Herr Righini, sung by Herr Fischer.
5. A movement from a symphony.
6. A new aria by Herr Kapellmeister Mozart, sung by Herr Fischer.
7. Mad. Lang will sing a Rondo by Herr Sarti.
8. Herr Fischer will sing a romanze: *Zu Stephen sprach im Traume*: by Herr Kapellmeister Umlauf.
9. A symphony by Herr Kapellmeister Mozart.

The prices are those prevailing at the Imperial Royal National Court Theatre.
To begin at 7 o'clock.

Source *A-Wn* Theatersammlung. Cited but not reproduced in *Dokumente* 252, *Documentary Biography* 286.
Commentary The bass Johann Ignaz Ludwig Fischer (1745–1825) was the first Osmin in *Die Entführung aus dem Serail*; his performance in the opera was singled out by Zinzendorf (*Dokumente* 180, *Documents* 203). Mozart composed the scena 'Alcandro, lo confesso/Non so, d'onde viene' K512 expressly for Fischer's concert.

80 *Staats- und gelehrte Zeitung des hamburgischen unpartheyischen Correspondenten*, Hamburg 9 November 1787

Prague, 1 November. . . . On the 29th of last month, a new opera, Don Giovanni (Don Juan, or the Stone Guest), was presented here by Herr **Mozard**, who also composed it. It is excellent beyond measure, and its equal has never before been given in Prague.

Source *US-PRu* 0902.873 (1787) [unpaginated].

81 Programme of a concert at the Burgtheater, Vienna 15 February 1788

Today, Friday 15 February 1788, at the Imperial Royal National Court Theatre, a grand musical academy will be given for the benefit of Herr Mandini. The pieces to be performed at this academy are the following:

1. A grand symphony by Herr Mozart.
2. A recitative and aria by Herr Kapellmeister Albertini, sung by Herr Mandini.
3. A scena and aria from *Olimpiade*: 'Se cerca', by Herr Cimarosa, sung by Mad. Morichelli.
4. Herr Calvesi will sing an aria by Herr Paisello.
5. The trio from *I due Litiganti*: 'Che vi pur Dorina', sung by the above.
6. Mlle. Josepha Ringbauer will be heard in a violin concerto.
7. A symphony by Herr Hayden.
8. A canon for three voices, without instrumental accompaniment, by Herr Martini.
9. The aria: 'L'impressario', by Herr Cimarosa, sung by Herr Mandini.
10. A scena with rondo by Herr Bianchi, sung by Mad. Morichelli.
11. A farewell aria, after *Biscroma's* from the opera: *Axur*, sung by Herr Mandini (NB. [The text of] this farewell aria, printed in German and Italian, will be distributed gratis at the entrance to the theatre.)
12. A *terzetto serio* by Herr Guglielmi, sung by the above.
13. A concluding symphony.

For the grand parterre, the price is 1 fl. per person, without exception. The remaining places are as at the German spectacles.
To begin at 7 o'clock.

Source *A-Wn* Theatersammlung. Cited but not reproduced in *Dokumente* 273, *Documentary Biography* 310. Facsimile in Mary Sue Morrow, *Concert Life in Haydn's Vienna: Aspects of a Developing Musical and Social Institution* (Stuyvesant, NY, 1989), 145.

Commentary According to Deutsch, Mandini was the baritone Stefano Mandini (1750–*c*1810), who sang in the quartet 'Dite almeno, in che mancai' K479 and the trio 'Mandina amabile' K480, both composed for a performance of Francesco Bianchi's *La villanella rapita* at the Burgtheater on 28 November 1785. Later he sang in Salieri's *Prima la musica e poi le parole* – the companion piece to Mozart's *Der Schauspieldirektor* K486 – performed at Schönbrunn on 7 February 1786, and as Count Almaviva in the première of *Le nozze di Figaro*. Morrow, however, suggests that the concert may have been given by the tenor Paolo Mandini (1757–1842), also a singer at the court theatres (p.438).

82 Heinrich Philipp Bossler, *Musikalische Realzeitung*, Speyer 5 March 1788

Promotion. Vienna 12 February. His Royal Highness Archduke Franz has appointed Herr **Wolfg. Amad. Mozart**, whom we have to thank for so many excellent compositions, as his Kapellmeister with a stipend of 800 imperial gulden.

Payments. His Imperial Majesty has decided to divide the considerable salary of the late **Chevalier Gluk** . . . among Herr Kapellmeister **Mozart** and other worthy Viennese musicians.

Source Facsimile edition, p.3.
Commentary Mozart was not engaged by Archduke Franz, but had been appointed Imperial Royal chamber musician on 7 December 1787; for other false reports on Mozart's appointment, see *Dokumente* 274, *Documentary Biography* 312.

83 Stendhal [M. H. Beyle], *Vie de Rossini* (Paris, 2/1824) [refers to 1787]

Le Nozze die Figaro (1787). Don Giovanni (1787)
In 1813, when I was in Dresden, I once met Luigi Bassi, that wonderful old buffo, for whom, twenty-six years earlier, Mozart had written the roles of Don Giovanni, and of Almaviva in le Nozze di Figaro. If I were to tell of the respectful curiosity with which I tried to induce this kindly old man to talk, no one would take me seriously. 'Mr Mozart', he would answer (how entrancing to hear someone who still said Mr Mozart!) 'Mr Mozart was an extremely eccentric and absent-minded young man, but not without a certain spirit of pride. He was very popular with the ladies, in spite of his small size; but he had a most unusual face, and he could cast a spell on any woman with his eyes . . .' On this subject, Bassi told me three or four little anecdotes, which, however, I must refrain from including at this point.

Source [M. H. Beyle], *Life of Rossini*, trans. and ed. Richard N. Coe (New York, 2/1970), 476.
Commentary Luigi Bassi (1766–1825) was the first Don Giovanni; from 1815 he was director of the Italian opera at Dresden. The first Almaviva was not Bassi, but Stefano Mandini. This passage is lacking in the first edition of

Stendhal's *Vie de Rossini*, also published in Paris (in 1824); in the second edition it was added between the *Préface* and the *Introduction*.
Literature John P. Harthan, 'Stendhal and Mozart', *Music and Letters*, xxvii (1946), 174–9.

84 [Amand Wilhelm Smith], *Philosophische Fragmente über die praktische Musik* (Vienna, 1787)

Prognosis. Concerning the imminent decline of music. . . . To come to our subject, the imminent decline of music: among the conditions that prove our accepted proposition, perhaps the following is the most likely. When an art is newly fashionable, it is acclaimed, partisans and admirers appear whose number is increased yet further by substantial reward from the great. Nature is not miserly in the distribution of its spiritual gifts to most of mankind, however, as many develop a particular spiritual capacity, and make of it their chief preoccupation, albeit not with equal success, so it is natural that this field, worked by too many, becomes more widely accessible, and thus arouses less curiosity: for only that which is rare excites them. Encouragement by the great by means of rewards diminishes, because the more common something is, the less its partisans see a prospect of benefit in its pursuit; it must also naturally be that in the future a Haendel, Gluc, Gasmann, Paisello, Sarti, Naumann, Salieri, Hayden, Dittersdorf, Mozart, and so on, can hardly be expected. For great courts, which could support the sciences and arts, do not particularly relish this kind of entertainment and pastime; and consitutions which are based on the iron law of metals leave little time for imbibing this nectar of the gods. Small eminent courts, however, which might know to treasure them, lack the essential conditions without which, in this world, nothing can be undertaken or supported.

Source *A-Wgm* 991/7, pp.96–7.
Commentary Although reviews of Smith's *Philosophische Fragmente* published in Bossler's *Musikalische Realzeitung* (*Dokumente* 314–15, *Documentary Biography* 358) and Johann Nikolaus Forkel's *Musikalischer Almanach für Deutschland auf das Jahr 1789* (Document 159) mention Mozart in connection with the chapter 'Von jungen, unzeitigen Virtuosen', the composer is not actually mentioned there. A copy of Smith's work was among the books in Mozart's estate (*Dokumente* 498, *Documentary Biography* 588).

85 *Verzeichnis der Brüder und Mitglieder der gerechten und volkomenen St. Johannes* [ ] *zur gekrönten Hoffnung im Orient zu Wien*, [Vienna] auf Johannes 5788 [1788]

Brothers in attendance . . . 70. Mozart. Wolfgang. K. K. Kapellmeister. III.

Source *US-Cn* Case °HS 602.V54 1788 [unpaginated]. [*See plate 5*]

86 Carl Ditters von Dittersdorf to Artaria, Johannisberg 18 August 1788

Sirs!

For some time now, friends, connoisseurs and amateurs of music have been telling me that I should write six quartets. For a long time I could not make up my mind to do so, since I did not want to write quartets according to the common taste, and writing good quartets seemed too laborious to me. A friend (I can rightfully call him a true connoisseur of music since his chief idea is that music theory and practice must always go hand in hand and that in no work should one take precedence over the other) encouraged me for a long time until I undertook the task, and after a period of 13 to 14 months I had composed 6. This same friend – who admires Pleyel's quartets for their trimness, pleasantness and expression, and Haydn's most recent ones published by you, not only for these qualities but even more for their art and novelty – this same friend has heard my quartets not once, but several times already and each time (I really should not say this myself, since self-praise sounds poor) he says: Now not only Pleyel's quartets but even Haydn's are surpassed! And I may boldly say without blushing that they turned out better than I had at first believed they would.

Now – I offer you the original manuscript or, more accurately, my own score of them for the same price you paid for Mozart's and in addition for the first ten prints or copies, and I am certain that you will do better with mine than you did with Mozart's (which, indeed, I and still greater theorists consider to deserve the highest praise, but which because of their overwhelming and unrelenting artfulness are not to everyone's taste) . . .

Source Eva Badura-Skoda, 'Dittersdorf über Haydns und Mozarts Quartette', in *Collectanea Mozartiana*, ed. Cordula Roleff (Tutzing, 1988), 42–7; *Carl Ditters von Dittersdorf: Six Symphonies*, ed. Eva Badura-Skoda (New York, 1985 = The Symphony 1720–1840. ser.B.i), pp.xxii–xxiv (facs. of second page only and English translation by Leo Balk).
Commentary Presumably Dittersdorf's quartets are those published by Artaria as plate number 221 and advertised in the *Wiener Zeitung* for 31 January 1789. According to a letter of 8 September 1788, he received 30 ducats for the works and asked for 60 copies of the print (Artaria had offered 50 prints).
Literature Jan LaRue, 'Dittersdorf Negotiates a Price', in *Hans Albrecht in Memoriam* (Kassel, 1962), 156–9.

87 Joseph Anton Stephan [Josef Antonín Štěpán], Ritter von Riegger, *Materialien zur alten und neuen Statistik von Böhmen* (Leipzig and Prague, 1788)

Attempt at a **list** of the most eminent **musicians** in or from Bohemia
. . . **Bauer** (Franz) from Gitschin, studied theology in Prague and

became a subdeacon; however, because he did not want further to take holy orders, and could not easily expect a dispensation from the subdeaconry he already held, he left for Russia. Since his youth he had devoted himself entirely to the violin and had made such progress, particularly with regard to speed, intensity of expression and precision, that Mozart himself praised him when in Prague he heard him play a concerto.

Source   *US-CAw* Slav 7270.30, p.138.

Commentary   Little is known about Franz Bauer (*b* 1748). Sometime after 1788 he and his wife, a virtuoso on the psaltery, travelled to St Petersburg and from there throughout Germany, Italy, France, Spain and Portugal, arriving in Lisbon in 1792. That autumn they performed in Hamburg and in 1793 in Weimar and Berlin. Bauer apparently retired from public life in 1798 (Gustav Schilling, *Encyclopädie der gesammten musikalischen Wissenschaften oder Universal Lexikon der Tonkunst*, i, Stuttgart 2/1840, 480-81). Mozart was first in Prague from 11 January to 8 February 1787 and later that year from 4 October to about 13 November; consequently this notice must have been written only shortly after the event it describes. Although the list is not attributed in Riegger, it was written by Gottfried. Johann Dlabač and later served as the basis for his *Allgemeines historisches Künstler-Lexikon für Böhmen* (Prague, 1815). The report on Bauer's acquaintance with Mozart was taken over by Ernst Ludwig Gerber in his *Historisch-biographisches Lexicon der Tonkünstler* (Leipzig, 1790–92), i, col.117.

Literature   Cliff Eisen, 'Some lost Mozart Editions of the 1780s', *Mitteilungen der Internationalen Stiftung Mozarteum*, xxxii (1984), 68.

88   Isabelle de Charrière to Jean-Pierre de Chambrier d'Oleyres, about 5 November 1788

I flatter myself, Monsieur, that the conclusion of my *Pheniciennes* has reached you. I wrote to Spineux to send it to you when it was printed. Should M. Prevost have the first rights to the *Pheniciennes* in manuscript, you have them for the published *Pheniciennes*. Today I sent it to Mosart, at the Archbishop of Saltzbourg. I would like to send it to Sarti who, I believe, is in St Petersburg.

Source   *Oeuvres complètes: Isabelle de Charrière (Belle de Zuylen)*, ed. Jean Daniel Candaux and others (Amsterdam, 1979–84), iii, p.111.

Commentary   Isabella Agneta de Charrière, *née* Tuyll (1740–1805), was a well-known author. Her *tragédie-lyrique Les Pheniciennes* was published in 1788. Charrière's correspondent, Jean-Pierre de Chambrier d'Oleyres (1753–1822), was the Prussian ambassador to the court at Turin from 1780 to 1798. In addition to considering Mozart and Sarti as possible composers for her work, Charrière also considered Graun, Cimarosa, and Salieri (*Oeuvres complètes*, iii, pp.112–14). Apparently she was unaware that Mozart had permanently left Salzburg in 1781, and when she had no reply from him she wrote on 12 January 1789 to Dudley Ryder, the future Count Harrowby: '*Les Pheniciennes* was sent to Cimarosa at Petersburg & Mosart at Salzburg. This last to whom I wrote has not had the courtesy to answer me' (*Oeuvres complètes*, iii, p.124). In the end, Charrière was advised against Mozart. *See* Document 89.

89 Isabelle de Charrière to Jean-Pierre de Chambrier d'Oleyres, 13 January 1789

Yesterday I received a letter from M. Stahl. . . . He offered me his services with regard to Cimarosa & he is precisely the person to whom you would want to speak. Furthermore, he spoke to me concerning Martini, who is also at St Petersburg & who had great success at Vienna, but in a genre that is not, I believe, what we require. At Vienna M. Stahl knows Salieri & he believes that the *Pheniciennes* would not do badly in his hands. . . . Certainly there are some fine numbers in *Tarare* & he knows French perfectly. As for Mosart, whom he also knows, he does not find his genius sufficiently regulated by taste and experience.

Source *Oeuvres complètes: Isabelle de Charrière (Belle de Zuylen)*, ed. Jean Daniel Candaux and others (Amsterdam, 1979–84), iii, p.127.
Commentary Stahl is Philipp Stahl (1762–1831), from 1788 to 1792 private secretary to Count Johann Ludwig Cobenzl, Austrian ambassador to Russia. Mozart had earlier dedicated the sonatas K333/315c, 284/205b and 454 to Cobenzl's wife, Countess Therese. *Les Pheniciennes*, finally, was composed by none of the composers originally considered by Charrière.

90 *Magazin der Sächsischen Geschichte aufs Jahr 1789*, Dresden April 1789

Noteworthy Events in Dresden. . . . On the 13th, two virtuosos from Vienna, or more precisely from the Kapelle of Prince Esterhazy, by the name of **Kraft**, father and son, a student of Haydn, performed double sonatas for violoncello for his Imperial Highness Duke Karl. The same day, the father played a concert at his Electoral Highness's, where a few days later the famous **Mozart** was also heard at the keyboard, so masterfully that he surpassed all who have been heard previously, including **Himmel** and even **Häsler**, according to the latter's own admission. Mozart received 100 ducats from the Elector, Kraft 50.

Source *US-CAw* Ger 45.3.3 (1789), p.245.
Commentary Mozart performed before Elector Friedrich August III of Saxony on 14 April. His pupil Johann Nepomuk Hummel ('Himmel') had performed in Dresden the month before; see the *Magazin der Sächsischen Geschichte aufs Jahr 1789*, Part VI, no.63, pp.178–9: 'This month the musical public saw and heard two great rarities, namely: at his Imperial HighnessDuke Karl's, an English virtuoso on the violin by the name of Weichsel, a pupil of Kramer, who according to the verdict of connoisseurs seemed to work magic in cadenzas, double-stops, double-trills and dexterity. Also, from Vienna, a young nine-year-old lad, a Hessian by the name of **Hommel**, a pupil of Mozart, well-known as one of the greatest of our German keyboard players, who with regard to his

years and unprecedented dexterity found universal approbation.' Anton Kraft (1749–1820) was first cellist in the orchestra of Prince Nikolaus Esterházy from 1778 to 1790; his son Nikolaus (1778–1853), was a cellist in the orchestra of Prince Lobkowitz from 1796. Both were pupils of Haydn, and were among the greatest cellists of the period. At Dresden, Nikolaus Kraft, who was then nine years old, performed with Mozart on 14 April (*Dokumente* 297, *Documentary Biography* 339). Charles Weichsell (*b* c1766; *d* after 1805) was a violin virtuoso. Johann Wilhelm Hässler (1747–1822) met Mozart in Dresden; on 15 April they played organ and piano competitions. *See* Document 91.

91 Alexander Mikhailovich Beloselski, *Dialogue sur la Musique* (?Dresden, ?1789)

The Marquise: – . . . I am still not convinced by everything you say concerning the superiority of German composers, one of the most famous of whom I heard in Vienna: Mozzart.

The Prince. – Mozzart is very learned, very difficult, and consequently very esteemed by instrumentalists: but he appears never to have had the good luck to love. Not a single melody emanates from his heart. Tell me rather about the musicians of Saxony, of Tuscany, of Germany: the names of Seidelman, of Nauman, are not unknown to you.

Source André Mazon, *Deux Russes écrivans français* (Paris, 1964), 363–4.
Commentary Prince Alexander Mikhailovich Beloselski (1757–1809) was Russian ambassador to the Turin court, a member of the Bologna Accademia Filarmonica, and later ambassador to Dresden. Mozart had lunch with him in Dresden on 15 April; in the afternoon he played in a contest against the organist J. W. Hässler at the court church, and later on the pianoforte at Beloselski's residence. Beloselski's three *Dialogues* may have been written about this time.
Literature Heinz Wolfgang Hamann, 'W. A. Mozart – J. W. Hässler: der Dresdener Orgelwettstreit im Jahre 1789', *Musik und Kirche*, xxxiii (1963), 126–8; Jacques Chailley, 'Les *Dialogues sur la Musique* d'Alexandre Belosel'skij', *Revue des études slaves*, xlv (1966), 93–103; Rudolph Angermüller, 'Italienische und französische Musik, wie sie 1778, als Mozart in Paris weilte, diskutiert würde: Beloselskys "De la musique en Italie"', in *Mannheim und Italien – Zur Vorgeschichte der Mannheimer: Bericht über das Mannheimer Kolloquium im März 1982*, Beiträge zur Mittelrheinischen Musikgeschichte, xxv, ed. Roland Würtz (Mainz, 1984), 208–22; Neal Zaslaw, *Mozart's Symphonies: Context, Performance Practice, Reception* (Oxford, 1989), 422–3.

92 *Theater-Zeitung für Deutschland*, Berlin 18 April 1789

Berlin. The 8th, **Belmonte und Constanze**, Opera in 3 Acts by **Bretzner** and **Mozart**. The music of this opera is so individual and varied that on first hearing it is not entirely understandable even to a trained ear. However, as a result of this very circumstance, it produces new fascination with each repeated hearing. So many beautiful, noble thoughts are crammed into each aria that a more economical composer could have produced perhaps six [arias] out of [each one of] them. Whether the music loses some of its effect from this almost extravagant over-abundance of ideas is a question worthy of detailed investigation; this much, however, seems certain, that many parts would have benefited immeasurably if they were not so long. So, for example, the duet between Belmonte and Constanze would be an incomparable masterpiece if it were somewhat shorter. Yet these observations should by no means lessen the worth of this excellent music: it is and remains a work that can be considered a model of the noble style and which does the German genius honour.

The role of Constanze is a true touchstone for a singer. In order to sing this role really **well** requires an exceptional, infallible certainty of intonation, great precision in diction, a light upper register, uncommon facility of the throat, and a profound feeling for passionate song. So if it is said that Mlle. **Hellmuth** sang this part faultlessly, then it is certainly unnecessary to add to her well-deserved praise. In addition, her acting was surprisingly good and correct, and showed a talent for noble roles. The part of Belmonte, although it is much less brilliant than that of Constanze, nevertheless has its own great difficulties; and a tenor who overcomes them as successfully as Hr. **Lippert** deserves to be called an excellent singer. His acting in this role is as expressive and good as one is accustomed to expect from him. As Osmin, Herr **Frankenberg** is so excellent and faultless in both his singing and his acting that one does not know which to praise him for first. The malicious Turkish child – rude when he gives orders, grovelling when he must obey – is recognizable in every expression and gesture; in short, because of him this role is the most outstanding in the entire piece.

Source   *D-Mth* Per 229, pp.121–2.
Commentary   Mozart saw this production on 19 May; the opera was also given on 13 April and on 7 and 28 May. Mozart may also have attended a performance by his pupil Hummel in Berlin, on 23 May. An advertisement for this concert, with reference to Mozart, appeared in the *Berlinische Nachrichten von Staats- und gelehrten Sachen* for 21 May, p.456: 'On Saturday 23 May at the Corsika Concert Room a ten-year-old virtuoso, Mons. Hummel from Vienna, will be heard on the fortepiano in a concert with full orchestra. He is a pupil of the famous Herr **Mozart**, and surpasses in dexterity, accuracy and delicacy all expectation. Tickets at 16 groschen per person are available from Herr Corsika, from Herr Toussaint in the Poststrasse at the Golden Eagle, and at the entrance. To begin at 4 o'clock.'

93   *Berlinische musikalische Zeitung*, Berlin 1805 [refers to April and May 1789]

Recollection of Mozart's visit to Leipzig. A. M. Mozart came to Leipzig in April and May 1789. He was praised for his generosity and was not so stingy with his art as many other artists. His forte-piano playing enchanted private gatherings, as at D. Platner's. Nor was he miserly in distributing free tickets for his concert to impecunious friends of music. On 22 April he played the organ at the Thomaskirche, without previous notice and without payment. He played very finely and artfully for an hour to a large audience. The then organist Görner and the late Cantor Doles were near him and pulled the stops. I saw him in person, a young fashionably-dressed man of medium height. Doles was completely enchanted by the artist's playing, and believed that his teacher, old Seb. Bach, was resurrected, for whom Mozart had also expressed the most profound admiration at the Thomasschule, when he heard one of his motets and saw his works. He applied all the harmonic arts and improvised most magnificently, with very good decorum and the greatest ease, on the themes, including the chorale *Jesu meine Zuversicht*.

Source Facsimile edition, p.132. Editions: Otto Jahn, *The Life of Mozart*, trans. Pauline D. Townsend (London, 1891), iii, 228–9 (extract); Warren Kirkendale, *Fugue and Fugato in Rococo and Classical Chamber Music* (Durham, North Carolina, 1979), 161 (extract); cited but not reproduced in *Dokumente* 298, *Documentary Biography* 340.

Commentary Mozart was in Leipzig from 20 April to about 23 April and from 8 to 17 May 1789. He improvised on the organ at the Thomaskirche on 22 April and gave a public concert on 12 May. Ernst Platner (1744–1818) was Rector of the University. Johann Friedrich Doles (1715–97), Cantor at the Thomaskirche, later dedicated his motet *Ich komme vor Dein Angesicht* to Mozart.

94 *Berlinische Nachrichten von Staats- und gelehrten Sachen*, Berlin 9 May 1789

Available at Rellstab's music shop by the *Garnisonskirche*, for 14 groschen, arranged for keyboard . . . the ballet from the opera Medea by Naumann, in which the Sibyls permit Medea to see her fate. Also the complete works of Mozart.

Source *D-AN* If 26, p.418.

Commentary Johann Friedrich Carl Rellstab was Berlin's leading music publisher and one of the city's most important impresarios. Although there is no evidence that Mozart met Rellstab, it would be surprising if he did not. Possibly Mozart himself was Rellstab's source for his works, few of which had previously been advertised in Berlin.

Literature Cliff Eisen, 'Contributions to a New Mozart Documentary Biography', *Journal of the American Musicological Society*, xxxix (1986), 628–30.

95 Karl August Varnhagen's manuscript notice concerning Mozart, n.d. [refers to May 1789]

Wolfgang Amadeus Mozart.
Born 1756, on 27 January, in Salzburg.

Died 1791, on 5 December, around midnight, in Vienna.

In May 1789 he came twice from Leipzig to Berlin. He stayed here at the inn *Zur Stadt Paris,* in the Brüderstrasse, and played double sonatas with the daughter of the landlady, Dlle Dacke, later the wife of Privy Councillor Selle.

Source Wolfgang Rehm, 'Mozartiana in der Sammlung Varnhagen', in *Festschrift Rudolf Elvers zum 60. Geburtstag*, ed. Ernst Herttrich and Hans Schneider (Tutzing, 1985), 409 (facs.) and 415 (transcription).

Commentary Karl August Varnhagen von Ense (1785–1858), who knew both Beethoven and Schubert, was a diplomat; his wife, Rahel Varnhagen (*née* Levin; 1771–1833), had a prominent literary salon in Berlin. Mozart was in Potsdam from about 25 April to about 6 May and in Berlin from 19 to 28 May 1789. Because some letters from the concert tour of 1789 are lost, not all of his activities at this time are known; it is possible that he travelled to Berlin while at Potsdam, which would account for his otherwise unknown stay at the inn Zur Stadt Paris. Evidence for other contact in Berlin before his visit there is suggested by an advertisement for Mozart's music published by Johann Friedrich Carl Rellstab in the *Berlinische Nachrichten von Staats- und gelehrten Sachen* for 9 May 1789 (*see* Document 94). 'Dlle Dacke' cannot be identified.

Literature K. Varnhagen von Ense, *Denkwürdigkeit des eignen Lebens* (Leipzig, 1840).

96 *Allgemeine musikalische Zeitung*, Leipzig 1812 [refers to May 1789]

Leipzig. A few weeks ago, the concert and theatre orchestra here lost its universally admired veteran *Carl Gottlieb Berger* . . . Berger's life proceeded entirely uniformly, actively and pleasantly until his death: and he himself, it seems, remembered only a few exceptional high points of it. . . .

The second of these was when Joseph Haydn's quartets first became well known and later, together with Mozart's earlier quartets, the two Bergers, and two of their friends, worthily performed them at the house of the art dealer Herr Rost.

The third was when for several years the (at the time) truly excellent Italian opera company of Herr Guardasoni gave exquisite performances in Leipzig during the summer, and we all became acquainted and familiar with Mozart's dramatic masterpieces in particular.

The fourth, finally, was when this great and immortal master came for several weeks to Leipzig, and in particular came to know, respect and be fond of our Berger. There was daily music, sometimes at this, at other times another, distinguished house, mainly quartets. Berger played the first violin, Mozart the pianoforte or viola; and later, whenever someone performed one of these quartets, he would whisper with sincere pleasure in the ear of a close acquaintance: Ah, I once had the honour of accompanying Mozart in that! It may be noted, as proof of the master's satisfaction with Berger, that on the evening of his public concert, he took him aside: 'Come with me, good Berger; I will play for you a bit longer. You understand better than most who applauded me today.' So he took him with him and, after a brief meal, improvised for him until midnight when finally, as was his custom, he sprang up suddenly and cried out: 'Well, Papa, did that please you? Only now have you really heard Mozart; others can do what you heard earlier!'

Source Vol.xiv (issue of 12 February 1812), cols.102–6.
Commentary Details concerning the life of Carl Gottlieb Berger are unknown, although according to the obituary, he was at least 80 at the time of his death. *Don Giovanni* was given at Leipzig in 1788 by the impresario Domenico Guardasoni (*c*1731–1806), who had mounted the opera at Prague in 1787. Mozart himself was in Leipzig from 20 April to about 23 April and from 8 to 17 May; he gave a public concert at the Leipzig Gewandhaus on 12 May. The reliability of this document cannot be verified; Berger is not mentioned in the Mozart letters or other contemporary documents.

97 *Allgemeine musikalische Zeitung*, Leipzig 1830 [refers to 12 May 1789]

In the second part of a concert Mozart gave here in Leipzig on 12 May 1789, he performed, among other things, an entirely new symphony in C major, the last movement of which is in 6/8. [In this movement,] after a pause by the bass instruments, the double bass enters unexpectedly with a new theme in 3/4. The double bassist Herr Wach, who is still among us, played in the performance. Mozart said to him: 'When the 3/4 begins, be guided only by the movement of my left hand.' We and also others inquired which it was: no one knows anything more concrete about this symphony. Nothing has been seen of it since that time. Has it been completely lost, or is anyone able to say something more about it?

Source Vol.xxxii (issue of 20 October 1830), col.687. Edition: Neal Zaslaw, *Mozart's Symphonies: Context, Performance Practice, Reception* (Oxford, 1989), 425–6 (translation).
Commentary Probably this anecdote is apocryphal. Although Mozart's concert at the Leipzig Gewandhaus on 12 May 1789 included symphonies in both the first and the second parts, none of his known C major symphonies with 6/8 finales includes a passage that fits Wach's description, and no other convincing interpretation of the document can be advanced.

98   Receipt of Elisabeth Rothmann, Vienna 10 August 1789

N° 3.

Madame Rothmann's receipt

This day I have received from my much-beloved brother-in-law Martin Rothmann, and in the presence of the executors Messrs. Imperial Exchequer Councillor Ignatz von Kunnersdorf, Imperial Kapelle Director Amadeus Mozart, and Imperial Councillor Jost v. Spaugh, a sum of two thousand florins hard cash. Given at Vienna, 10 August 1789.

Elisabeth Rothmann
widow Born

Witnesses present

Ign. v. Kunnersdorff   Mozart   v Spaugh

Source   Privately owned (Stockholm, Sven Hansson).
Commentary Mozart had signed a similar receipt on 10 July (*Dokumente* 305–6, *Documentary Biography* 348). The exact nature of his relationship to Elisabeth Rothmann is unknown.
Literature 'Enskilda arkiv. Per Wilhelms Hanssons brevsamling', *Svenskt musikhistoriskt arkiv: Bulletin*, vii (1971), 24–37.

99   From the account books of the Hoftheater, Vienna 20–26 February 1790

Extra Expenses. Music Charges.
to Wolfgang Mozart for composing the music to the opera *Così fan tutte* . . . . 450 [gulden]

Source   Dexter Edge, 'Mozart's Fee for *Così fan tutte*', *Journal of the Royal Musical Association* (in preparation).
Commentary According to a letter of late December 1789 to Michael Puchberg, Mozart expected to receive 200 ducats for the composition of *Così*, twice the usual payment for new operas (*Briefe* iv.99–100; *Letters* 934–5). The discovery of the long-lost account of the payment to Mozart shows, however, that (officially at least) he received only the standard fee of 450 gulden, the equivalent of 100 ducats at the prevailing rate. The sum is identical to the payment for *Die Entführung aus dem Serail*, 426 gulden 40 kreuzer, which in 1783 was the equivalent of 100 imperial ducats. Possibly Mozart had a private arrangement with the Emperor, who died on 20 February 1791 (about the time of this payment), for the other 100 ducats. *Così* had its première on 26 January 1790.
Literature Julia Moore, 'Mozart in the Market-Place', *Journal of the Royal Musical Association*, cxiv (1989), 18–42; Rudolph Angermüller, '"sein Fehler waren, da er das Geld nicht zu dirigieren wuste": Mozarts finanzielle Verhältnisse', *Collectanea Mozartiana*, ed. Cordula Roleff (Tutzing, 1988), 19–39.

100 *Verzeichnis der Mitglieder der gerechten und vollkommenen St: Johannes zur gekrönten Hofnung im Orient von Wien,* Vienna 5790 [1790]

Brothers present . . . 56. Mozart Wolfgang I. R. Kapellmeister III

Source H. C. Robbins Landon, *Mozart and the Masons: New Light on the Lodge 'Crowned Hope'* (New York, 1983), 65–72.

Commentary The Roman numeral 'III' designates a brother of the Third Degree (Master Mason). On the basis of this register and iconographical evidence, Landon argues that Mozart is the seated figure in the front right corner of an anonymous oil painting showing a meeting of a Viennese Lodge. The painting was first reproduced in Otto Erich Deutsch, 'Innenansicht einer Wiener Freimaurer-Loge', in *Studien aus Wien*, Wiener Schriften, v (Vienna, 1957), 96–102.

101 Benedikt Pillwein, *Biographische Schilderungen oder Lexikon salzburgischer, theils verstorbener, theils lebender Künstler, auch solcher, welche Kunstwerke für Salzburg lieferten* (Salzburg, 1821) [refers to 1790]

Wölfl (Joseph), born at Salzburg in 1772, studied with **Leopold Mozart** and **Michael Haydn**. . . . Because (Joh. Chrysost. Wolfg. Amadäus) **Mozart's** reputation was at that time known all over Germany, **Wölfl's** father decided to send his son to perfect his musical training with this immortal composer. He was Wölfl's most faithful friend and recommended the 18-year-old youth to the Polish Count Orginsky as Kapellmeister.

Source *A-Smi* 701 A1 Pil 80 p.262.

Commentary Joseph Wölfl (1773–1812) studied the violin and keyboard with Leopold Mozart from 1783 to 1786, first as a choirboy and later, after his voice broke in 1785, privately. Michael Haydn was an instructor at the Kapellhaus from 1782. Apparently on his father's advice, Wölfl sought out Mozart in Vienna in 1790. The exact nature of their relationship, however, and whether Wölfl studied with Mozart, remains uncertain. In a letter of early May 1790 to Michael Puchberg, Mozart wrote that he had two (unidentified) students (*Briefe* iv.108, not in *Letters*); and Nissen stated in his *Biographie W. A. Mozarts* (Leipzig, 1828) that 'In 1791, at the same time Mozart was in Prague, the keyboard player W** was with him, in order to be heard on the pianoforte. When Mozart was given the concert bill, which advertised W** as his pupil, he said: "The young man plays very well, but I am not responsible for that; perhaps he profited somewhat from [lessons with] my sister."' Possibly 'W**' is Wölfl, a supposition strengthened by the reference to Nannerl Mozart and by Wölfl's dedication of his three piano sonatas (1797) to 'Madame Anne de Sonnenburg, née Mozart'. However, Nissen also suggests that Nannerl's pupils were exclusively women (p.14). Orginsky is probably Count Michel-Kasimir Orginsky (1731–1803), Grand Field-Marshall of Lithuania.

Literature Richard Baum, *Joseph Wölfl, 1773–1812: sein Leben und seine Klavierwerke* (Kassel, 1928); Heinz Wolfgang Hamann, 'Mozarts Schülerkreis', *MJb 1962–3*, 115–39, esp. 127; Ernst Hintermaier, 'Michael Haydns Salzburger Schülerkreis', *Österreichische Musikzeitschrift*, xxvii (1972), 14–24, esp. 22.

102 Rudolf Hommel, *Briefe über die Kaiserwahl während derselben aus Frankfurt geschrieben*, Leipzig 1791 [refers to 1790]

Frankfurt 2 October. . . . More splendid and various here than Thalia's events, however, are the joys of Polyhymnia. Rejoice with me: I have heard Vogler, Häßler and Mozart. Above all, Vogler's organ concerto made a profound impression on me.

Source *US-NYpl* ED, p.93. Edition: Ursula Mauthe, 'Die Hebstreise', in *34. Deutsches Mozartfest Schwetzingen* [programme book] (Schwetzingen, 1985), 21.

Commentary Thalia is a reference to theatrical, as opposed to purely musical, performances. According to Mauthe, the following additional reference to Mozart occurs under the date 11 October: 'Yesterday I was convinced, finally, to visit the operetta *Figaro*. The music was well-cast and tolerably performed. . . . However, the chattering of the large crowd was so severe that one could understand only a little: a sure indication that the audience found the piece boring.' This passage is lacking in the New York Public Library copy of the work.

103 Felix Joseph Lipowsky, *Baierisches Musik-Lexikon* (Munich, 1811) [refers in part to October 1790]

Beecke (Ignatz von). . . . This well-known, excellent artist made several journeys to Italy and France and acquired a broad musical knowledge. His keyboard playing was unique, and his compositions ingenious. He was in touch with all the great artists of his time, and carried on an enthusiastic correspondence concerning art with Ritter Gluck. The former Kapellmeister at Stuttgard, Jomelli, was his friend and teacher in musical composition. Mozart, who used to call him the father of keyboard players, visited him often in Vienna. At the last coronation in Frankfurt they played a keyboard concerto for four hands. He died at Wallerstein in 1802.

Source *US-ATS* ML 106 G3L7, pp.15–16. Mentioned but not reproduced in A. Hyatt King, *Mozart in Retrospect: Studies in Criticism and Bibliography* (London, 1955), 258, and *Dokumente* 330, *Documentary Biography* 376.

Commentary Ignaz von Beecke (1733–1803) was music director to Count Philipp Karl of Oettingen-Wallerstein. He first became acquainted with Mozart in Paris in 1766; they met again at Hohenaltheim in 1777. King asserts that Beecke and Mozart performed one of Mozart's own concertos arranged for four hands. It is possible, however, that the reference is to a concerto for two keyboards, such as K242 or 365/316a, or a work by another composer altogether. Mozart composed a cadenza (K624/626aII[K]) for an unidentified concerto in D major by Beecke. For an entry from Lipowsky's *Baierisches Musik-Lexicon* that refers to Mozart and Benedikt Schack, see *Dokumente* 532, *Documentary Biography* 514.

104   From the diary of Wilhelm Backhaus, Mannheim 24 October 1790

Kapellmeister Motzard was here on the 23rd and gave numerous tempos at the rehearsal of Figaro. I embarrassed myself with Motzard. I took him for a journeyman tailor. I was standing at the door during the rehearsal. He came and asked me if one could listen to the rehearsal. I sent him away: 'But surely you would let Kapellmeister Mozart listen?', he said. Then I was more embarrassed than ever.

Source   Roland Würtz, 'Die Erstaufführungen von Mozarts Bühnenwerken in Mannheim', in *Das Mannheimer Mozart-Buch*, ed. Roland Würtz (Wilhelmshaven, 1977), 181; idem, 'Die Erstaufführungen von Mozarts Bühnenwerken in Mannheim', *MJb 1978–9*, 170.
Commentary   Mozart was in Mannheim from about 23 to 25 October. According to Würtz, a hand-written notice on a playbill for this performance reads: 'Mozart himself directed, and departed from here the next day.' Wilhelm Backhaus played Antonio at the Mannheim première of Figaro on 24 October.

105   *Wiener Zeitung*, 26 January 1791

Organ for sale. A good organ by a famous master is for sale at 970 Rauhensteingasse, first floor (rear staircase).

Source   Hans-Josef Irmen, *Mozart – Mitglied geheimer Gesellschaften* (Neustadt an der Aisch, 1988), 279.
Commentary   Mozart had moved to 970 Rauhensteingasse, first floor (entrance from the rear staircase) on 30 September 1790 (in fact, Constanze had moved first, during Mozart's absence), and remained there until his death. It is likely, then, that this advertisement, although unsigned, was placed by Mozart. His ownership of an organ was previously unknown.
Literature   H. C. Robbins Landon, *1791: Mozart's Last Year* (London and New York, 1988), 201–8.

106   Correspondence of Friedrich Wilhelm Gotter, Heinrich Beck, Friedrich Hildebrand von Einsiedel, Gottfried August Bürger and August Wilhelm von Schlegel concerning *Die Geisterinsel*, 24 March 1791 to 7 January 1792

[Gotter to Einsiedel, 24 March 1791]   [Beck] longs no less impatiently for the musical completion of our opera. He inclines, however, to *Mozart*, who at the moment is to be found at Vienna. And I confess to you – much as I am a musical novice – that the samples from the most recent works of this modern Amphion that he had me listen to also decided me in his favour.

[Beck to Einsiedel, 7 April 1791]   As far as I remember having heard from Mozart himself, he will hardly compose any more

German subjects; the reason is that he composes everything for Vienna where German opera is not given, only Italian opera. I would recommend Ditters. . . . Mozart is permanently settled in Vienna. He is in very straitened circumstances and supports himself by teaching.

[Gotter to Einsiedel, 14 May 1791] I spoke with Schröder about the opera and asked his advice concerning the choice of a composer. He is of the opinion that *Mozart* is not to be counted on, for he has too much work for the opera buffa, while *Ditters* would not measure up to a subject of this sort. Instead, he praised highly the talents of a certain *Schwenke*, Bach's successor in Hamburg.

[Bürger to Schlegel, 31 October 1791] Gotter has made a marvellous free adaptation of Shakespeare's The Tempest under the title Die Zauberinsel. . . . Mozart is composing the piece.

[Gotter to Einsiedel, 3 November 1791] The edifice is all ready to receive Mozart's heavenly choruses . . . we may with certainty be allowed to anticipate a prompt and obliging answer from Mozart. . . . After a joint revision of the work, a letter, with the first act, goes immediately to Vienna. . . . In the unhoped-for case, however, that he is overburdened with work, I would be in favour of Reichard above all.

[Gotter to Einsiedel, 15 December 1791] I know Mozart's moral character too little to judge the extent to which his discretion can be relied upon. However, the more distant I am in general from distrust, so the more willingly I agree with your suggestion that the entire work be sent to him immediately.

[Gotter to Einsiedel, 7 January 1792] In his most recent letter, Beck, who sincerely grieves with us for the irreplaceable *Mozart*, recommends the composer of *Oberon*, a certain Wranitzky, as a promising musical genius. I have never heard his name. Do you know anything about him? – Beck also reminded us of Haydn. But Haydn is in London, and is as little to be counted on as Schulz in Stockholm.

Source *Briefe von und an Gottfried August Bürger*, ed. Adolf Strodtmann (Berlin, 1874) iv, 136 (letter of 31 October); Werner Deetjen, 'Der *Sturm* als Operntext bearbeitet von Einsiedel und Gotter', *Shakespeare-Jb*, lxiv (1928), 82–4 (extracts); Alfred Einstein, 'Mozart and Shakespeare's *The Tempest*', in *Essays on Music*, trans. Ralph Leavis (London, 2/1958), 200 (letter of 31 October); Otto Erich Deutsch, 'Mozart und Shakespeares *Sturm*', *Wiener Figaro*, xxxiv (1966), April, 1–3.

Commentary Einstein, who knew only Bürger's letter of 31 October, suggested that Mozart may have agreed to set *Die Geisterinsel*, as the work was eventually called, although there is no evidence for this; as the other letters show, the text was not sent to him before his death on 5 December 1791. The essential facts are also recounted in the preface to *Gedichte von Friedrich Wilhelm Gotter*, ii (Gotha, 1802), p.xlii: 'It was decided to have *Die Geisterinsel* set to music by Mozart; the famous artist died, however, before the manuscript could be sent to him. Since its publication, *Die Geisterinsel* has been set by several distinguished composers, whose musical arrangements of the work are of great value; but it never once had good fortune, and did not receive its deserved success.' The opera was later set by Friedrich Fleischmann (Regensburg, 1796), Friedrich Haack (Stettin [Szczecin], 1798), Johann Friedrich Reichardt (Berlin, 1798), Johann Rudolf Zumsteeg (Stuttgart, 1798), and Johann Daniel Hensel (Hirschberg [Jelenia Góra], 1799). Johann Friedrich Wilhelm Gotter (1746–97) was private secretary to the Duke of Saxe-Gotha, and author of the text to Georg Benda's melodrama *Medea*, which Mozart heard in Mannheim in November 1778. The poet Gottfried August Bürger (1747–94) was the author of *Lenore*; from 1789 he was an unpaid professor of literature, philosophy, philology and history in Göttingen. His correspondent, the author and scholar August Wilhelm Schlegel (1767–1845), was a pupil of Bürger.

Literature Thomas Bauman, Introduction to Johann Rudolf Zumsteeg: *Die Geisterinsel* (New York and London, 1986).

107 Domenico Guardasoni's contract with the Bohemian Estates, 8 July 1791

Specification of the points which I the undersigned agree to maintain in respect of the High Estates of Bohemia . . . concerning a grand opera seria to be put on in this National Theatre for the occasion of the coronation of Their Imperial Royal Majesties, to take place within the first days of September next; for which purpose I shall be given and assigned six thousand florins, or six thousand five hundred if the castrato Marchesi is engaged.

First. I obligate myself to engage a first castrato, of leading quality, such as for example Marchesini, or Rubinelli, or Crescentini, or Violani, or another, but always of leading quality.

And equally I obligate myself to engage a prima donna, also of leading quality, and certainly the best of that level who is free, and I agree that my company shall provide the remaining singers.

Second. I agree to have the libretto written either on the two subjects given to me by His Excellency the Count of the Castle, and to have it set to music by a celebrated master; but in case it will prove to be impossible to do this because the time is so short, I obligate myself to procure an opera newly composed on the subject of *Tito* by Metastasio.

Third. I obligate myself to have made for this opera two new changes of scenery.

And equally I obligate myself to have new costumes made, and specifically for the leading parts of this opera.

Fourth. I obligate myself to illuminate and to provide the theatre with garlands, to mount in every detail the said opera and to perform it gratis for one evening, at the disposition of the said High Estates, within the time specified.

Urgent requirements:

First. That I shall be advanced the sum of six hundred florins for my trip to Vienna and to Italy, on an order payable by a banker in Vienna and in Italy, and that I shall be given a draft for some two thousand florins in case the singers require some monies in advance.

Second. That the remaining honorarium be paid to me on the day that the opera is executed.

Third. That if within the space of 14 days after the day I shall leave for Italy, the opera is cancelled, then only the expenses of the trip shall be paid.

Fourth. Guardasoni will announce at once the day on which he engages a singer; from that day, should the opera not be given, said singer will be reimbursed if he or she has already left Italy.

Fifth. In case the said opera is not given, those items purchased with the money which has been advanced shall be retained, whereas those for which no contract has been issued shall be returned; and a remuneration shall be made to Guardasoni if he can show that the expenses of the trip prove to be greater than the sum advanced.
Prague, 8 July 1791

Henrico Conte di Rottenhan [Count of the Castle]
Casparo Ermanno Conte Kinigl
Giuseppe Conte di Sweerth
Giovanni Conte Unwerth
Giovanni Baron d'Hennet

Domenico Guardasoni
Impresario

Source Tomislav Volek, 'Über den Ursprung von Mozarts Opera "La Clemenza di Tito"', *MJb 1959*, 281–2; *Eibl* 67–8; H. C. Robbins Landon, *1791: Mozart's Last Year* (London and New York, 1988), 88–9 (English translation).
Commentary According to this document, the original contract for the coronation opera was between Guardasoni and the Bohemian Estates, not the Bohemian Estates and Mozart.

108 Antonio Salieri to Prince (Paul) Anton Esterházy, [Vienna August 1791]

Your Highness! Immediately upon the return of the Italian opera company, which had the honour to serve Your Highness in the last magnificent fête at Esterhaza, I was informed that someone had written to Your Highness that I had refused the Imperial court prompter permission to leave for Esterhaza which caused some discomfort at the rehearsals for this fête and also casts the most humiliating suspicions on me.

Surely the person who suggested such things must have been unaware that for the last seven years I have been the teacher of the young Weigl for whose talent and habits I can take credit, in that I myself gave him and got him to compose a poem by a famous poet for the opera at Esterhaza which I myself had started to put into music. Moreover, in order to allow my pupil more opportunity to finish his music in the allotted time and to do himself credit on such a wonderful occasion for him and for his master, for more than two months I myself took over his duties at the court theatre, to the point of attending the minor rehearsals of the opere buffe myself whenever the other work of my own situation did not prevent me. And furthermore, without regretting it, however, I had to decline to write the opera which is being prepared for the coronation in Bohemia, for which opera the impressario came five times from Prague to Vienna to press the commission on me to the point of showing me 200 zecchini, a commission which I could not accept since I alone was attending to the affairs of the court theatre.

Such sacrifices stand singularly opposed to the accusations brought against me. That similar details were disregarded or intended to be disregarded by the person who cast me as the author of the possible or actual upheaval would not upset me much or even at all, but it is my duty to explain my actions in this instance to Your Highness, because an honest man, an artist, and head of a family who spends the few free hours which his occupation leaves him doing good to his neighbour, without any ulterior motives, the same good which he has unreservedly received from others, cannot and must not remain indifferent to this kind of judgment passed on him.

I know through the troupe that the real author of this intrigue was finally discovered, but I am in doubt if that fact is known to Your Highness and that is the reason I have taken the decision to write to you respectfully this justification which I beg Your Highness to receive as a mark of the profound respect with which I beg to subscribe myself as Your Highness's

Most humble and obedient Servant
Antonio Salieri
First Kapellmeister at the
Imperial Court of Vienna

Source 'The Acta Musicalia of the Esterhazy Archive (Nos.101–52)', *Haydn Yearbook*, xv (1984), 153–6 (Italian original and English translation); H. C. Robbins Landon, *1791: Mozart's Last Year* (London and New York, 1988), 86–7 (translation).

Commentary Because the installation of Prince Anton Esterházy as Lord Protector was celebrated on 3 August 1791, this letter must date from after that time. It shows that Salieri, not Mozart, was Guardasoni's first choice to compose the coronation opera for Leopold II. Guardasoni may have visited Salieri before the signing of the contract with the Bohemian Estates, which included an escape clause, permitting him to engage another composer to compose Metastasio's *La clemenza di Tito*, the text eventually set by Mozart (*see* Document 107). The inclusion of this clause suggests that by mid-July Guardasoni may already have had, or expected, Salieri's refusal. Probably Mozart received the commission only about this time.

109 Empress Maria Luisa to Maria Theresa, Prague 7 September 1791

. . . in the evening to the theatre, the gala opera was not much and the music very bad so that almost all of us fell asleep. The coronation went marvellously.

Source John Rice, 'Emperor and Impressario: Leopold II and the Transformation of Viennese Musical Theater 1790–1792' (diss., U. of California, Berkeley, 1987), 334–5 and 352.
Commentary Maria Theresa was Empress Maria Luisa's daughter-in-law. The opera was Mozart's *La clemenza di Tito*, the coronation opera first given on 6 September.
Literature Joseph Heinz Eibl, '". . . Una porcheria tedesca"? Zur Uraufführung von Mozarts "La Clemenza di Tito"', *Österreichische Musikzeitung*, xxxi (1976), 329–34.

110 *Staats- und gelehrte Zeitung des hamburgischen unpartheyischen Correspondenten*, Hamburg 4 October 1791

Vienna, 24 September. . . . Herr **Mozart** has composed a new opera, *Die Egyptische Geheimnisse*, which is one of the most excellent compositions of this outstanding artist. The new sets and costumes for the opera cost 5000 Gulden.

Source *US-PRu* 0902.873 (1791), *Beylage* [unpaginated].
Commentary *Die Zauberflöte* was first given on 30 September at the Theater auf der Wieden.

111 *Staats- und gelehrte Zeitung des hamburgischen unpartheyischen Correspondenten*, Hamburg 14 October 1791

Letter from Vienna, 5 October. . . . Some days ago a new machine comedy called *Die Zauberflöte* was performed at the theatre here. The sets cost 7000 Gulden, and the music was composed by the famous Kapellmeister Mozart. For this reason, and because of the marvellous sets, the piece would have won universal approval, if only the text had also met the minimum expectations.

Source *US-PRu* 0902.873 (1791) [unpaginated].

Commentary A review in the Berlin *Musikalisches Wochenblatt* for December 1791 also cited the high cost of the production and the mediocre quality of the text: '*Vienna*, 9 October. The new comedy with machines, *Die Zauberflöte*, with music by our Kapellmeister *Mozard*, which is given at great cost and with much magnificence in the scenery, fails to have the hoped-for success, the contents and the language of the piece being altogether too bad' (*Dokumente* 358, *Documentary Biography* 409).

112 *Das Wienerblättchen*, Vienna 26 November 1791

On the 17th, the Viennese Lodge 'New-Crowned Hope' celebrated the inauguration of its temple with an oration, procession, and a cantata composed by Herr Mozart. Printed, public admission tickets were distributed.

Source *A-Wsl* A 9316, p.401. Discovered by Dexter Edge.
Commentary Neither Deutsch nor Eibl gives a source for the assertion that this event took place on 18 November (*Dokumente* 361, *Documentary Biography* 413; Eibl, *Chronik* 113). The cantata, *Laut verkünde unsre Freude* K623, was completed on 15 November.

113 *Allgemeine musikalische Zeitung*, Leipzig 1825 [refers to 3 or 4 December 1791]

Brief Contribution to Salieri's Biography, by Anselm Hüttenbrenner. . . . One day I asked Salieri to show me the house where Mozart died, whereupon he took me to the Rauhensteingasse and showed it to me. If I remember correctly, it is marked by a Madonna. Salieri visited him only the day before he died, and was one of the few to accompany his remains [at the funeral procession].

Source Vol.xxvii (issue of 30 November 1825), col.797.
Commentary Anselm Hüttenbrenner (1794–1868), from 1825 director of the Steiermärkischer Musikverein, was Salieri's pupil in Vienna from 1815 to 1818. Salieri's visit to Mozart cannot be confirmed. The rumour that Mozart was a victim of Italian composers in Vienna apparently circulated at the time of his death, if a reminiscence by the author Georg Ludwig Peter Sievers (*b* 1775) is to be believed: 'I was having a composition lesson with Schwanenberg, the worthy, late Kapellmeister at Brunswick, just at the moment that he received a letter from Vienna, informing him of Mozart's death. I mentioned in passing the rumour that Mozart had fallen victim to the Italians in Vienna. "*Pazzi*", answered Schwanenberg ironically (now and then he very gladly spoke Italian), "that's ridiculous; he did nothing to merit such an honour"' (*Allgemeine musikalische Zeitung*, xxi, 24 February 1819, col.120). Johann Gottfried Schwanenberger [Schwanberg, Schwanberger] (*c*1740–1804) was Kapellmeister at the court of the Duke of Brunswick from 1762 to 1802.

114 From the diary of Wenzel Müller, Vienna December 1791

5 December 1791. The great Kapellmeister Amade Mozart died +++ 36 years of age.

Source Karl Pfannhauser, 'Epilegomena Mozartiana', *MJb 1971–2*, 277.
Commentary Wenzel Müller (1767–1835) was music director at the Leopoldstadt Theatre from 1786. [*See plate 6*]

115 *Franckfurter Kayserliche Reichs-Ober-Post-Amtszeitung*, Frankfurt 16 December 1791

Vienna 7 December. . . . Mozart, Imperial Royal court chamber composer, a man who ascended to a high rank among musicians and artists, and whose name will be forever celebrated by friends of music, died in the night of the 5th, of dropsy of the heart, in his 34th year. All Vienna mourns the early death of this man who was so great and virtually inimitable in his art, and who so often enchanted connoisseurs and friends. A few weeks before his death he composed another 4 quartets [*Quadros*], in which he nearly surpassed even himself in art, modulation and intensity of expression.

Source *D-Rtt* Publ. 820/34 [unpaginated]. An abbreviated version of this notice, dated Vienna 10 December, also stating that Mozart composed four quartets shortly before his death, appeared in the *Staats- und gelehrte Zeitung des hamburgischen unpartheyischen Correspondenten* for 20 December 1791 [unpaginated].
Commentary Almost certainly the reference to four quartets, and to their recent composition, is an error. In the *Musikalische Korrespondenz der teutschen Filarmonischen Gesellschaft* for 28 December 1791 (p.411), Heinrich Philipp Bossler reported that 'only a few weeks before his death, he composed 4 quartets, which were engraved by Artaria in Vienna'. The reference here must be to the *three* quartets K575, 589 and 590 published by Artaria in December. Other notices concerning Mozart published in the *Franckfurter Kayserliche Reichs-Ober-Post-Amtszeitung* on 17, 20, 23 and 26 December are reprints from the Viennese manuscript newspaper *Die heimische Botschafter* of 13, 16 and 18 December (*Dokumente* 373–4, *Documentary Biography* 423–6).

116 *Staats- und gelehrte Zeitung des hamburgischen unpartheyischen Correspondenten*, Hamburg 16 December 1791

Vienna, 7 December. Wolfgang Mozart, Imperial Royal court chamber composer, died here during the night of the 4th–5th of this month. Known throughout Europe in his childhood because of his rare musical talent, he rose to the rank of a great master through the felicitous development of his exceptional natural gifts and assiduous industriousness; this is shown by his universally loved and admired works and it gives the measure of the irreplaceable loss which music has suffered because of his death.

Source *US-PRu* 0902.873 (1791 *Beylage*) [unpaginated].

117 Johann Haibel to Wolfgang Heribert von Dalberg, Vienna 10 December 1791

Concerning the *Egyptische Geheimnisse*, which is known here as *Die Zauberflöte*, I must respectfully report that I have not yet been able to obtain the opera inasmuch as Herr Mozart has died and during his lifetime he asked 100 ducats for the score. In the meantime I will send Your Excellency the libretto.

Source Formerly in the archives of the Nationaltheater, Mannheim, now lost. Edition: Friedrich Walter, *Archiv und Bibliothek des Grossh. Hof- und Nationaltheaters in Mannheim 1779–1839* (Leipzig, 1899) i, 460 n.1.
Commentary Johann Petrus Jakob Haibel (1762–1826) was a tenor in Schikaneder's company at the Freihaus-Theater auf der Wieden from about 1789. His correspondent, Wolfgang Heribert, Reichsfreiherr von Dalberg (1749–1806), was Intendant of the Nationaltheater at Mannheim from 1778 to 1803. Although Haibel sent Dalberg the score of *Die Zauberflöte* on 29 February 1792, the opera was not produced in Mannheim until 29 March 1794. A review of the performance appeared in the *Gothaische gelehrte Zeitungen* on 24 May 1794 (p.384). The 100 ducats Mozart asked for a copy of *Die Zauberflöte* was as much as he had received from the court for the composition of *Die Entführung* in 1782 and *Figaro* in 1786. After Mozart's death, Constanze also asked 100 ducats for scores of *Die Zauberflöte* and *La clemenza di Tito*. See her letter (of 28 December 1791) to Luigi Simonetti in Bonn (*Dokumente* 377, *Documentary Biography* 428).

118 *Musikalische Korrespondenz der teutschen Filarmonischen Gesellschaft*, Speyer 4 January 1792

Mozart! This favourite of the Muses is dead! His services to music are too important for us to be satisfied with a simple announcement of his passing away. Accordingly, we communicate the following biographical notices concerning him:

    Wolfgang Amadeus Mozart was the son of the famous Kapellmeister to the Prince of Salzburg, Leopold Mozart, whose Violin School is a lasting monument to his fame and merit. Mozart was born in the year 1757 at the place of his father's residence. Aware of the obvious and precociously marvellous talents of his son, [Leopold Mozart] had already taken over his training and education in those years when so many fathers allow the spirits of their children to lie dormant in carefree idleness and ignorance. Mozart had a sister who was only two years older than he. Both children were the darlings of their father, who devoted the time left over from the fulfilment of his duties to their education; the boy was trained as a keyboard player and composer and the daughter as a singer. The father was so diligent that even in his seventh year the young Mozart not only flowered, but produced full blossoms, which astounded Germany, France, England and Italy. In 1764, a French artist immortalized these children in a pretty copper engraving. The still-very-young composer, however, established a more splendid monument with his sonatas, which were engraved in Paris in 1767. Two years later he extended his fame to Italy, where he was made a Knight of the Golden Spur by the Pope. From there he travelled via Naples to Milan where he composed his first commissioned opera, for the wedding of the Archduke; it was received with such approval that he was commissioned to write the opera for the next Carnival.

Undoubtedly these trips had a profound influence on the development of the immortal Mozart's taste, which catapulted him to the position of Germany's favourite composer; for in addition to a profusion of ideas which rules in his works, they are also distinguished by the pairing of his serious native Muse with Italian grace.

After his return from Italy he became Konzertmeister to his sovereign, the Archbishop of Salzburg. Mozart, however, felt within himself a calling, and in order to expand his career and advance his services, he left his native city in 1781 and moved to Vienna as a private music teacher and composer for the National Theatre. In the imperial city he earned all that a man of such merits can earn, fame, honour, attention and a satisfactory income; in the year 1783 he was paid 1600 gulden for a single opera. In 1788 Joseph rewarded his services in particular by appointing him to the position of actual Kapellmeister and I[mperial] R[oyal] court composer, with an annual salary of 6000 gulden. The first opera that he composed in Vienna was *Belmond und Konstanze, oder die Entführung aus dem Serail*, a keyboard version of which was published in Mainz in 1785. This opera can rightly be considered the pedestal upon which Mozart firmly erected his reputation. It was followed by several operettas, mostly made known through Viennese prints, namely: *Le Nozze di Figaro*; *Der Schauspieldirektor*; *Il Don Giovanni*; *Die Maurerfreude*; *Semiramis*; and *Die verstellte Gärtnerin*, among others. In addition to being active for the theatre-loving Viennese public, Mozart was also busy for the rest of the musical public. He furnished Germany, France and England with numerous instrumental works which audibly testify to his solid understanding, the fire of his imagination, and the fecundity and inventiveness of his great genius. His compositions are like pictures that deserve more than a passing glance if all their beauties are to be seen. Mozart's musical genius was fully ripe; but, alas! so was he – for the grave!! In the middle of the glorious course of his life, he was surprised by death, and he passed away on 5 December 1791. On the 14th of the same month, at 11 o'clock, a solemn obsequy was held for him at the small side parish church of St Niklas in Prague; the ceremony was entirely worthy of the great master and did the greatest honour to the orchestra of the Prague National Theatre, directed by Herr Jos. Strobach, and all the musicians who took part.

The day before, a printed announcement was distributed to the nobility and the entire public. On the day itself, all the bells of the parish church were rung uninterruptedly for a full half-hour. Almost the entire city turned out, so that the Italian Square could not accommodate the carriages, nor the church, with room for nearly 4000 people, those who came to honour the deceased. The Requiem was by the famous Kapellmeister **Rosetti** (we patriots call him by his proper name, **Rössler**) and it was so admirably performed by 120 of the best musicians, first among whom was the famous singer **Duschek**, that Mozart's great spirit in Elysium must have rejoiced. In the middle of the church stood a finely illuminated catafalque; three choirs of timpani and trumpets played in muffled tones. The Mass was celebrated by his Excellency, the parish priest Herr Rudolph Fischer; he was assisted by twelve students from the small side Gymnasium, who carried torches, wore mourning-crapes draped diagonally across one shoulder, and carried white cloths in their hands. A solemn silence reigned on all sides and, what is more, a thousand tears flowed for the worthy Mozart, who with his heavenly harmonies had so often filled all hearts with the most tender feelings. So was Mozart still honoured in Prague after his death. All hail to a nation that acts and thinks so nobly, honouring a foreign artist so. And seven times hail that great humanitarian, **Baron von Swieten**, who immediately after the death of his friend Mozart, and in recognition of his services, declared himself ready to embrace as his own Mozart's children, who through the lack of an estate would be destitute, without shelter and education, and to replace their father and care for their future lives!

Source Albi Rosenthal, 'Der früheste längere Nachruf auf Mozart', in *Collectanae Mozartiana*, ed. Cordula Roleff (Tutzing, 1988), 134–6; cited but not reproduced in *Dokumente* 377, *Documentary Biography* 428.

Commentary Despite numerous factual errors – Mozart was born in 1756, not 1757; he never completed a *Semiramis* (he had apparently begun such a work in Mannheim in November 1778); and he did not receive 1600 gulden for *Die Entführung* or 6000 gulden as Imperial Royal Court Composer – this obituary, the most extensive biographical notice of Mozart up to that date, is so detailed about some aspects of Mozart's life as to suggest that the author was personally acquainted with Mozart, or had some authentic source of information. More striking still is a parallel between one sentence of the obituary and a *later* reminiscence of Mozart's sister: '[Leopold Mozart] entirely gave up his violin-instruction and his composing so as to devote all the time remaining to him after his princely duties, to the education of his two children' (*Dokumente* 398, *Documentary Biography* 454). Possibly the author of the obituary was Heinrich Philipp Bossler, publisher of the *Musikalische Korrespondenz der teutschen Filarmonischen Gesellschaft*. Bossler had possibly known Mozart as early as 1783 and published several of the composer's works during the 1780s; they may have met again at the coronation of Leopold II in Frankfurt in 1790, and in Vienna in 1791. Although Bossler was in Prague on 14 December 1791, the description of the obsequies performed at the St Nikolaus church probably is not original; it is virtually identical to a report published in the *Prager Oberpostamtszeitung* for 17 December (*see* Document 179) and the *Wiener Zeitung* for 24 December (*Dokumente* 375–6, *Documentary Biography* 427). The printed invitation to the obsequies is given in *Dokumente* 374, *Documentary Biography* 424.

119 *Salzburger Intelligenzblatt*, Salzburg 7 January 1792

Anecdotes.

I.) Concerning Mozart – Some months before his death he received an unsigned letter, asking him to write a Requiem and to ask for it what he wanted. Because this work did not at all appeal to him, he thought, I will ask for so much that the patron will certainly leave me alone. A servant came the next day for his anwer – Mozart wrote to the unknown patron that he could not write it for less than 60 ducats and then not before 2 or 3 months. The servant returned immediately with 30 ducats and said he would ask again in 3 months and if the mass were ready he would immediately hand over the other half of the money. So Mozart had to write it, which he did, often with tears in his eyes, constantly saying: I fear that I am writing a Requiem for myself; he completed it a few days before his death. When his death became known, the servant came again with the remaining 30 ducats, but did not ask for the Requiem and since then there has been no further inquiry. When it has been copied out, it will be performed at the St Michael's Church in his memory.

Source Ernst Hintermaier, 'Eine frühe Requiem–Anekdote in einer Salburger Zeitung', *Österreichische Musikzeitschrift*, xxvi (1971), 436–7; Karl Pfannhauser, 'Epilegomena Mozartiana', *MJb 1971–2*, 291–2; H. C. Robbins Landon, *1791: Mozart's Last Year* (London and New York, 1988), 160 (English translation); Paul Moseley, 'Mozart's Requeim: a Revaluation of the Evidence', *Journal of the Royal Musical Association*, cxiv (1989), 212.

Commentary Deutsch cities only a later version of this anecdote, published in the *Zeitung für Damen und andere Frauenzimmer*, Graz, on 18 January 1792 (*Dokumente* 526, *Documentary Biography* 439).

120 John Owen, *Travels into different parts of Europe in the Years 1791 and 1792, with familiar remarks on Places-Men- and Manners* (London, 1796) [refers to 1792]

Vienna, Oct. 13, 1792

The second theatre to which I was conducted is stiled the Wiedner. This is in the fauxbourgs. It can boast of no great beauty. Its principal excellence arises from the musicians and singers, who support the whimsical performances here exhibited. The pieces presented in this theatre are usually of a metaphorical description and abound in magic and metamorphose. I was much entertained with the representation of the favorite burletta of the Magical Flute. The scenery was varied in a thousand grotesque forms, and the wonderful powers of the magical flute gave birth to many humourous events. The stile of the composition, though perfectly unnatural, and even monstrous, was yet, by the ingenuity of the author, neither uninteresting nor inelegant. The music was simple and characteristic, assorted well with the composition and added to the enchantment of the action the more potent magic of sweet sounds. This species of dramatic entertainment is novel and delicious. Founded upon the fictions of imagination, it sets probability at defiance, and justifies the wildest caprice of genius.

Source *US-CAw* KF 1531, vol.II, pp.430–31.
Commentary John Owen (1766–1822) undertook a grand tour of France, Switzerland and Austria from the spring of 1791 to early 1793. The letters are addressed to his friend W. Belsham, probably the political writer and historian William Belsham (1752–1827).

121 *Allgemeine musikalische Zeitung*, Leipzig 1799

Some anecdotes from Mozart's life, reported to us by his widow.

1

A Polish count was present for a Sunday musical gathering at which Mozart performed and, like the entire audience, he was completely enchanted by a new quintet for piano and winds. He told Mozart as much, and expressed his wish that Mozart would some time compose for him a trio for flute. He promised to do so when he had the chance. As soon as the Count returned home, he sent Mozart 100 gold half-sovereigns (150 imperial ducats) and a very complimentary note, thanking him for the great pleasure. Mozart was grateful and in return sent him the original score of the quintet, which he otherwise never did, and recounted to his friends with enthusiasm this pleasant experience. The Count was [subsequently] away, but a year later came to Mozart again, asking for his trio. Mozart answered that he had not yet felt himself inclined to compose something worthy of the Count. The Count replied: And perhaps you will not feel inclined to return my 100 gold half-sovereigns, which I paid to you in advance for the trio. It will be remembered that, in the above-cited letter, the money was given as nothing more than a token of his admiration and thanks for his great pleasure. Mozart – angry but noble – paid him the money. The Count kept the original score [of the quintet] and some time later it was published by Artaria as a quartet for piano, violin, viola and violoncello, without Mozart's authorization.

2

He promised the violin player Strinasacchi, now Mad. Schlick in Gotha, a sonata with obbligato violin, but because such minor works were distasteful to him, he postponed finishing it until the day before the concert at which it was to be performed. It was at the court theatre. Now he wrote her part, but did not find time for his own. Emperor Joseph, peering out of his private box, thought he saw that Mozart had no notes in front of him; he had him come, in order to see the score, and was amazed to find nothing but bar lines on his manuscript.*

3

The day before the première of *Don Juan* in Prague, when the dress rehearsal was already over, Mozart said to his wife in the evening, that he would write the overture in the night, and that she should make punch for him, and stay up with him, in order to keep him awake. She did this, telling him fables from Aladin's Lamp, from Eschenputterln, and so on, which made him laugh to tears. The punch, however, made him so sleepy, that he dozed off when she paused and only worked when she recited. Because the strain of drowsiness and the frequent naps and starting up again made the work much too difficult for him, his wife urged him to sleep on the sofa, promising to wake him up in one hour. He slept so soundly, however, that she could not bring herself to do this, and only woke him after two hours. This was at five o'clock. The copyist was ordered for seven, and at seven the overture was finished. Some will recognize the dozing off and starting up again in the music of the overture.

4

When, under Emperor Joseph, he had to declare his income for tax purposes, he wrote on the official notice: too much for what I do, too little for what I could do. That is, in his capacity as chamber composer (for which he was paid 800 florins), the court never gave him a commission.

5

It is a demonstration of his kindness, that he immediately took over and completed the following commission: A person, who according to his employment was to compose twelve violin duets yearly, lost the desire and ideas to write the last two and asked Mozart to write them. After some years it became known that they were Mozart's work; but he did not give them back.

* Note. The sonata is in B flat major and begins with an Adagio.

6

When his wife was seriously ill, he greeted each guest with a finger held up to his lips and a quiet sshh! This became so natural for him that at first, during the period after her recovery, he would greet acquaintances in the street with a finger to his lips, whispering sshh! and doggedly move on.

7

When his wife was ill or weak, he would rise at 5 o'clock in the morning to go for a solitary walk, but never without leaving a note, written like a prescription, by her bed. This included the following loving words: Good morning, dear little wife. I hope that you slept well, that nothing disturbed you, that you did not wake up too suddenly, that you are not cold, bent over or in need, that you do not quarrel with your maid, and do not trip over the doorstep in the next room. Save domestic annoyance until I return, so that nothing happens to you. I will come at – o'clock, etc.

More trifles from Mozart's life, reported by his widow.

1

When Mozart was composing the second of the six quartets dedicated to Haydn, his wife was in labour for the first time. He worked in the same room where she lay. Whenever she gave voice to her suffering, he came to her in order to console her and cheer her up; and when she was calmer, he returned to his manuscript.* The Menuet and Trio were composed exactly at the time of the delivery.

2

Now and then these quartets had a curious fate. When the late Artaria sent them to Italy, he received them back 'because the engraving was so very faulty' – that is, the many unfamiliar chords and dissonances were taken there for engraving errors. Even in Germany Mozart's work now and again did not fare better. The late Prince Grassalkowich, for example, once had these quartets performed by some players from his Kapelle. Time and again he cried out, 'You are not playing correctly!' and when he was convinced to the contrary, he tore up the music on the spot.**

---

* That is, he never composed at the keyboard, but wrote music like letters, and tried out a movement only when it was finished.
** Saint Hieronymus threw Lykophron's *Cassandra* in the flames with equal zeal and for the same reason – because he did not understand her. The saint, however, was honourable enough to acknowledge this candidly, which was not always the case with Mozart's detractors.

3

Mozart's wife had a dog, who was very fond of her. While they were taking a walk in the Augarten, chatting about the faithful animal, she said: Pretend that you are beating me; he will attack you angrily! – As Mozart was following this good suggestion, the sociable Emperor Joseph came out of a summer house –

Ey, ey, married only three weeks and already fighting? Mozart told him [what they were doing] and the Kaiser laughed. During the conversation, which Joseph then pursued, he asked Mozart:

Do you still remember the anecdote with Wagenseil***, that I played the violin and that you, among the listeners in the ante-chamber cried out now: '*Pfui,* that was out of tune', at other times: 'Bravo'.

*** This can be found in the biography of Mozart in Schlichtegroll's *Nekrolog.* That is, as a child of six years, Mozart was brought by his father to the court at Vienna and played before Emperor Franz I. The Emperor came over to turn the pages for him – No, said the little one, let Herr Wagenseil do it: he understands!

Source Vol.i (issue of 6 February 1799), cols.289–92 and (issue of 11 September 1799), cols.854–6.

Commentary The truthfulness of these anecdotes, or that they do in fact derive from Constanze, has never been fully established. In a letter to Gottfried Christoph Härtel of 18 May 1799, Haydn's biographer Griesinger wrote that 'It is said that Mozart's widow will not vouch for the authenticity of the anecdotes published in the *Music-Zeitung*' (Günter Thomas, 'Griesingers Briefe über Haydn: aus seiner Korrespondenz mit Breitkopf & Härtel', *Haydn-Studien,* i, 1966, p.56). While this probably refers to Friedrich Rochlitz's Mozart anec-dotes, also published in the first year of the *Allgemeine musikalische Zeitung* (10 October 1798, cols.17–24; 24 October 1798, cols.49–55; 7 November 1798, cols.81–6; 21 November 1798, cols.113–17; 5 December 1798, cols.145–52; and 19 December 1798, cols.177–83), it is not out of the question that it also refers to the first instalment of Constanze's anecdotes, published in the *Allgemeine musika-lische Zeitung* in February. Furthermore, the very first anecdote raises problems. Less than five years later, Rochlitz reprinted a garbled version of the anecdote (*Allgemeine musikalische Zeitung,* vi, 1803–4, issue of 21 December 1803, col.196) stating that it came from a source in Paris (actually Carl Friedrich Cramer's *Anecdotes sur W. G. Mozart,* 1801), and was probably apocryphal; in short, he did not recognize a story he himself had published, from a supposedly unimpeach-able witness, only shortly before, and this must cast some doubt on the claim that Constanze Mozart was the source of the original anecdote. Artaria did, in fact, publish an arrangement for piano, violin, viola and cello of the quintet K452, but not until 1794, after Mozart's death (see Alexander Weinmann, *Vollständiges Verlagsverzeichnis Artaria & Comp.,* Vienna, 1952, p.35). There are echoes in other documents elsewhere in the Mozart literature: the story of Mozart composing two violin duets, for example, is clearly related to the claim that he composed duets for violin and viola for Michael Haydn (*see* Document 52), and the anecdote concerning Wagenseil derives from Friedrich Schlichtegroll's widely-known *Mozarts Leben* (Graz, 1794), 12. The apparent confused reception of the six quartets dedicated to Haydn, at least, is confirmed elsewhere. According to Giacomo Gotifredo Ferrari's *Aneddoti piacevoli e interes-santi occorsi nella Vita di Giacomo Gotifredo Ferrari da Roveredo* (London, 1830), '[Attwood] arrived in the metropolis [Vienna] at the time when Mozart had just published his six quartets dedicated to Joseph Haydn. He made me a present of a copy, which he sent to me in Naples, with a letter in which he urged me not to pass judgment until I had heard them several times. I tried them . . . with various *dilettanti* and teachers, but we could not play anything but the slow movements, and even these only with difficulty' (Georges de Saint-Foix, 'A Musical Traveler: Giacomo Gotifredo Ferrari (1759–1842)', *The Musical Quarterly*, xxv, 1939, p.460). Similarly, the claim that Mozart composed the quartet к421/417*b* during Constanze's first pregnancy is also reported in the Vincent and Mary Novello travel diaries (*A Mozart Pilgrimage: being the Travel Diaries of Vincent and Mary Novello in the Year 1829*, ed. Nerina Medici di Marignano and Rosemary Hughes, London, 1955, 112); Alan Tyson's paper studies confirm a date for the quartet of June 1783, about the time of the birth, on 17 June, of the Mozarts' first child, Raimund Leopold. The account of Mozart's composition of the overture to *Don Giovanni* is similar to that given by Niemetschek in 1798:

> Mozart wrote this opera [*Don Giovanni*] in October 1787 in Prague. It was quite complete, had been rehearsed and was to be performed two days later; only the overture was still lacking. His friends were in a great state of agitation, which increased every hour, but this seemed merely to amuse him; the more embarrassed they became, the more light-hearted Mozart appeared. At last, on the evening before the day of the first performance, when he had been frivolous long enough, he went into his room towards midnight, began writing, and in a few hours had completed this admirable masterpiece, which connoisseurs rank even higher than the overture to *Die Zauberflöte*. The copyists were only just ready in time for the performance, and the opera orchestra, whose skill Mozart well knew, played it excellently *a prima vista* (Franz Niemetschek, *Life of Mozart (Leben des K. K. Kapellmeisters Wolfgang Gottlieb Mozart, 1798)*, trans. Helen Mauther, London, 1956, p.64).

Rochlitz's claim that Mozart never composed at the piano, however, is suspect: in a letter from Paris of 5 April 1778, Maria Anna Mozart wrote to Leopold: 'The entrance and stairs [to our room] are so narrow that it is impossible to carry up a harpsichord [*Clavier*]; consequently, Wolfgang must go to Monsieur Le Gros's in order to compose, because there is a harpsichord there' (*Briefe* ii.330, *Letters* 520); similarly, Wolfgang wrote to his father on 1 August 1781: 'Right now I am going to borrow a *Klavier*, because I cannot live in my room until I have one; I have things to write and not a minute to lose' (*Briefe* iii.144, *Letters* 756). Rochlitz's annotation is apparently an effort to project a particular view of musical genius and personality, which he did elsewhere, inventing the infamous (and spurious) 'Letter by Mozart to the Baron von . . .' describing Mozart's creative process (*Allgemeine musikalische Zeitung*, xvii, 1814–15, cols.561–6). It may be that all of the anecdotes said to derive from Constanze, even if they are based on fact, were filtered through Rochlitz's fertile imagination and interpreted according to his own lights.

Literature Maynard Solomon, 'Beethoven's Creative Process: a Two-Part Invention', in *Beethoven Essays* (Cambridge, Mass., and London, 1988), 126–38; Alan Tyson, 'Mozart's "Haydn" Quartets: the Contribution of Paper Studies' and 'The Origins of Mozart's "Hunt" Quartet, K458', in *Mozart: Studies of the Autograph Scores* (Cambridge, Mass., and London, 1987), 82–93 and 94–105; Neal Zaslaw, review of *Briefe*, in *Journal of the American Musicological Society*, xxxi (1978), 371–2.

Apocrypha

Apocrypha

122 From the diary of Mrs Hester Lynch Thrale (Mrs Piozzi), London [August–September] 1777 [refers to 1764]

A Boy who played in a surprizing Manner upon the Hautboy was called to perform before King George the 3:ᵈ and beginning with a slow movement which his Majesty took for Bashfulness don't be afraid my little Fellow says he, don't be afraid I say: Afraid! cries the Lad with a wide Stare, why I have played before the Emperour. [marginal gloss in the hand of Mrs Thrale] It was young Mozart, the Instrument not a Hautbois but a Forte Piano or Harpsichord.

Source *US-SM* HM 12138, vol.I, p.239. Editions: *Thraliana: the Diary of Mrs Hester Lynch Thrale (later Mrs Piozzi) 1776–1809*, ed. Katharine C. Balderston (Oxford, 1942), i, 141; Cliff Eisen, 'Mozart Apocrypha', *The Musical Times*, cxxvii (1986), 685.

Commentary Hester Lynch Thrale (1741–1812) was a friend of Dr Johnson. This anecdote is a bowdlerization of a story first reported in Daines Barrington's 'Account of a very remarkable young musician', published in 1771 in the *Philosophical Transactions of the Royal Society* in London: 'This notice taken of him by so great a personage [the empress dowager at Vienna, Maria Theresa], together with a certain consciousness of his most singular abilities, had much emboldened the little musician. Being therefore the next year at one of the German courts, where the elector encouraged him, by saying, that he had nothing to fear from his august presence; Little Mozart immediately sat down with great confidence to his harpsichord, informing his highness, that he had played before the empress' (*Dokumente* 87, *Documentary Biography* 95–6). Mrs Thrale's anecdote, then, does not refer to Mozart's performances before George III on 27 April or 19 May 1764. Possibly her source was Charles Burney, for although the story is not explicitly credited to him, Burney first appears only shortly before it in the *Thraliana*, where he is represented by a series of musical anecdotes. [*See plate 7*]

123 C. F. Barbieri, *A New Treatise on the Theori-Practical, Fundamental & Thorough Bass, also on Composition. Respectfully Dedicated to Mʳˢ Geoᵉ Clerk Craigie of Dumbarnie, By C. F. Barbieri. Piano Forte Master to his Royal Highness the Duke De Berri, and Member of several Philharmonic Societys. Second edition greatly augmented & Improved. – 1ˢᵗ was Pubᵈ in Paris . . . Edinburgh Printed for the Author, & Sold by Robt Purdie 70. Princes Sᵗ J.* [word or words obliterated] *and all the Principal Music Sellers in London* (Edinburgh, n.d.)

Vienna 6 June 1791

My estimed friend,

It was with much satisfaction and pleasure that I received from Mʳ le Comte de Sᵗ Genois six copies of the Theory of the Art of Music and Composition.

I have studied it all with great attention; it gave me much pleasure and it seems to me that you have not forgotten the instruction I once gave you. I have sent [it] to my friends, all of whom praised it highly. Should an opportunity present itself, would you be so kind as to send me an additional twelve copies?

I hope to see you in Paris after the affairs of my late father are settled. Farewell my dear friend. Believe that I am always

Your devoted friend,
A. Mozart

Source   *US-NYp* Drexel 3015 [unpaginated].

Commentary   Little is known about Barbieri, who on the title-page claims to be pianoforte master to the Duc de Berry, a position he can have held only until 1789 when the younger duke, Charles-Ferdinand d'Artois, had to flee Paris. Apparently he was in London during the 1790s; his *Ouverture et trois airs de ballet pour le piano forte* op.13 were published by Longman & Broderip about 1795. However, there is no reference to him in the Scottish Record Office; nor is he mentioned in the Mozart letters. The alleged intermediary, François-Joseph, Count of Genois, is also unknown in the Mozart literature, although he did spend some time in Vienna during the 1780s. Furthermore, Mozart never signed his name 'A. Mozart' and his French orthography – which he occasionally exercised in letters to Constanze – was considerably better than the original publication of the letter suggests:

Viene le 6 Juin 1791

Mon Estimabel Ami,
    J'ai recu avec bocoup de satisfaction et plesir: six copiés de la Théorie de l'art de la Musique et de composition, par la main de M^r le Comte de St Genois.
    J'ai tout examiné avec bocop d'atention, elle ma fait bocoup de plesiers, il me paroit que vous n'avez pas oublié mes instructions que j'ai vous ait donné dans son tems. J'ai distribuoit a mes confrers, touts ils ont fait des grands éloges. Si une occasion se presente; ayes la bonté de m'anvoier douze copies de plus.
    J'ai-sper de vous voire a paris, aprés que mes affairs de mon pere defunct seront terminée. Adieu mon cher. Craiez [*recte*: Croiez] moi pour toujours.

Votre Devoué Ami
A. Mozart

The matter is apparently clinched by the reference to Leopold Mozart, who had died in May 1787 and whose estate was settled by the end of that year. Elsewhere in the treatise, Mozart is mentioned once, in connection with fundamental bass (pp.57–8):

> The fundamental bass is so called because it only makes the fundamental sounds, and proves that Harmony is complete, and the chords are in order. [I]t is as ancient as music itself, and never was separated, but has been greatly improved of late years, by Mozart, Haydn, Bocherini, Martini tedesco[,] Cherubini, Mehul, and Kozeluch, and many other masters of eminence; the present treatise is composed after the model of the Celebrated Mozart.

Presumably the reference here is to the doubtful *Kurzgefaßie Generalbaßschule*, KAnh.C30.04, published in 1817 by S. A. Steiner of Vienna, and in an English translation by Preston of London in 1823. The appearance of these publications suggests that Barbieri's otherwise undated treatise may have appeared in the mid- to late 1820s. The Scottish publisher Robert Purdie (*fl* 1809–*c*1837) had established his printing shop in 1809.

Literature Cliff Eisen, 'Mozart Apocrypha', *The Musical Times*, cxxvii (1986), 684–5; Jamie Croy Kassler, *The Science of Music in Britain 1714–1830* (New York and London, 1979) i, 52.

Reception Documents

German-speaking Europe

124 *Catalogus über die sämtliche Musicalische Werck und derselben Authorn, nach Alphabetischer Ordnung: Welche von Ihro Hochfürstl. Durchlaut dem . . . Fürsten und Herrn Carl Friedrich Erbprinzen zu Hohenzollern angeschafft worden seynd. Consignirt von mir dem Expeditions Rath, und Music-Directore Schindele Ao. 1766* (Sigmaringen, 1766)

Mozzart.
Sinfonia in D à 2. VV. 2. Corn. 2. Clarini. Timp. Viola. et Basso.

Divertimento à Flautotr. Violin. et Basso –

Concerto à 2. Corni con. 2. V.V. Viola et Basso.

Concerto à 2. Corni – 2. V.V. alto Viola con Basso.

Source *D-SI* without shelfmark, p.91.

Commentary The symphony is KAnh.219/Anh.C11.06, a work by Leopold Mozart (Eisen D11), composed not later than 1751. An authentic copy, without the trumpet and timpani parts listed in the Sigmaringen catalogue, survives in *D-HR* 4°536. In July 1786 the Hamburg music dealer Johann Christoph Westphal advertised manuscript copies of the symphony, also in an expanded version, attributed to Mozart (Document 73). The divertimento and the concertos for two horns are otherwise unknown. Presumably they are also meant to be attributed to Leopold Mozart, although their authenticity is uncertain; elsewhere in the Sigmaringen catalogue the concertos are attributed to 'Reluzzi', who was active in Prague *c*1760, according to Ernst Ludwig Gerber's *Historisch-biographisches Lexicon der Tonkünstler* (Leipzig, 1790–92), i, col.267. An authentic concerto for two horns by Leopold Mozart survives in *D-HR* 4°421.

Literature Cliff Eisen, 'The Symphonies of Leopold Mozart: their Chronology, Style and Importance for the Study of Mozart's Early Symphonies', *MJb 1987–8*, 181–93.

125   *Unterhaltungen*, Hamburg May 1767

Music. Paris. In April, **J. G. W. Mozart**, from Salzburg, a child of
nine years and son of the famous violinist, who was uncommonly
applauded here recently for his excellent keyboard playing, published *VI. Sonates pour le Clavecin avec l'Accompagnement d'un Violon*. Price
7 L. 4 S.

Source   *S-Uu* Tidskrifter/Tyska (1767), p.460.
Commentary   The sonatas are K26–31, first published by Hummel at The
Hague and Amsterdam in 1766 and reissued in Paris by Le Menu & Boyer. In
the index to the volume, the announcement is given as 'Mogart, der jungere, hat
Sonaten gesetzt'.

126   *Supplemento II. dei Catalogi delle Sinfonie, Partite, Overture, Soli,
Duetti, Trii, Quattri e Concerti per il Violino, Flauto Traverso, Cembalo ed
altri Stromenti. Che si trovano in manoscritto nella Officina Musica di
Breitkopf in Lipsia 1767* Leipzig 1767

II. Partite, Divertimenti, Cassationes, Concertini.

I. Divert. di MOZART, a Quattro Instrum. Conc. *a Viol. Violonc.* 2
Corn. B.

Source   *The Breitkopf Thematic Catalogue: the Six Parts and Sixteen Supplements
1762–1787*, ed. Barry S. Brook (New York, 1966), 267.
Commentary   K*deest*. Although this early listing probably refers to a work by
Leopold Mozart, it is not entirely out of the question, as Neal Zaslaw suggests,
that the divertimento is by Mozart and one of the '*6 Divertimenti à 4.* für
verschiedene Instrumenten: als Violin, clarino, Corno, flautotrav: fagotto,
Trombone Viola, Violoncello etc:', K41*a*, listed in Leopold Mozart's *Verzeichniß
alles desjenigen was dieser 12jährige Knab seit seinem 7ten Jahre componiert, und in
originali kann aufgezeiget werden* of 1768.
Literature   Neal Zaslaw, 'Leopold Mozart's List of his Son's Works', in *Music
in the Classic Period: Essays in Honor of Barry S. Brook* (New York, 1985), 342.

127   Karlsruhe thematic catalogues, Baden or vicinity, about the
third quarter of the 18th century

27 Sinfonia del: Singore Mozartt

27

Source   *D-KA* Inventar 4, p.19.
Commentary   K*deest*. Almost certainly the Mozart referred to here is Leopold.
Not only do the Karlsruhe catalogues preserve the record of a mid-century
repertory – other works listed on the same page are attributed to Sammartini,

Chiesa, Richter, Cröner, Zach and Gluck – but the musical style of the incipit is similar to Leopold Mozart's symphonies A1 (*D-Asa* MG II 47) and A2 (*D-Mbs* Mus.mss.5427, dated 1751). The origin of the Karlsruhe catalogues is uncertain although two possibilities seem likely: that they derive from the Catholic line of the house of Baden at Rastatt, which died out in 1771 and whose possessions passed to the Margrave of Baden-Durlach; or from a Baden monastery secularized during the early years of the 19th century.

Literature Cliff Eisen, 'Leopold Mozart Discoveries', *Mitteilungen der Internationalen Stiftung Mozarteum*, xxxv (1987), 6.

128 Martin Gerbert, *De Cantu et Musica Sacra a prima ecclesiae aetate usque ad praesens tempus* (St Blasien, 1774)

Johann Zach . . . brilliantly expressed the character of his nation without the admixture of the current international Italian style, as did Ernst Eberlin (successor to Sigismund Biechteler and Heinrich Biber, prefects of the Salzburg Cathedral in this century), an illustrious musician in all respects. . . . A Swabian, he was succeeded by another Swabian, Leopold Mozart, born at Augsburg. Famous for his violin school, he was best known, however, on account of his precocious son . . . who was the wonder of almost all of Europe, led as he was by his father from one country to another.

Source Cliff Eisen, 'Leopold Mozart Discoveries', *Mitteilungen der Internationalen Stiftung Mozarteum*, xxxv (1987), 7–8.

Commentary Johann Ernst Eberlin (1702–62), Kapellmeister at Salzburg from 1749 to 1762, was succeeded by Giuseppe Francesco Lolli (1701–78), not Leopold Mozart, who never advanced beyond the post of deputy Kapellmeister (*see* Document 45). Matthias Siegmund Beichteler von Greiffenthal (*c*1668–1743) was Kapellmeister from 1706 to 1743; Karl Heinrich Biber (1681–1749), son of the violinist Heinrich Franz Biber, was Kapellmeister from 1743 to 1749.

129 *2 Thematischer Cathalog von verschiedener Compositionen von verschiedener Meistern* ['Quartbuch'], central Austria *c*1775

The keyboard must bring you your first acquaintances and make you popular with the great. After that you can have something engraved by subscription, which is slightly more profitable than composing six quartets for an Italian gentleman and getting a few ducats, and perhaps a snuff-box worth three, for your pains. Vienna is even better in that respect, for at least it is possible to get up a subscription for music to be copied for private circulation. You and others have had experience of both (*Briefe* ii.295–6, *Letters* 492).

Source Original destroyed; copy, *A-Wn* S.m. 9040, Book I, pp.4, 8, 14, 18, 23 and 28.

Commentary The works are Mozart's quartets K169, 172, 170, 173, 171 and 168, respectively. The independent transmission of the quartets lends weight to the assertion that the six quartets offered for sale by Torricella in the *Wiener Zeitung* for 10 September 1785, about the same time as Artaria's advertisement for the six quartets dedicated to Haydn, were in fact K168–173 (*Dokumente* 220–22, *Documentary Biography* 251–3, K[6] p.188). The previously unknown dissemination of the works may also explain a passage from Leopold Mozart's letter of 23 February 1778:

> The keyboard must bring you your first acquaintances and make you popular with the great. After that you can have something engraved by subscription, which is slightly more profitable than composing six quartets for an Italian gentleman and getting a few ducats, and perhaps a snuff-box worth three, for your pains. Vienna is even better in that respect, for at least it is possible to get up a subscription for music to be copied for private circulation. You and others have had experience of both (*Briefe* ii.295–6, *Letters* 492).

Possibly, then, the Mozarts had offered the quartets K168–173 on subscription in Vienna in 1775.

Literature Cliff Eisen, 'Contributions to a New Mozart Documentary Biography', *Journal of the American Musicological Society*, xxxix (1986), 625–6; Jens Peter Larsen, 'Haydn und das "kleine Quartbuch"', *Acta musicologica*, vii (1935), 111–23 (and the subsequent exchange with Adolph Sandberger, *Acta musicologica*, viii, 1936, pp.18–29, 139–54 and ix, 1937, pp.31–41; *idem*, 'Evidence or Guesswork: the "Quartbuch" Revisited', *Acta musicologica*, xlix, 1977, 86–102.

130 Christoph Gottlieb von Murr, *Journal zur Kunstgeschichte und zur allgemeinen Litteratur*, Nuremberg 1776

Sketch of a list of the best living musicians in Europe. . . . **Violin**. . . . **Salzburg**. The famous **Mozarts**, father and son.

1. Extract from Charles Burney's notebook (Yale University, Osborn shelves c100)

ordered to play on his bad fiddle just without the door of the Room; when Puteveri suddenly sprang up, seized two candlesticks, placed them on the floor, & danced his Country dance. He next gave us the French opera, which was the most natural & admirable Parody I ever heard, accompanied with all its proper gestures. I thought at the time of trying the power of Italian Musick, but we wanted opportunity & how could we get it properly executed at Paris?"

I passed lately some days at Salsburg — we had a great deal of Musick at the Archbishops who is a Dilettante & plays well on the fiddle. He takes pains to reform his Band, which, like others, is too harsh. He has put Bischietti at the head of it, Composer of il mercato di malventile & il Dottore &c. There is among them an excellent Composer for the Bassoon & other wind Musick, Secchi & Rainer (for so Reiner is to be called for the future by my direction) are to go there on purpose to play before him, that he may learn their stile & write for them. Young Mozhart is too of the band, you remember their prodigy in England. He composed an Opera at Milan for the marriage of the archduke, & he is now to do the same this Carnaval tho' but sixteen years of age. He is great master of his Instrument; for I went to his fathers house to hear him & the & his Sister play together on the same Harpsicord. but she is

2. *Extract from a letter to Charles Burney from Louis De Visme (Yale University, Osborn files)*

3. *Leopold Mozart's petition to Archbishop Colloredo to succeed Lolli as Kapellmeister (Landesarchiv, Salzburg; GA XXVM 26 no.9)*

Augsburgisches Intelligenz = Blatt.

Montag den 12. Dec. 1785.

Allerley Avertissements.
Bey dem Buchhändler Stage in Augsburg auf dem Obstmarkt, ist zu haben.

Josephs und seiner Väter Leben, zur Förderung einer heitern Frömmigkeit und der häuslichen Glückseligkeit für Bibelfreunde in 14 Predigten entworfen, von Joh. Dan. Gotthilf Weilern, erster Diakon der Evang. Barfüßer Gemeinde allhier. 5tes und des 2ten Theils 2tes Bändchen, über 1. Buch Mose 42stes bis 46stes Kap. gr. 8. Augsburg. 1785.

Diejenigen Herren Liebhaber welche fl. 2 24 kr. voraus bezahlt haben, zahlen beym Empfang dieses 5ten Bändchens noch 36 kr. nach, und bekommen das 6te und letzte Bändchen, so gegen Ostern künftigen Jahrs herauskommt, unentgeldlich. Wer aber 30 kr. pränumerirt hat, läßt solches abholen, und zahlt 30 kr. aufs 6te Stück.

Das erste bis 4te Bändchen enthält 47 Predigten über 1. Buch Mose 24stes bis 41stes Kap.

Zum Besten meiner lieben Mitbürger, welche den Pränumerations Termin versäumt haben, will ich diese 6 Bändchen noch bis aufs neue Jahr um fl. 3 geben. Nach diesem aber kostet das ganze Werk fl. 4 30 kr. Augsburg im Monate Dec. 1785.

Conrad Heinrich Stage, als Verleger dieser Predigten.

Die Entführung aus dem Serail ein komisches Sing-Spiel in 3 Aufzügen. Die Musik ist von dem vortreflichen Herrn von Mozart, der Klavier Auszug von Herrn Abbé Starck, Gestochen und herausgegeben von B. Schott, Kurfürstl. Hof - Musikstecher in Mainz,

queer Fol. 1785. fl. 7. 12 kr.
Mémoires Authentiques pour servir à l'histoire du Comte de Caglioftro, 8. à Londres, 1785. 20 kr.

Grabschriften (Launige) 8. Lindau, 1786 6 kr.

Herrn Overbecks Lehrgedicht und Lieder für junge empfindsame Herzen, 8. Lindau, 1786. 36 kr.

Ephemeriden über Aufklärung, Litteratur und Kunst, 1stes und 2tes Bändchen 8. Marburg, 1785. fl. 1. 30 kr.

Zangen (Carl Georg von) Abhandlung von der Zunftfähigkeit der Schäfer, 8. Gießen, 1785. 20. kr.

Gelehrte Sachen.
Kopenhagner Gesellschaft für Bürgertugend.

Es ist bekant, daß in gegenwärtiger Zeit sich an manchen Orten in mehrern Ländern besondere Gesellschaften formiren, und nach gewissen Planen, zu gewissen Absichten vereinigen. Eine solche Gesellschaft ist kürzl ch zu Kopenhagen zur Aufnahme der Bürgertugend zusammengetretten, und die Haupttugend derselben ist keine andere als Sparsamkeit, und eine nach der angenommenen Convenienz unsrer Zeiten eingerichtete Enthaltsamkeit. Ihr allgemeiner Zweck erstreckt sich auf alle die einzelnen Tugenden, die der Begriff des Worts Bürgertugend, umfaßt. Unter diesen giebt das Bedürfnis unserer Zeit der vernünftigen Sparsamkeit de

4. Page from the 'Augsburgisches Intelligenz Blatt', 12 December 1785 (Universitätsbibliothek, Munich)

VERZEICHNIS

DER

BRÜDER UND MITGLIEDER

DER

GERECHTEN UND VOLKOMENEN

ST. JOHANNES □

ZUR

GEKRÖNTEN HOFFNUNG

IM ORIENT ZU WIEN.

N^{ro.} 61

AUF JOHANNES 5788. *(Wien 1788)*

69	Metz Joſeph von.	Official bei dem niederländiſchen Departement.	II.
70	Mozart Wolfgang.	K. K. Kapellmeiſter.	III.
71	Münſterfeld Georg Brachtrupp v.	Kanzelliſt bei der k. k. Staatsrathskanzley.	II.
72	Nevery Alexius Leopold von.	Hofſecretär bei der k. ungariſch - ſiebenbürgiſchen Hofkanzley.	III.

5. Cover of the members' list for the masonic lodge to which Mozart belonged (Newberry Library)

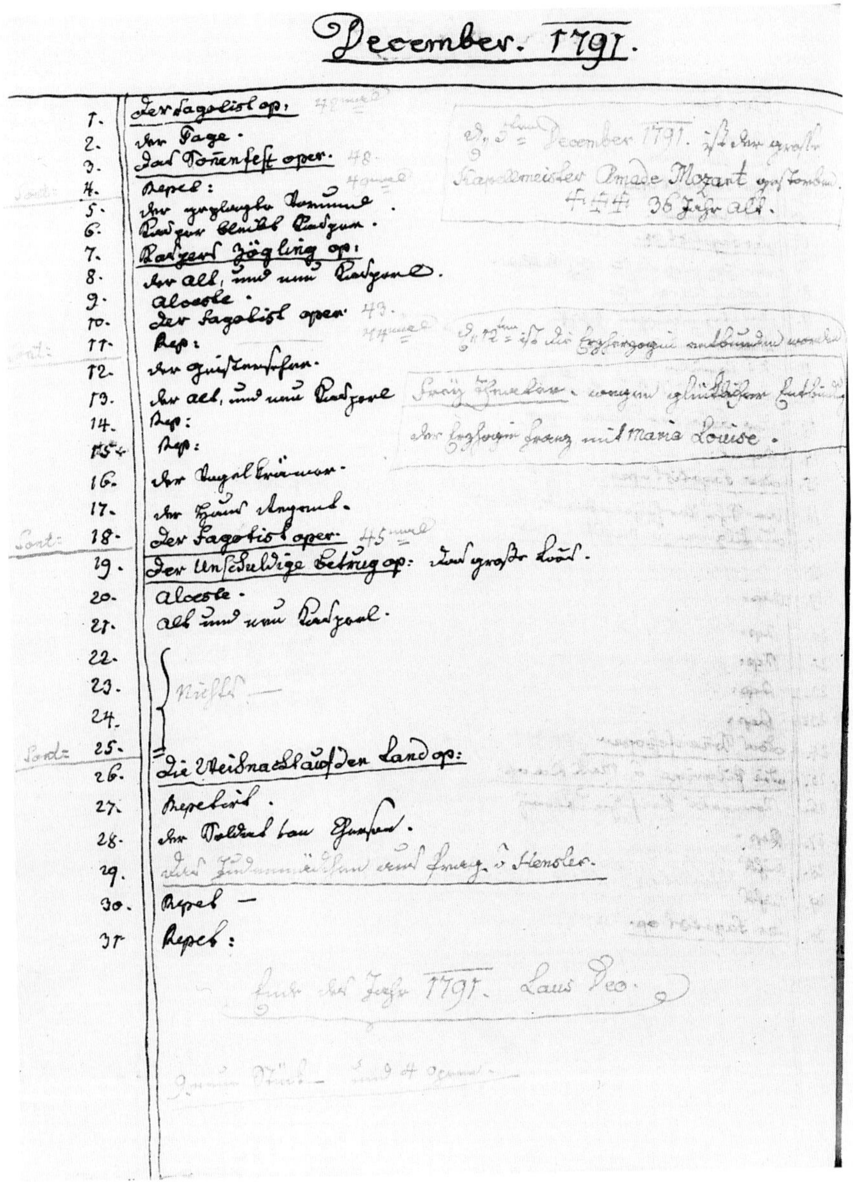

December. 1791.

a Boy who played in a surprizing manner upon the Hautboy was called to perform before King George the 3.d and beginning with a slow movement which his Majesty took for Bashfulness don't be afraid my little Fellow says he, don't be afraid I say: afraid! cries the Lad with a wide Stare, why I have played before the Emperour.

In a conversation the King of Prussia had once with Marshal Keith the latter quoted Scripture: why Keith have you been reading the Bible lately: Yes Sir, re=plies the Marshal, & whatever your Majesty may think of the Book in general, one must allow that Joshua understood a Line of Battle special well.

In a Conference between the Emperor & the King of France concerning the affairs of Europe —— Et pour les Anglois said the latter —— on n'en peut rien decider, replies the Emperour; ce sont un Troupeau de Lions, avec une veritable ane a leur Tête.

Two Scotsmen went to Sir Robert Walpole to apply for a Place for a Third; Sir Robert would not consent —— says Gordon to Campbell, Wully- whistle to Sir Robert. Campbell was it seems a very famous Whistler; but the Scots could not in those Days get Places for Whistling.

no; but it seems they might "whistle for Places"

7. *Page from vol. 1 of Hester Lynch (Salusbury) Thrale Piozzi's 'Thraliana' (Huntington Library)*

8. *Frontispiece and Dance of Turkish Soldiers from Stephen Storace's 'Siege of Belgrade'*

Source *US-CAw* PGerm 247.1, pt. II, p.22.

Commentary The writer Christoph Gottlieb von Murr had probably known the Mozarts since the time of his visit to Salzburg about 1760–61. It is noteworthy that Mozart is described here as an eminent violinist. In a letter to his father of 6 October 1777, he described one of his performances at Munich: 'I played as if I *were* the greatest violinist in all of Europe'; Leopold replied: 'I am not surprised that when you played your last Cassation they all opened their eyes. You yourself do not know how well you play the violin, if you will only do yourself credit and play with energy, with your whole heart and mind, yes, just as if you were the foremost violinist in Europe' (*Briefe* ii.41 and 72, *Letters* 300 and 331).

131   Christian Friedrich Daniel Schubart, *Ideen zu einer Ästhetik der Tonkunst* (Vienna, 1806) [written *c*1784–5, refers to 1770s]

Concerning musical genius. . . . All great musical geniuses are, accordingly, self-taught . . . for the fire that inspires them propels them irresistibly in search of an individual path. The **Bachs**, a **Galuppi**, **Jomelli**, **Gluk** and **Mozart**, already distinguish themselves in childhood through the most magnificent products of their spirits. Harmony is in their souls, and they soon throw away the crutch of art.

Source *GB-Lbl* Hirsch 5463, pp.368–9. Edition: Richard W. Harpster, 'Genius in the 18th Century: C. F. D. Schubart's "Vom musikalischen Genie"', *Current Musicology* (1973), no.15, p.75 (translation).

Commentary Christian Friedrich Daniel Schubart (1739–91) was organist at Geisslingen and Ludwigsburg early in his career, but was a noted journalist, and editor of the *Teutsche Chronik*, from 1774. His *Ideen zu einer Ästhetik der Tonkunst* was written in about 1784–5 but not published until 1806.

132 Johann Georg Meusel, *Teutsches Künstlerlexikon oder Verzeichnis der jetztlebenden teutschen Künstler* (Lemgo, 1778)

Mozart (Leopold), deputy Kapellmeister of the Archbishop of Salzburg; born at Augsburg on 14 November 1719.§§. Six sonatas. 1740. *Der Morgen und der Abend, den Einwohnern der Hochfürstl. Residenzstadt Salzburg melodisch und harmonisch angekündigt; oder: Zwölf Musickstücke für das Klavier, wovon täglich eines in der Vestung Hohensalzburg auf dem Hornwerke Morgens und Abends gespielet wird.* Augsburg, 1759. Very many unpublished works. – See Marpurg's *Beyträge*, vol.3, p.184f. Burney's *Tagebuch*, vol.3, p.262. *Gel. Teutschl.*

Mozart (J. G. Wolfgang), son of the previous; musician in the Kapelle of the Archbishop of Salzburg: born . . . . *Six Sonates pour le Clavecin avec l'accompagnement d'un violon.* Paris 1767. (He composed these sonatas in his ninth year.) Two similar sonatas London . . . 2 similar. 6 similar. 6 Trios. Amsterdam.

Source *C-Tul* (reference), p.90.
Commentary The entry for Leopold Mozart makes reference to: *Sonate 6 per chiesa e da camera* (Salzburg, 1740); *Der Morgen und der Abend . . . oder 12 Musikstücke* (Augsburg, 1759), to which Leopold contributed seven pieces; Friederich Wilhelm Marpurg, *Historisch-kritische Beyträge zur Aufnahme der Musik*, iii (Berlin, 1757), 183–98, esp. 184–5: 'Nachricht von dem gegenwärtigen Zustande der Musik Sr. Hochfürstlichen Gnaden des Erzbischoffs zu Salzburg' (*Dokumente* 13, *Documentary Biography* 10–11); Charles Burney, *Tagebuch seiner musikalischen Reisen, Band III* (Hamburg, 1773); Georg Christoph Hamberger, *Das gelehrte Teutschland oder Lexikon der jetzlebenden teutschen Schriftsteller* (perhaps the second edition; Lemgo, 1767, p.278: 'Mozart (Leopold) chamber musician to the Bishop of Salzburg: born at Augsburg 1719.§§. Versuch einer gründlichen Violinschule. Augsburg 1756. 4.'). The entry for Mozart makes reference to: K26–31, K6–7 and K8–9, probably K301/293*a*, 302/293*b*, 303/293*c*, 304/300*c*, 305/293*d*, and 306/300*l*, published at Paris in 1778, and K10–15. Meusel's work-list apparently served as the basis for a similar account in Forkel's *Musikalischer Almanach für Deutschland auf das Jahr 1782* (*Dokumente* 176, *Documentary Biography* 199). For Meusel's revision of the Mozart entry for the second part of the *Teutsches Künstlerlexikon* (1789), *see* Document 167.

133 Christian Friederich Daniel Schubart, *Leben und Gesinnungen, von ihm selbst im Kerker aufgesetzt* (Stuttgart, 1791) [written 1779]

Each work must constitute a whole, be of individual character but not tarnished by caprice, and be straight-forwardly and clearly performed. Accordingly, the immortal **Schubart** (not Schubert, Schobert or Schober, as the French garble it), **Vogler**, **Ekardt**, **Beeke**, and in particular **Mozardt**, are great models to which budding virtuosos can aspire. . . . A keyboard player does very badly when he takes models that are not German – for what are foreigners such as **Marchand**, **Skarlatti** and **Jozzi*** compared to our **Bach**, **Händel**, **Wagenseil**, **Schubart**, **Beeke**, **Ekardt**, **Vogler**, **Fleischer**, **Müthel**, **Kozeluch**, **Mozardt** – the number of our *Menatseachs* can hardly be counted!

* **Clementi** is an important exception.

Source *US-CAw* 48565.10.14, pp.61–2.
Commentary For Schubart, *see* Document 131. In 1777, Schubart was imprisoned at Hohenasperg by Duke Carl Eugen of Württemberg, allegedly for insulting the duke's mistress. His autobiography was dictated during his imprisonment and, according to his son, completed on 21 April 1779.

134 Johann Nikolaus Forkel, *Musikalischer Almanach auf das Jahr 1782* (Alethinopel [?Berlin], [1781])

Sketch of a small, selected music library. . . . **Duos. For keyboard**. . . . Sterkel. Mozart. Riegel. Schmidt. Schobert. Schröter. Schumann.

Source *US-NYp* Drexel 622, p.112.
Commentary The *Musikalischer Almanach* has also been attributed to both J. F. Reichardt and C. L. Junker. The other composers named are Johann Franz Xaver Sterkel (1750–1817); Riegel, either Henri-Joseph (1741–99) or his brother Anton (?1745–after 1807); Johann Samuel Schobert (*c*1735–67); and Johann Samuel Schröter (*c*1752–88). Schumann is perhaps Frederic Theodor Schumann (*fl* London 1760–80). Schmidt cannot be identified. 'Duos' here means accompanied sonatas.

135 Carl Friedrich Cramer, *Magazin der Musik*, Hamburg 9 November 1783

Description of a mechanical keyboard instrument [*Clavier-Flügel*]**, invented and manufactured by the Court Mechanic and Member of the Musical Academy of His Electoral Highness of Pfalz-Bayern in Munich, P. J. Milchmeyer.** Because it consists only of strings and crow's quills, this instrument, newly-invented by me, can be maintained by any tuner and instrument maker. It is of normal length, but is three inches higher, and has three keyboards, each one set above the other, that are very low in order not to tire the arm because of their height. With regard to the mechanics and stops, these are entirely hidden, and cannot be seen from the inside or outside. They are controlled with the knees by two levers, with which one can produce true and fine musical expression, together with all the chief stops. . . . I flatter myself that it is in every respect original, and not in the least bit copied from another instrument. I have a collection of choice music, by the most famous composers, **Bach, Bocherini, Eckard, Edelmann, Eichner, Forckel, Gluck, Mozart, Schobert, Schroeter, Sterkel, Vogler** and other famous composers, as well as my own compositions, which I will gladly provide to purchasers of this instrument.

Source Facsimile edition, pp.1024–8.
Commentary Johann Peter Milchmeyer (*c*1750–1818) was active as a piano and harp teacher in Paris from 1770 to 1780, in Mainz from 1780 to 1798, and in Dresden thereafter. His invention, no example of which survives, is also described in the *Musikalischer und Künstler Almanach auf das Jahr 1783* (Kosmopolis [?Berlin], [1782]), 152–3. Milchmeyer's *Pianoforte-Schule oder Sammlung der besten für dieses Instrument gesetzten Stücke, aus den Werken der berühmtesten Tonkünstler ausgewählt* (Dresden, 1797–9) and *Kleine Pianoforteschule für Kinder, Anfänger und Liebhaber* (1801) both include examples by Mozart.

136 Carl Friedrich Cramer, *Magazin der Musik*, Hamburg 9 July 1784

Miscellaneous Reports and Opinions from Italian letters 1783.
. . . **Mozart's** sonatas with obbligato violin please me very much.

They are very difficult to play. Although the melodies are not entirely new, the accompaniment for the violin is masterly; it is well-fitted to the harmony and frequently introduces imitations at the proper times. The sonatas must be heard often.

Source Facsimile edition, p.60.

Commentary The sonatas are probably K296, 376/374d, 377/374e, 378/317d, 379/373a and 380/374f, published by Artaria in Vienna in 1781 and reviewed in Cramer's *Magazin der Musik* in April 1783 (*Dokumente* 190, *Documentary Biography* 214).

137 *Anhang zum Verzeichniss von Musikalien welche bey Johann Christoph Westphal & Comp. auf den grossen Bleichen in Hamburg zu haben sind. Anno 1785,* Hamburg 1785

In manuscript:
Mozart, W. A. I [Symphony] à 11 with timpani and trumpets ad
    libit. No. I. D major. New and original
— I dito à 13 with horns, timpani, trumpets and bassoons, No. 2.
    D major. New & original
— I dito à 14, similar. No. 3. D major. New and original

Source *B-Br* Fetis 5205/MN Mus. 103 [unpaginated].

Commentary Two of the advertised symphonies can be identified by comparison with Breitkopf & Härtel's early 19th-century *Alter handschriftlicher Catalog von W. A. Mozart's Original Compositionen Abschrift* (*A-Wgm* 4057/38): symphony no.1, listed in Breitkopf's catalogue as 'Westphal No.1' is K203/189b; symphony no.2, identified by Breitkopf as 'Westphal No.2', is K320. The third symphony, in D major, cannot be identified, although it may be K204/213a, 250/248b or 385. A comparison of Westphal's catalogues with advertisements for manuscript music published in Vienna suggests that the works may be identical to three symphonies advertised by Johann Traeg in the *Wiener Zeitung* for 16 February 1785 (*Dokumente* 210, *Documentary Biography* 237). Deutsch speculated that the symphonies offered by Traeg were perhaps K319, 338 and 385.

Literature Neal Zaslaw and Cliff Eisen, 'Signor Mozart's Symphony in A-Minor, KAnhang 220 = 16a', *The Journal of Musicology*, iv (1985–6), 195–7.

138 *Concert de M^rs les Amateurs,* Mannheim 15 May 1785

Overture by Gossec
Mademoiselle Crux, Violin Concerto by Stamitz
Mademoiselle Fränzl, Scene by Benda
Monsieur Wendling, Flute Concerto of his own composition
Monsieur Goes, Air by Piccini

Monsieur Fränzl, Violin Concerto of his own composition
Madame Wendling, Air by Holzbauer
Monsieur Baron Dalberg, canon, Keyboard Concerto by Mozart
Symphony by Hayden

Source   *Mannheim Geschichtsblätter*, x (1909), 186–7.

Commentary   Wolfgang Heribert von Dalberg (1749–1806) was Intendant of the Mannheim Nationaltheater from 1778 to 1803. Several concertos by Mozart had been published up to this time, including K175+382 (Paris, 1785) and K413/387a, 414/385p and 415/387b (Vienna, 1785); others circulated in manuscript copies. An account of *Concerts de M^rs les Amateurs* appeared in the *Pfälzische kleine Kalender* for 1784 (pp. 55–6):

> *Liebhaber* Concerts. These were established on 20 November 1778 by Konzertmeister Fränzl, and will be given throughout this winter in the same fashion as last year, under his direction. Other than visitors of rank, who must have a complimentary ticket, no one other than those who have subscribed will have entry. In addition to many of the famous masters from the Electoral court orchestra who have remained here, and many of their skilful students, numerous other amateurs of instrumental and vocal music (in all 82 persons) will be heard there; and because in addition to the refined taste displayed here only the most select new music will be performed, one can expect nothing less than the most pleasant entertainment from this company. The concerts will be given every Friday throughout the winter.

The violinist Ignaz Fränzl (1736–1811), from 1778 music director of the newly-founded Nationaltheater in Mannheim, first met Mozart at Schloss Schwetzingen in 1763. They met again at Mannheim in 1777 and it was for the *Concerts de M^rs les Amateurs* that Mozart began composing the fragmentary concerto for violin and piano KAnh.56/315f in 1778. On 12 November 1778 he wrote to his father: 'An academy of amateurs, like the one in Paris, is being founded here – H: fränzel directs from the violin – and I am now writing a concerto for keyboard and violin for them' (*Briefe* ii.506, *Letters* 631).

Literature   Roland Würtz, '". . . ein sehr solider Geiger": Mozart und Ignaz Fränzl', *Acta Mozartiana*, xvi (1969), 65–72.

---

139 *Staats- und gelehrte Zeitung des hamburgischen unpartheyischen Correspondenten*, Hamburg 1785

The following music has arrived at the Musical Warehouse here:

1)   Grand Concert pour le Clavecin avec l'Accompagnement de deux Violons, Alto & Basse, deux Hautbois & deux Cors, composé par W. A. Mozart, Oeuvre IV. Livre I. publié à Vienne chez Artaria & Compag.

2)   Dito Oeuvre IV. Livre II.

3)   Dito Oeuvre IV. Livre III.

The first concerto is in *A major*, the second in *F major* and the third in *C major*. All three are very well composed and include much that is new, as well as various brilliant passages. Each *Oeuvre* costs 4 Marks.

. . .

8)   Trois Sonates pour le Clavecin ou Piano forte, composées par W. A. Mozart. Oeuvre VI. Vienne, chez Artaria & Comp. (Costs 4 Marks.)

Three excellent sonatas, which, when properly played, make a good effect.

Source *US-PRu* 0902.873 (1785, *Beyträge zum gelehrten Artikel . . . Sechstes Stück*) [unpaginated].
Commentary The concertos are K413/387*a*, 414/385*p* and 415/387*b*. The sonatas are K330/300*h*, 331/300*i* and 332/300*k*. The concertos were published by Artaria in 1785, the sonatas in 1784.

140 *Staats- und gelehrte Zeitung des hamburgischen unpartheyischen Correspondenten*, Hamburg 1785

Available from the Musical Warehouse: . . . *Trois Sonates pour le Clavecin ou piano forte avec l'Accompagnement d'un Violon, composes par W. A. Mozart. Oeuvre I. à Amsterdam, chez J. Schmitt.*
These three sonatas are more original than the others by Herr **Mozart** that are known to us and for this reason we prefer them. The second, in *E minor*, pleased us particularly. The violin can by no means be omitted.

Source *US-PRu* 0902.873 (1785, *Beyträge zum gelehrten Artikel . . . Neuntes Stück*) [unpaginated].
Commentary The sonatas are K301/293*a*, 304/300*c* and 302/293*b*, published by Schmitt in Amsterdam about 1780. The works were originally published, together with the sonatas K303/293*c*, 305/293*d* and 306/300*l*, by Sieber in Paris in 1778.

141 *Premier Concert de M^{rs} les Amateurs*, Mannheim 23 November 1785

Overture by Rigel
Grand Chorus by Schweitzer
Mademoiselle Baroness Castell, Air by Mozart
Messieurs de Stengel, Concerto for two Flutes by le Prévôt de Stengel

Grand Chorus by Bach
Monsieur Danner jr, Violin Concerto of his own composition
Mademoiselle Schäfer, Scene by Jomelle
Grand Chorus by Bach

Source *D-Msa* Geheimes Hausarchiv, Korrespondenz-Akten nr.882/V/b.
Commentary Mademoiselle Castell cannot be identified, although she may be some relation to the Munich Privy Councillor Joseph Sebastian von Castell, who is mentioned by Mozart in a letter of 1 December 1780: 'Yesterday morning Mr. Raaff came to see me again in order to hear the aria in Act II [of *Idomeneo*, 'Fuor del mar']. . . . He said to Herr von Vierreck, Chief Equerry, and to Herr von Castel (I knew this from a reliable source and now I know it from him himself): *until now I have been accustomed to accommodate myself in my roles, both in the recitatives and the arias – here, however, everything remained as it was, there is no note that does not suit me, etc.*' (*Briefe* iii.40, *Letters* 677–8).

142 *Troisième Concert de M^rs les Amateurs*, Mannheim 9 December 1785.

Overture by Mozard
Monsieur Goes, Scene by Prati
Mademoiselle Crux, Violin Concerto by Jarnowick
Symphony by Hayden

Messieurs Franzel, Nicola, Dausch & de Villiez, Concertante by C. Stamitz
Madame & Mademoiselle Wendling, Duo by Cimarosa
Symphony by Jomelli

Source *D-Msa* Geheimes Hausarchiv, Korrespondenz-Akten nr.882/V/b.
Commentary The 'overture' by Mozart cannot be identified, although possibly it was K319 or K385, published by Artaria in 1785; K203/189*b* and K320 also circulated at this time in manuscript copies (*see* Document 137).

143 Hans Adolf Freiherr von Eschstruth, *Musicalische Bibliotek für Künstler und Libhaber* (Marburg, 1784–5)

Reviews. . . . X. *Journal de Musique Militaire ou Pieces d'Harmonie, composées et arrangées par les meilleurs maitres, pour deux Clarinettes, deux cors, deux Bassons obligées et deux Clarinettes, deux Trompetes, deux petites Flutes, Fifres, Tambour, Tambourin, Cimbales, Triangles, Serpent ou Contrebasson ad libitum . . . à Strasbourg chéz J. Reinhard Stork, Luthier, Marchand de Musique au concert des Cicognes, prés le pont du corbeau.*
An attractive copper-engraved title-page after the blue wrapper, with works by *Mozart*, *Gretri*, *Monsigny*, and *Müller*, clearly printed on writing paper; partly well-known opera arias and overtures; partly new marches and allemandes. Concertos, symphonies, rondos, variations on arias and the like are to follow, each volume about 41 pages.

Source *D-Mbs* Mus.Th.980, *II. Stück*, pp.235–6.
Commentary There is no evidence that Mozart met Johann Reinhard Storck (1766–1800), a prominent instrument manufacturer and music dealer in Strasbourg, during his visit there in October and November 1778. No copy of the *Journal de Musique Militaire* survives.
Literature Cliff Eisen, 'Some lost Mozart Editions of the 1780s', *Mitteilungen der Internationalen Stiftung Mozarteum*, xxxii (1984), 64–5.

144 Christian Gottlob Neefe, *Dilettanterien* (n.p., 1785)

In his instrumental works for several parts, the great Joseph Haydn – a genius who has made a sensation not only among his contemporaries, but will also do so for musical posterity – has produced elegant and expressive masterpieces and shown what a composer can bring to them, how powerfully and intelligently he can affect his listeners, when head and heart are united, and his audience is not among the *Pecus Campi*. Every one of his smallest notes is significant. Mozart, Kozeluch, Kraus, Pleyel, Reicha and Rosetti stand at his side, or laudably follow in his footsteps.

Source *A-Wgm* 2989/4, p.131.
Commentary Christian Gottlob Neefe (1748–98) had established himself in Bonn by about 1780, where he became Beethoven's piano and composition teacher.

145 *Septième Concert de M^rs les Amateurs*, Mannheim 20 January 1786
Overture by F. Danzi
Monsieur Bernay, Flute Concerto by Rosetti
Mademoiselle Baroness de Castell, Air by Giordaniello
Monsieur Streicher, Forté Piano Concerto by Hoffmeister

Symphony by Haydn
Monsieur Ferdinand Franzl, Violin Concerto by Jarnowick
Madame & Mademoiselle Wendling, Messieurs Danzi & Epp, Quartet by Mr. Mozart
Symphony by Franzl

Source *D-Msa* Geheimes Hausarchiv, Korrespondenz Akten nr.882/V/b.
Commentary Mozart was well acquainted with the Wendling family which included Johann Baptist Wendling (1723–97), a flautist in the Mannheim court orchestra from 1751 or 1752 and one of the intended soloists for the Sinfonia Concertante ΚAnh.9/297*B*; his wife Dorothea Wendling (1736–1811), a singer at the Mannheim court from 1752, for whom Mozart composed the recitative and aria 'Basta, vincesti . . . Ah non lasciarmi' Κ295*a* as well as the role of Ilia in *Idomeneo*; their daughter Elisabeth Augusta Wendling (1752–94), for whom Mozart composed some French songs, thought to include 'Oiseaux, si tous les ans' Κ307/284*d* and 'Dans un bois solitaire' Κ308/295*d* (see *Briefe* ii.265 and 305, *Letters* 468 and 498); and J. B. Wendling's sister-in-law, Elisabeth Augusta Wendling (1746–86), who sang Electra in *Idomeneo* and for whom Mozart may have composed the recitative and aria 'Ma, che vie fece, o stelle . . . Sperai vicino il lido' Κ368. Franz Danzi (1763–1826) was a member of the Nationaltheater orchestra at Mannheim from about 1778 and cellist in the Munich court orchestra from 1783. Epp is probably Friedrich Epp (1747–1802), who sang in early performances of *Die Entführung* at Mannheim (Document 146) and Tamino in the first performance of *Die Zauberflöte* there in 1794. Possibly the quartet by Mozart was one of the six 'Haydn' quartets published by Artaria in Vienna in September 1785.

146 *Pfalzbaierisches Museum*, Mannheim [1786]
Letters concerning the Mannheim stage. . . . Thursday, 26 January. Die Entführung aus dem Serail, a Singspiel in 3 Acts.

Mlle Schäfer, who was away for some time, and then ill after her return, appeared again today for the first time as Konstanze. The public loudly expressed its delight in seeing and hearing her again. She sang the first aria masterfully.

Herr Gern, as Osmin, overacted somewhat the comic aspects of his role.

Herr Epp sang to applause. I only wished that he made more of a distinction between the character of a nobleman, and that of a peasant; for he delivered some words too harshly, which may be appropriate to the role of a *Christliebchen*, but not to this one.

As the Bassa, Herr Renschüb wandered about the stage indifferently and delivered one speech just like the other.

I do not know why Herr Böck did not play this role; I believe he should not refuse to take this part, since it would be for the best of the whole here.

The public received the performance in the best possible way.

Source *D-Mbs* Per. 164m, Band II (1785–6), pp.193–4.
Commentary Mozart's *Die Entführung aus dem Serail* was first given at Mannheim on 18 April 1784.

147 Carl Friedrich Cramer, *Magazin der Musik*, Hamburg 21 November 1786

On Thursday, an advertisement was brought to me for a *Liebhaberkonzert* at an inn the next day, so I delayed my departure until Saturday. . . . The concert began with a new Symphony in D by **Mozart**, which was all the more welcome to me because I had long been eager to hear it. Herr chamber-musician **Lehritter** (a stepbrother of Abbé Sterkel) led the orchestra, which consisted of approximately 45 or 46 mostly young artists, with so much fire and solidity that I stood there full of astonishment. Everything hung together from one beat to the next: tempo, execution, forte, piano, and crescendo were in every respect perfect and I had nothing more to wish for, except that you were here with me. Mozart's symphony itself I consider a masterpiece of harmony.

Source Facsimile edition, p.954.
Commentary The symphony may have been K203/189*b*, 320 or 385, all of which circulated, in manuscript copies or printed editions, in 1785.

148 Christian Friedrich Daniel Schubart, *Musikalische Rhapsodien* (Stuttgart, 1786)

We still have great pillars in the temple of Harmony. There stands our Gluck, the inventor; there Benda, the intimate friend of elegant song; there our Naumann, Schuster, Hiller, Rolle . . . there Mozart and Haydn, the givers of music; there our immortal theorists, no less great in execution – our Bachs, Vogler, Reichardt, Schulz, Forkel.

Hohenasperg, in January 1786.

Source   Christian Friedrich Daniel Schubart, *Gesammelte Schriften und Schicksale*, ed. Ludwig Schubart (Stuttgart, 1839–40), 57.

Commentary   For Schubart, *see* Document 131.

149   Carl Friedrich Cramer, *Magazin der Musik*, Hamburg 17 December 1786

Praenumeration pour le Forte Piano ou Clavecin I. II. III. IV. Cahiers pour les Mois November. December. 1785. Janvier & Fevrier 1786. Publiée & se vend a Vienne au Magazin de Musique du Mr. Hoffmeister. The first four monthly instalments of this periodic music collection include quartets, terzetts, sonatas for four hands, fugues, concertos, and variations by Albrechtsberger, Mozard, Haydn, Wanhall and Hoffmeister, easy and difficult, galant and serious pieces. Each individual work by an author is also separately printed, and presumably will be sold individually. The best in the collection is a terzett by Haydn; then Mozart's compositions. The volumes could be very interesting if in future the editor is more careful in the selection of works. . . .

Taschenbuch für Freunde und Freundinnen der Musik, edited by J. F. Marpius in Erlangen. Volume 1, octavo, 3 Kreuzer. This small work consists of two parts. The first includes some new arias, minuets, English [dances], Schleiser and marches, by Mozart, Rosetti, Schubart, &c. In the second part are short items concerning music itself, namely: 1) short biographies of composers; 2) something from the theory and other material appropriate to the subject of music; 3) letters; 4) a short history and 5) anecdotes concerning music; 6) an alphabetical list of the best composers in Germany; 7) a sketch of a personal music library; 8) musical riddles. The entire volume, both notes and text, is engraved.

Source   Facsimile edition, pp.1042–3 and 1051–2.

Commentary   For Hoffmeister's subscription series, *see* Document 61. The second *cahier* included Mozart's piano quartet K478, the third the accompanied sonata K481. The terzett by Haydn is H XV:10, published by Hoffmeister in the third *cahier*, about January 1786. Jacob Friedrich Martius was organist at the Altstädter Kirche in Erlangen from 1781 and at the Neustädter Kirche from 1786. Although no copy of the *Taschenbuch* is extant, its contents are known from a review published in the *Oberdeutsche allgemeine Literaturzeitung* for 1791 (pp.313–15)

> The following songs are to be found in the first number: *Schlaf wohl, du Himmelsknabe, du &*. *Mein trauter Michel ist so gut &*. Text and melody by

Schubart; the charming Romanze, with abbreviated ritornello: 'Im Mohrenland gefangen' &. from Brezner's *Die Entführung aus dem Serail* by Mozart (a delightful vignette accompanies this last, Osmin hanging from a tree; Belmonte, however, must be stuck behind the house!). *Bild der Unschuld, schönste Blume &.* by Reichardt (the composer not named); three marches by Neefe, Hiller and Smith; three Menuets by Rosetti, Becke (the bass is faultily engraved here: in measures 2, 6, 14 and 15 the upper bass note must be F, not E♭), and Pleyel (from a symphony, presumably arranged by Herr Martius himself, and tastefully abridged); three contradances by Rosetti, Kellner and Muck (based on Mozart's 'O wie will ich triumphiren!'); and two Schleiser by Christmann und Marzius.

The second number includes the songs *Liebchen &c.* by Rosetti, charmingly set (although the interlude, so disagreeably separating the text *dann genießen wir – die Freuden alle ungestört*, is objectionable); *Sonst war ich so heiter &c.* by Much, set by Marzius (although it might have gained in naïveté through the use of the same metre; the end of the first part in G is not very good); *Lachet nicht, Mädchen &.* by J. Haydn, an excellent composition; *Holde Knospe, deiner Mutter Freude &c.* by Tank, agreeably set by Marzius; and *Sey wilkommen, feyerliche Stunde &c.* very well expressed; *Hier Schert des Herrn und Gideon &c.* by Rautenstrauch, set by Kellner; and a march, by Marzius, based on Mozart's overture to *Die Entführung aus dem Serail* (the beginning of the second part is surprising; the quick transition from D through G minor to C is striking); four undistinguished Menuets by Hayden, Pleyel and two unidentified composers whose work, however, is not correct; two charming Andantes by Schmidt and Naumann (from his opera *Orpheus und Euridice*); and four dances by Breitkopf, Marzius, and two unidentified composers.

Ernst Ludwig Gerber described 'a selection of pretty trifles by Schubart, Neefe, Hiller and Rosetti' in his *Historisch-biographisches Lexicon der Tonkünstler* (Leipzig, 1790–92), i, cols.895–6.

Literature Cliff Eisen, 'Some lost Mozart editions of the 1780s', *Mitteilungen der Internationale Stiftung Mozarteum*, xxxii (1984), 66–7 (*Taschenbuch* by Martius).

150 *Tagebuch der Mannheimer Schaubühne*, Mannheim 1786–7

8 February [1787]. *Die Entführung aus dem Serail* . . . for the 14th time. This work continues to be a favourite of our public, and today again the house was full. It was acted and sung with warmth. Mademoiselle Schäfer as Konstanze, Herr Epp as Belmonte, and Herr Gern as Osmin rightly deserved, and received, the loudest applause. Mademoiselle Jacquemin as Blonde somewhat slighted the beautiful music; over the years, one demands that a singer or actress constantly improve.

Source D-Mth Per 00009, p.189.
Commentary *Die Entführung aus dem Serail* was first given at Mannheim on 18 April 1784.

151 *Anhang zum Verzeichniss von Musicalien, welche in der Musicalischen Niederlage bey Johann Christoph Westphal & Comp. in Hamburg zu haben sind. März 1787*, Hamburg March 1787

In manuscript
Mozart,   I Symphony à 13. D major,
              No.5, with timpani and trumpets. New
_____   [Symphony] à 9, with obbligato bassoon, F major
Mozart,   I Trio, with I violin and violoncello, G major

Source   B-Br Fetis 5205/MN Mus. 103 [unpaginated].
Commentary   The symphony in D major is probably K250/248*b* or 385 ('Haffner'); the symphony in F major is KAnh.C.11.08. Westphal's advertisement for KAnh.C.11.08 includes the previously unknown information that the work included an obbligato bassoon part. The trio in G major may be K496.
Literature   Neal Zaslaw and Cliff Eisen, 'Signor Mozart's Symphony in A-Minor, K.Anhang 220 = 16a', *The Journal of Musicology*, iv (1985–6), 195–7.

152   Carl Friedrich Cramer, *Magazin der Musik*, Hamburg 9 April 1787

Cassel, 21 March 1787. . . . The music performed this winter was mostly by the best masters including symphonies chiefly by **Haydn**, but also often by **Pleyel**, **Ditters**, **Zimmermann**, **Rosetti** and the like. The keyboard works were by **Mozart**, **Kozeluch** or **Haydn** and the arias by **Sacchini**, **Päsiello**, **Naumann**, **Piccini** and **Gretry**.

Source   Facsimile edition, p.1276.

153   From the diary of Count Karl von Zinzendorf, 21–5 September 1787

[Schwarzenberg Castle, Český Krumlov, 21 September] The opera *Figaro* played on wind instruments, I didn't listen.
[Frauenberg, 25 September] After dinner, music from *Figaro*. . . .

Source   H. C. Robbins Landon, *Mozart: the Golden Years* (London and New York, 1989), 33 and 239 n.11.
Commentary   Count Karl von Zinzendorf (1739–1813) was a high state official; he had first met Mozart in Vienna in 1762 and there are numerous references to the composer in his diaries of the 1780s. It is likely that the selections from *Figaro* given at Frauenberg on 25 September were also played by a wind band.

154   *Donaueschinger Wochenblatt*, Donaueschingen 26 September 1787

Donaueschingen, 25 September. The day before yesterday the opera *Der Lustige Tag oder Figaros Hochzeit* was so accurately and well performed that, together with the excellent music and sets, it was universally praised and admired by the very numerous audience.

Source Manfred Schuler, 'Die Aufführung von Mozarts "Le Nozze di Figaro" in Donaueschingen 1787: ein Beitrag zur Rezeptionsgeschichte', *Archiv für Musikwissenschaft*, xlv (1988), 128.

Commentary *Figaro* had its first performance in Donaueschingen on 23 September. The performance was first announced in the *Donaueschingener Wochenblatt* on 12 September: 'On Sunday the 23rd of this month *Der Lustige Tag, oder Figaros Hochzeit*, a Singspiel in 4 acts, with excellent music by the famous Herr Mozart, will be performed at the court theatre here.' The version of the opera given in Donaueschingen apparently derived from sources related to the 1787 Prague, not the 1786 Viennese, performances.

Literature Alan Tyson, 'Some Problems in the Text of *Le nozze di Figaro*: Did Mozart Have a Hand in Them?', *Journal of the Royal Musical Association*, cxii (1987), 99–131; idem, 'The 1786 Prague Version of Mozart's "Le nozze di Figaro"', *Music and Letters*, lxix (1988), 321–33; Manfred Schuler, 'Das Donaueschinger Aufführungsmaterial von Mozarts *Le nozze di Figaro*', in *Florilegium Musicologicum: Hellmut Federhofer zum 75.Geburtstag*, ed. Christoph-Hellmut Mahling (Tutzing, 1988), 375–88.

155 Christian August von Bertram, *Annalen des Theaters* (Berlin, 1788) [refers to December 1787]

Concerning the Bellomo Theatrical Company. Weimar, 24 May 1788. . . . 15 [December 1787]. *Die Entführung aus dem Serail*. Opera in 3 acts with Mozart's music. Herr Pfeifer, a newly-arrived member of the company, appeared for the first time in this work. He sang and acted excellently, and was universally applauded. Madame Bellomo sang very beautifully as Konstanze. Madame Ackerman played Blondchen coquettishly, Herr Pleisner Pedrillo superficially, and Herr Ackermann Osmin well.

Source *D-B* Yp 1953, Heft 2, p.45.

Commentary Mozart's operas were especially popular at Weimar. During the period 1784–91, *Die Entführung aus dem Serail*, first given there in September 1785, was performed 15 times, more than any other opera or play; Paisiello's *Die eingebildeten Philosophen* and Shakespeare's *Hamlet* were given nine times each, while Schiller's *Der Räuber* was given seven times. From 1791 to 1794 the most frequently performed operas were *Die Zauberflöte* (14 times), *Die Entführung* (nine times), Dittersdorf's *Hieronimus* and *Das rothe Käppchen* (eight times each), and *Don Giovanni* and Grétry's *Richard Löwenherz* (seven times each). *Figaro* was given only twice. See the anonymous 'Chronologie des Theaters zu Weimar: Vom 1. Jan 1784. bis zum 31. Dec. 1794', *Annalen des Theaters*, xx (1797), 43–74.

156 *Schlesische Provinzialblätter*, Breslau April 1788

Report on the works performed at the Breslau winter concerts. . . . X. On 8 February. In the first part: Symphony. Aria with concertante violin by Naumann. Aria by Anfoßi. Duet by Sacchini. In the second part: Keyboard Concerto by Mozart. Recitative and Aria by Sarti. Quartet by Trajetta. Symphony.

Source *US-CAw* PGerm 340.1, VII/4, p.357.
Commentary This performance was directed by Johann Adam Hiller (1728–1804), from 1787 municipal director of music in Breslau. He organized a series of 16 weekly concerts there between 7 December 1787 and 20 March 1788. Haydn is the only other composer of instrumental music identified in the review; selections from the *Seven Last Words* were performed on 15 and 28 February and 7 March. Mozart's *Die Entführung aus dem Serail* was given in Breslau the previous August, but the performance was not reviewed in the *Schlesische Provinzialblätter.*

157 *Grätzer Zeitung*, Graz 2 August 1788

Saturday the 9th, the second part of the *Barbier von Sevilien*, a new Singspiel in 4 acts, called: *Die Hochzeit des Figaro.* The music is by the famous Herr Mozard, composer of Die Entführung aus dem Serail.

Source Hellmut Federhofer, 'Frühe Mozartpflege und Mozartiana in Steiermark', *MJb 1957*, 142 n.16.
Commentary Federhofer speculates, on the basis of an announcement published in the *Grätzer Zeitung* for 25 November 1795, that the 1788 *Figaro* performance was not complete: 'On Tuesday, 25 November, the universally admired Singspiel, *Die Hochzeit des Figaro*, complete, with all four acts, will be performed at the Provincial Theatre. The music is by the popular Herr Mozart and the complete libretto can be had for 12 kreuzer.' Contemporary reviews of this performance are unknown.

158 Heinrich Philipp Bossler, *Musikalische Realzeitung*, Speyer 12 November 1788

Bibliothek der Grazien [*Library of the Graces*], a monthly publication for lovers and friends of singing and the keyboard. . . . I flatter myself in advance that the very names of the composers whose works appear in the *Bibliothek der Grazien* will excite a favourable impression of the intrinsic excellence of this work: Anfossi, Bertoni, Capelli, Cimarosa, Gluk, Gretry, Guglielmi, Haydn, Martin, Mozart, Naumann, Paisello, Piccini, Pleyel, Prati, Reichardt, Sacchini, Salieri and Sarti, among others. . . .

Speier, 11 November 1788.
Bossler, Princely Brandenburg Councillor

Source Facsimile edition, cols.158–60.
Commentary 'Vedrai carino' and 'In quali eccessi . . . Mi tradi quell' alma ingrata', both from *Don Giovanni*, appeared in issues of the *Bibliothek der Grazien* in 1789 (*Jg.1*, January and February). The contredanse 'La bataille' к535 and the overture to *Le nozze di Figaro* appeared in 1790 (*Jg.2*, February and June). *See also* Document 5.

159 Joseph Anton Stephan [Josef Antonín Štěpán], Ritter von Riegger, *Materialien zur alten und neuen Statistik von Böhmen* (Leipzig and Prague, 1788)

Appendix. Karl Helmer, a native of Prague, the most famous lute and instrument maker not only in Prague, but also, as far as is known, in all of Bohemia. In addition to being himself a virtuoso on the lute and mandolin, he manufactures not only both those instruments, but also violins of all sorts, for 4, 5 and 6 ducats. He is also a music publisher, and perhaps still the only one in the country.*

* The following copper-engraved music is available from him: symphonies by **Haydn**, **Mozart** and **Rosetti**; quintets by **Haydn**, **Boccherini**, **Kreith**; concertos by **Boccherini** and **Lem**; quartets by **Boccherini**, **Capuzzi**, **Fiala**, **Haydn**, **Hofmeister**, **Mozart**, **Müller**, **Pleyel**, **Rosetti**, **Tig**, **Vanhal**, **Schmitbauer**, and **Paisiello**; trios by **Boccherini** and duets by **Breunig**, **Rosetti**, **Sirmen**, **Tig**, **Vanhal** and **Stad**, for the violin, viola and cello; further, for keyboard, with and without accompaniment, concertos by **Haydn**, **Hofmeister**, **Kozeluch**, **Mozart**, **Zimmerman**; sonatas with accompaniment by **Haydn**, **Kozeluch**, **Mozart**, **Sardi**, **Sterkel**, **Vanhal**, **Zimmermann**; sonatas for solo keyboard by **Auenbrug**, **Bohdanowics**, **Bengraf**, **Clementi**, **Haydn**, **Kozeluch**, **Kauer**, **Mozart**, **Martin**, **Rauch**, **Riegler**, **Schroter**, **Sterkel**, **Vanhal**, **Zimmermann**; further, sonatas for two persons at one keyboard by **Kozeluch**, **Mozart**, and **Vanhal**; similarly, Italian arias, duets and trios, also German arias and songs, as well as melodramas, operas, oratorios, minuets and German dances by the most famous masters.

Source Cliff Eisen, 'Some lost Mozart editions of the 1780s', *Mitteilungen der Internationalen Stiftung Mozarteum*, xxxii (1984), 68.
Commentary Karl Joseph Hellmer (1739–1811) was a virtuoso on the lute, guitar and mandolin and a prominent manufacturer of musical instruments. The statement that he was also a publisher was a mistake that Dlabač corrected in the *Allgemeines historisches Künstler-Lexikon* (Prague, 1815) i, 608–9: 'Some years ago, a music-selling business was founded by this man who served music so well, and in the year 1787 the following copper-engraved works were available from him: [here follows an abbreviated list from that given in Riegger].'
Literature Karl Jalovec, *Encyclopedia of Violin Makers*, i (London, 1968), 388.

160 Johann Nikolaus Forkel, *Musikalischer Almanach für Deutschland auf das Jahr 1789* (Leipzig, 1788)

Philosophical fragments concerning practical music. At the author's cost. Vienna, 1787. Octavo, 164 pages. In order to show that the author intends to discuss the most important and interesting [aspects] of the art, we have only to cite some of the rubrics of his work. . . . Concerning young, premature virtuosos; they are unnatural products of art and are more likely to regress than progress (this is in many, but not all, cases true, for example Mozart).

Source *US-NYp* Drexel 625, pp.30–31.
Commentary A review of Smith's *Philosophische Fragmente* published in Bossler's *Musikalische Realzeitung* for 25 November 1789 makes similar reference to Mozart (*Dokumente* 314–15, *Documentary Biography* 358); possibly it was copied

from this notice. For a passage from Smith that does refer to Mozart, *see* Document 84.

161   *Staats- und gelehrte Zeitung des hamburgischen unpartheyischen Correspondenten*, Hamburg 29 April 1789

Three Sonatas for keyboard . . . by *C. F. G. Schwenke*. Halle, at the author's expense, printed on commission by J. C. Hendel, 1789.

With these three keyboard sonatas, **Herr Schwenke**, a respected son of our excellent musician and bassoonist of the same name, appears before the public for the first time as a musical author, and fulfils the expectations which all friends of music who know him rightly have of him. Devoted to music from childhood, he studied under the supervision of his father. . . . Above all he dedicated himself to the keyboard, and he plays this instrument with such a degree of perfection that he is a virtuoso. The present sonatas give very favourable evidence of his taste and manner of composition. He has chosen **Bach**, **Haydn** and **Mozart** as models, and has understood so well the way these famous men think that their manner of treatment – for example, that of **Bach** in the first sonata, and of **Haydn** in the second – can be found without difficulty, although Herr **Schwenke** is not merely a slavish imitator but remains a true original, his models notwithstanding.

Source   *US-PRu* 0902.873 (1789) [unpaginated].
Commentary   Christian Friedrich Gottlieb Schwenke (1767–1822) succeeded C. P. E. Bach as *Stadtkantor* at Hamburg. His father, the bassoonist Johann Gottfried Schwenke (1744–1823), was a town musician in Hamburg. The influence on Schwenke of Haydn and Mozart, as well as C. P. E. Bach's instruction, was also noted by Ernst Ludwig Gerber (*Historisch-biographisches Lexicon der Tonkünstler*, ii, Leipzig, 1792, col.437). Schwenke later made copies of Mozart's symphonies K200/189k, 204/213a, 250/248b, 297/300a, 320, 338, 385, 425, 504, 543, 550 and 551, all of which survive in *D-B*.
Literature   Hans-Günter Klein, ed., *Wolfgang Amadeus Mozart: Autographe und Abschriften* (Kassel, 1982), 256–7.

162   *Staats- und gelehrte Zeitung des hamburgischen unpartheyischen Correspondenten*, Hamburg 10 July 1789

Hamburg. *Die Entführung aus dem Serail*, composed by **Mozart**, was performed at the theatre here last Tuesday. On this occasion, the incomparable music of the opera was seen in a new light thanks to Madame **Lange** from Vienna, who played the role of Constanze. This excellent singer, who some years ago enchanted the music lovers of Hamburg with her charming voice and characteristically tasteful execution, has since gained still more strength of voice; as

Constanze on Thursday she won the greatest applause of the full and numerous audience for her enchanting singing, a true virtuoso. We hear with pleasure that this opera, one of the pre-eminent musical masterpieces, will be repeated today, Friday.

Source *US-PRu* 0902.873 (1789), *Beylage* [unpaginated].
Commentary *Die Entführung aus dem Serail* was first given at Hamburg on 18 June 1787. 'Madame Lange' is Mozart's sister-in-law, Aloysia Lange.

163 Heinrich Philipp Bossler, *Musikalische Realzeitung*, Speyer 11 November 1789

Hamburg, the 30th of October. This week the opera **Don Juan**, excellently composed by Mozart, was performed three times at the playhouse here to great approval. Everyone who knows the difficulty of the music of this opera will gladly cry 'Bravo' for our singers, in particular Madame **Langerhans** in the role of Donna Elvira, Mademoiselle **Kalmus** in the role of Donna Anna, and Herr **Ambrosch** and **Eule** in the roles of Ottavio and Leporello, and also concede that our orchestra accompanied this opera masterfully.

Source Facsimile edition, col.367.
Commentary *Don Giovanni* was first given at Hamburg on 27 October 1789 and repeated on 28 and 30 October, 4, 10 and 27 November, and 8 December; see *Annalen des Theaters*, vi (Berlin, 1790), 81–2.

164 *Grätzer Zeitung*, Graz 28 November 1789

On Monday the 30th will be performed an entirely new Singspiel in two acts with the title Don Juan, recently translated from the Italian and not yet performed on any German stage. The music is composed with great art by the famous Herr Mozart.

Source Hellmut Federhofer, 'Frühe Mozartpflege und Mozartiana in Steiermark', *MJb 1957*, 142 n.16.
Commentary There is some doubt as to whether this performance took place.

165 Johann Gottlieb Portmann, *Leichtes Lehrbuch der Harmonie, Composition und des Generalbasses, zum Gebrauch für Liebhaber der Musik, angehende und fortschreitende Musici und Componisten* (Darmstadt, 1789)

The design or outline of a musical work is the skilful setting out of chief and secondary keys and their arrangement, what is to be set out first, and what should follow second, third, fourth etc. As an example, I will give the plan of an allegro of a keyboard sonata in D major. Accordingly, I firmly establish the tonic, D, in which I begin and present an idea; from here I proceed, via the dominant to the secondary key of the fifth, present a new idea, and close in it: this is the outline of the first part of the allegro. In the other part, I begin a new idea with loud passing material. A minor, the fourth of E minor, is my point of departure; from A minor I have B, the dominant of E minor. – E minor itself – then G major; then C♯, the dominant of F♯ minor; F♯ minor itself; then D, the dominant of G major – instead of G major however, B, the dominant of E minor, then E minor itself; again, C, the dominant of F major, but instead of F major, A, the dominant of D minor; D minor itself; then A, the dominant of D minor, but instead of D minor, B♭, the tonic of the sixth; then F, the dominant of B♭ major, but instead of B♭ major, the tonic of the sixth, G minor; from G minor the substitute dominant E of D minor, and in this orderly way A, the dominant of D minor; this minor dominant, however, is transformed into a major dominant and this leads me again to D major, the tonic, in which key I repeat the theme, as well as the melodies and phrases I had presented in the secondary key of the fifth, G, remain [in the tonic], and close. . . .

Reading or performing a work by Mozart, however, should make one forget my sonata, the basic harmonic plan of which, with careful forethought, I borrowed from him, in order, by comparison, to bring his work – which like all of his compositions should be in everyone's hands – to my reader's attention. . . .

Most composers of operettas have taken simplicity in the choice of basic harmonies as their first principle, as well as the frequent repetition of easily appreciated, singable melodies which can, accordingly, be learnt without difficulty and easily imitated. My assertion can be confirmed by looking at the [selection of] songs with keyboard accompaniment from the newest German, Italian and French operettas, published by Herr Kapellmeister André in Offenbach. However, some of our national composers depart from this entirely, including Herr Benda, Mozart and Wolff, who prefer greater richness of harmony and dispense with frequent repetitions.

Source   *D-Mbs* 4° Mus.th.1246, pp.50, 52 and 53.

Commentary   Johann Gottlieb Portmann (1739–98) was active as a tenor and music teacher in Darmstadt from 1766. His sonata movement, published as fig.98 in the *Beilage* to his *Leichtes Lehrbuch der Harmonie* (pp.43–9), is reproduced here (*see* fig.1). It is modelled on the first movement of Mozart's sonata K284/205*b*, also published in the *Beilage* (as fig.99, pp. 50–56).

166   Daniel Gottlob Türk, *Klavierschule, oder Anweisung zum Clavierspielen für Lehrer und Lernende* (Leipzig and Halle, 1789)

Introduction. . . . When students have progressed sufficiently, then the sonatas of **Gressler**, **Gruner**, **Blum**, **G. Benda**, **Sander** (the

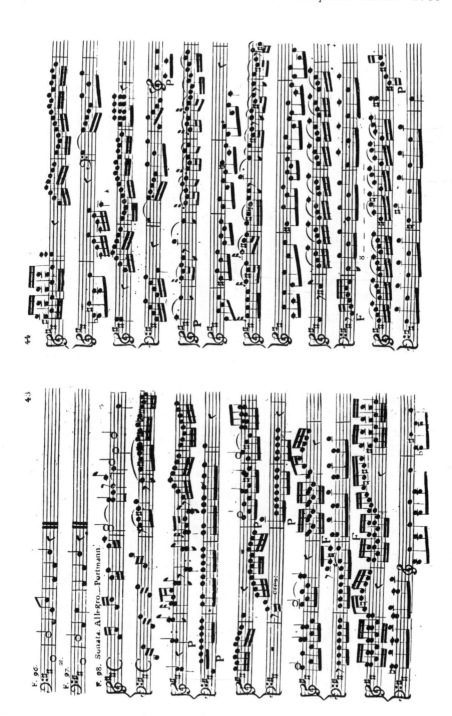

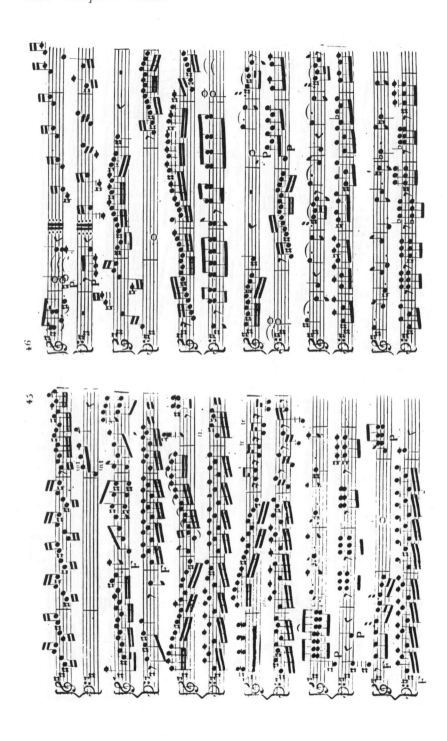

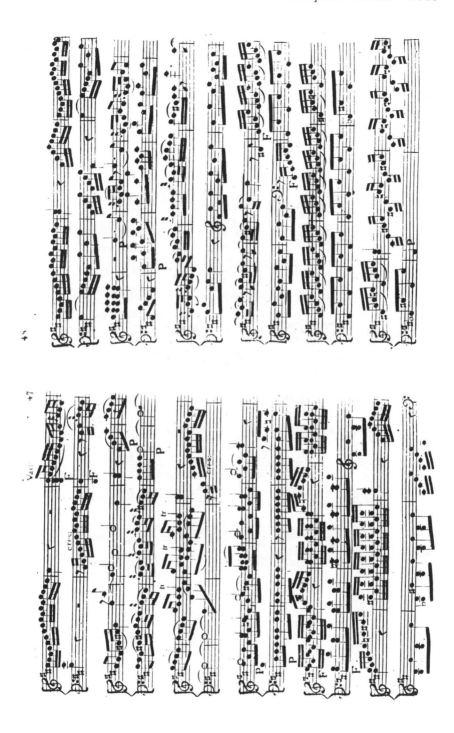

longer ones), **Zink, Vierling, Haydn, E. W. Wolf, Hässler, C. P. E. Bach**, etc. may be studied with them. One should also study with his students trios, quartets, concertos etc., by accomplished masters, which is necessary for [practice in counting] measures and rests. Duo sonatas for two keyboards, or sonatas for four hands at one keyboard, for example by **P. Schmidt, Mozart, Seydelmann, Kozeluch, Vanhall, E. W. Wolf** etc., are also suitable for this practice. . . .

Concerning weighty and light execution. . . . In general, a composition written to the Italian national taste requires a medium execution. The performance of a French composition must be lighter. On the other hand, the works of German composers for the most part require a weightier and more robust execution.

Similarly, the style of the composer also requires an individual manner of treatment. A composition by Händel, Sebastian Bach, etc., must be more emphatically performed than, for example, a modern concerto by Mozart or Kozeluch, among others.

Source *D-Mbs* 4° Mus.Th.1575, pp.16–17 and 364. Translation in Daniel Gottlob Türk, *School of Clavier Playing*, trans. and ed. Raymond H. Haggh (Lincoln, Nebraska, and London, 1982), 352.

Commentary Daniel Gottlob Türk (1750–1813), a pupil of Johann Adam Hiller, was cantor at the Ulrichskirche in Halle from 1774 and director of music at the university from 1779. A review of his *Clavierschule* in the *Staats- und gelehrte Zeitungen des hamburgischen unpartheyischen Correspondenten* for 8 January 1791 described the work as 'in every respect a classic, and to this time unquestionably the only and most perfect work of its kind'.

167 Johann Georg Meusel, *Teutsches Künstlerlexikon oder Verzeichnis der jetztlebenden teutschen Künstler* (Lemgo, 1789)

Mozart (Wolfgang Amadäus), from 1788 Kapellmeister to Archduke Franz in Vienna. – born at Salzburg 1758.§§. *Die Entführung aus dem Serail*, an operetta by Bretzner, the frequently-published score of which has become well known. It was first performed in Vienna in 1782, and printed in 1785. Six sonatas for keyboard or pianoforte with violin accompaniment, Opus II, 1783. Divertimento for solo keyboard, four hands. . . . Grand concerto for keyboard, with accompaniment, Opus IX, Spire 1787. Sonata for keyboard with violin accompaniment, Spire 1788, quarto.

Source *C-Tul* (reference), p.144.

Commentary The works referred to are *Die Entführung aus dem Serail*; the accompanied sonatas K376/374*d*, 296, 377/374*e*, 378/317*d*, 379/373*a*, 380/374*f* (Vienna, 1781); the concerto K453 (Speyer, 1787); and the accompanied sonata K481 (Speyer, before 1788). The 'Divertimento per il Cembalo solo a quattri mani' may be the sonata K381/123*a*; a contemporary copy of the work now at St Peter's, Salzburg, has a title-page that reads: 'in D/Divertimento/per il/Clavis

Cembalo/a/4 Mani/Del Sige: Wolfgang Mozart' (*A-Ssp* Moz 332.1). Another divertimento, Κ*deest*, is listed in Breitkopf & Härtel's *Alter handschriftlicher Catalog von W. A. Mozart's Original Compositionen Abschrift* (*A-Wgm* 4057/38, p.62):

Mozart was born in 1756, not 1758. For the confusion concerning his appointment, see *Dokumente* 274, *Documentary Biography* 312. The first part of Meusel's *Teutsches Künstlerlexikon* had appeared in 1778; *see* Document 132.

Literature Wolfgang Plath, 'Kleine Mozartiana', in *Festschrift Rudolf Elvers zum 60. Geburtstag*, ed. Ernst Herttrich and Hans Schneider (Tutzing, 1985), 397–402 (concerning the divertimento Κ*deest*).

168 *Journal des Luxus und der Moden*, Weimar January 1790

Continuation of the letters concerning the Mannheim theatre. . . . Among the operas, Mozart's *Don Juan* has had exceptional success. Donna Anna is a master role of our **Beck**. Orchestra, singing and acting were all very fine; the more one hears this music, the more it pleases. It is a pity that Madame **Müller's** indisposition created a gap in the cast. Otherwise this performance would have been a perfect whole.

Source *F-Pn* M.22274/300 (1790), p.50.
Commentary *Don Giovanni* was first given at Mannheim on 27 September 1789, in a German translation by C. G. Neefe.

169 Georg Forster, *Ansichten vom Niederrhein, von Brabant, Flandern, Holland, England und Frankreich in April, Mai und Junius 1790* (Berlin, 1791)

Before I hurry on with my tale, I will describe to you briefly the theatre, which we visited on the evening of our arrival in Dunkirk. Troupe, orchestra and public – all of them seemed to us as caricatures. The stalls, the balcony, and almost all the boxes were filled with officers, for there are two occupying regiments here. You have no idea of the noisy conversation that rang in our ears; one would have thought that tomorrow an eternal silence was to be imposed on these gentlemen and that here they took the last opportunity to exercise the freedom of their tongues. When the performance began it was still more annoying; the entire herd sang or howled along with all the arias of the operetta. As luck would have it, the cast was so bad that it was really of little consequence who whiled away our time. . . . Mozart's and Paesiello's art is wasted on these Midas ears, which are open only for Ditters street songs.

Source Gerhard Steiner, ed., *Georg Forsters Werke: sämtliche Schriften, Tagebücher, Briefe*, ix (Berlin, 1958), 237–8.

Commentary The naturalist Georg Forster (1754–94) was librarian to the Elector of Mainz from 1788 to 1792. 'Midas ears' is a reference to the Greek myth in which King Midas judged Pan's musicality superior to Apollo's. Apollo punished Midas by transforming his ears into ass's ears.

170 Franz Friedrich Siegmund August von Böcklin, *Beyträge zur Geschichte der Musik, besonders in Deutschland* (Freiburg im Breisgau, 1790)

Fifteenth letter. To Herr v. W. Freyburg. The concerts here are quite good and agreeable. Works by Pugnani, Paisello, Sacchini, Salieri, Gluck, Mozart, Piccini, Pleyel, Haide and other great composers are played with genuine taste.
Sixteenth letter. To Herr. D. in W. [Ettenheimmünster.] The chamber music and symphonies include works by Gassec, Gretry, Ditters, Filz, Mozart, Stamitz, Schmidt, Handel, Hasse, Hofmann, Eichner, Vanhall, Bach, Hayde, Salieri, Piccini, Pugnani, Sacchini, Lang, Storkel, Davauch, Eisemann, Pichel, Pleyel, Rosetti &c.

Source *GB-Lbl* Hirsch I.637, pp.110 and 124–5.

Commentary The statesman Franz Friedrich Siegmund August von Böcklin (1745–1813) studied music with Schobert, Jommelli and F. X. Richter as a youth. For his reports on Vienna and Salzburg, see *Dokumente* 335–6, *Documentary Biography* 381–2.

171 *Annalen des Theaters* (Berlin, 1791) [refers to October 1790]

Review of the most noteworthy events at the Mannheim theatre during the year 1790. . . . On 24 October, for the first time: **Die Hochzeit des Figaro**, an operetta in four acts, with music by **Mozart**. Only Mozart's music makes this caponized Figaro bearable, it has suffered such mutilation; well-adapted to the characters and sentiments of the singers, it is, for the ear and the heart, full of expression and truth. These qualities characterize Mozart's work, and him, as a thoughtful artist. Mlle. **Keilholz the elder**, for all the excellence of her singing, lacks the vivacity necessary for **Susanna**, just as Herr **Gern** lacks the cleverness and facility of Figaro. In Mlle.

Keilholz the younger, as Cherubino, one missed the mischievousness and frivolity that belongs to the portrayal of this role. Herr **Epp**, as Count Almaviva, and Madame **Beck**, as the Countess, competed in agreeable execution and skilful singing.

Source *D-B* Yp 1953 (vii), p.47.

172 *Musikalische Korrespondenz der teutschen Filharmonischen Gesellschaft,* Speyer 2 February 1791

Corrections and additions to the musical almanachs for the years 1782, 1783 and 1784.`. . . Wolf in Weimar. It was to be wished that he had never had occasion to compose operettas. As excellently as this private music teacher in Jena, who rose to be Kapellmeister in Weimar, composes for the chamber and church, his works for the lyric stage are mediocre. Theatrical compositions must not be tried out at the keyboard or in the concert hall, but in the pit. There it is apparent how much is lacking and that in operettas Wolf very nearly approaches **Hiller**. For he stands as far below **Benda** as **Hiller** himself does below **Dittersdorf** and **Wolfgang Mozart** and D. **Schubauer**.

Source Facsimile edition, p.37.
Commentary Ernst Wilhelm Wolf (1735–92) was court Konzertmeister at Weimar from 1761, court organist from 1763 and Kapellmeister from 1772.

173 *Staats- und gelehrte Zeitung des hamburgischen unpartheyischen Correspondenten,* Hamburg 31 August 1791

Marches, Angloises, Menuets & Ballets, tiré de l'Opera, les noces de Figaro, par Mozart, & arrangés pour le Clavecin. Berlin, ches Rellstab. 8 Gr. Whenever possible, a music lover will want to have for himself those works which in concert gave him so much pleasure, or which many never have the opportunity to hear publicly. This is the reason for the keyboard and various other arrangements of great works which do not fail in their purpose of giving the amateur the opportunity to amuse himself so much with them, when time and inclination allow, according to his abilities and Muse. The above-mentioned work is very much to be recommended for such private entertainment, for the reputation of the composer is well known, and the selection and arrangement of the pieces is good and tasteful. The marches, arranged for wind instruments, are also available in manuscript copies from the publisher, each at 1 Thaler.

Source *US-PRu* 0902.873 (1791, *Beyträge zum gelehrten Artikel*) [unpaginated].
Commentary Johann Carl Friedrich Rellstab (1759–1813) had studied in Berlin with J. F. Agricola from 1773 and C. F. C. Fasch from 1776 to 1778. He

took over the family publishing business in 1779 and issued his first music prints about 1785. His edition of arrangements from *Le nozze di Figaro* probably appeared in early 1791. The opera was first given in Berlin on 24 September 1790.

Literature Rudolf Elvers, 'Die bei J. F. K. Rellstab in Berlin bis 1800 erschienenen Mozart-Drucke', *MJb 1957*, 152–67.

174 *Musikalische Korrespondenz der teutschen Filarmonischen Gesellschaft*, Speyer 23 November 1791

Further concerning the Electoral orchestra at Cologne. . . . On the first day I heard table music, which is played every day while the Elector is in residence at Mergentheim. It consists of 2 oboes, 2 clarinets, 2 bassoons, 2 horns. These 8 players can rightly be called masters in their art. Rarely does one find an ensemble of this sort that plays so well together, with such agreement, and in particular can sustain tones to such high degrees of accuracy and perfection, as this one. They also distinguish themselves from similar ensembles by performing larger works, as, at that time, they then performed the overture to Mozart's *Don Juan*. . . . The other morning at 10 o'clock there was a rehearsal for the festive court concert, which began about 6 o'clock in the evening. . . . The court concert began an hour after the table music. It opened with a symphony by Mozart.

C. L. Junker

Source Facsimile edition, cols.374–6, continued in the following issue, 30 November 1791, cols.379–82.

Commentary *Don Giovanni* was first performed at Cologne on 7 October. In a letter of 23 January 1782 to his father Mozart wrote of the then Archduke Maximilian Franz: 'He puts me forward at every occasion – and I might say with near certainty that if he were already Elector of Cologne, I would also already be his Kapellmeister' (*Briefe* iii.194, *Letters* 677–8). Shortly after Mozart's death, Maximilian Franz is said to have given Constanze 24 gold ducats (*Dokumente* 379, *Documentary Biography* 430). Carl Ludwig Junker (1748–97), composer and writer on music, was court chaplain at Kirchberg (Hohenlohe) from 1779.

175 *Musikalische Korrespondenz der teutschen Filarmonischen Gesellschaft*, Speyer 23 November 1791

[from a review of Josef Lipavsk's *12 Variazioni per il Forte-Piano dedicati al Sign. W. A. Mozart*, Vienna 1791] This first attempt by the composer at keyboard composition already bespeaks an educated composer and gives well-founded hope that he will contest the superiority of many of his contemporaries in the galant keyboard style. This work can already be set beside the variations of Mozart, Kozeluch and other famous composers. . . . The only fault we can find with them is the obvious imitation of Mozart's variations. Imitating good models deserves praise rather than reproach. However, such imitation can become detrimental, so that the spirit of the composer is shackled; because of it a work inevitably loses its intrinsic worth, that is, its originality. If Herr L. will indeed copy models, we recommend to him in similar works the variations of Herr Abt. Vogler, recently published in Speier.

Source   Facsimile edition, col.370.
Commentary   Josef Lipavský (1772–1810) studied in Vienna with Georg Pasterwiz, Johann Baptist Vanhal and possibly Mozart. His variations op.1 were published by Hoffmeister and advertised in the *Wiener Zeitung* on 13 July 1791. Bossler in Speyer first advertised the work in the *Musikalische Korrespondenz der teutschen Filarmonischen Gesellschaft* for 17 August 1791 (p.264). No copy of the print appears to be extant.
Literature   Alexander Weinmann, *Die Wiener Verlagswerke von Franz Anton Hoffmeister* (Vienna, 1964), 128.

176   *Allgemeine deutsche Bibliothek*, Berlin and Stettin 1791

Die Entführung aus dem Serail, a Singspiel in three acts, freely adapted from Bretzner. Set to music by Herr Mozart. Frankfurt and Leipzig, 1791. . . . . Thanks to Mozart's music, which is full of individual beauties (although here and there it is written in too artful or serious a style), this work has been successful at our theatre. Otherwise, it is to be commended neither for its invention nor its poetic adaptation. Still, one is exceptionally indulgent these days with regard to the Singspiel, and this work is still of greater worth than the numerous nonsensical, taste-corrupting Italian farces that parade as excellent compositions.

Source   *US-CAw* BP 361.1 (vol.99, part 1), pp.124–5.
Commentary   According to Thomas Bauman, the author of this review was Adolf Knigge, who had already written extensively on *Die Entführung* in his *Dramaturgische Blätter* (*Dokumente* 287–8 and 292, *Documentary Biography* 353–6).
Literature   Thomas Bauman, 'The Music Reviews in the *Allgemeine deutsche Bibliothek*', *Acta musicologica*, xlix (1977), 83.

177   *Allgemeine Literatur-Zeitung*, Jena 18 February 1792

Deaths. The famous Imperial and Royal Kapellmeister Mozart, 34 years old, died at Vienna on 15 December. His last opera, *Die Zauberflöte*, was given 33 times at Vienna last year, and continues to be gladly seen.

Source   *US-CAw* BP 361.2 (1792), *Intelligenzblatt*, xxiv, p.187.
Commentary   '15 December' should read '5 December'.

178   *Allgemeine deutsche Bibliothek*, Berlin and Stettin 1792

Deaths. Herr Wolfgang Amadäus Mozart, Kapellmeister to Archduke Franz, died at Vienna on 5 December, barely 34 years old.

Source   *US-CAw* BP 361.1 (vol.106, part 1), p.615.
Commentary   For the confusion concerning Mozart's appointment, see *Dokumente* 274, *Documentary Biography* 312.

179   *Prager Oberpostamtszeitung*, Prague 17 December 1791

Prague, 15 December. Yesterday at the Nicolai Church here a solemn funeral ceremony was celebrated for Mozart, who died in Vienna, which was worthy of the pre-eminent virtuoso, as well as the orchestra in Prague, which he founded, and all of our famous musicians, who participated. The ceremony began with the ringing of bells. People came out in such numbers that neither the church nor the adjacent, so-called Italian Square, could accommodate all of them. A Requiem, given by 120 persons under the direction of the famous singer Frau Duschek, was so nobly performed that Mozart's spirit in Elysium must have rejoiced. In the middle of the church stood a masterfully illuminated catafalque. Three choruses of trumpets and timpani were heard in muffled tones. The Requiem was celebrated by Father Fischer. Twelve schoolboys dressed in mourning crapes with white cloths carried torches. There was a profound silence during the ceremony, and a thousand tears flowed for our Mozart, whose heavenly harmonies so often moved and filled our hearts with tender feelings. His loss is irreplaceable. There are, and always will be, masters of music, but to bring forth a master above all others – for this Nature needs centuries. His creative spirit reveals itself in his works, and even his enemies (for how could such a man not have enemies?) admit his unequalled greatness. After all, they could accuse him of only a single fault, a fault that they rather should envy, that he was too rich in ideas. If only the unforgettable man could have left one of his friends this defect as a legacy. Everything that he wrote carries the clear stamp of classical beauty. For this reason he pleases each time even more, for one beauty evolves from another, and so he will always please for he will always seem new; advantages which accrue to a classic. Is this not proved by his operas? Are they not heard the eightieth time with as much pleasure as the first time?

Source   *Eibl* 75; Norbert Tschulik, 'Neue zur Mozart-Bericherstattung', *Österreichische Musikzeitschrift*, xxxi (1976), 337–9.
Commentary   According to Eibl, this notice was taken over in the *Stockholms-Posten* for 5 January 1792. For another report, published in the *Wiener Zeitung* for 24 December, see *Dokumente* 375–6, *Documentary Biography* 427. See also Document 118.

180 *Musikalische Korrespondenz der teutschen Filarmonischen Gesellschaft,*
Speyer 16 May 1792

Review. *Concert pour le Forte-Piano avec l'accompagnement de deux Violons,*
Viola, 1 Flute, 2 Obois, 2 Cors, 2 Fagottes, 2 Clarin, Timp. & Basse,
compos. par W. A. Mozart. Speier, Bossler (Pr. 3 fl. 30 kr.)

For friends and admirers of the Mozartean muse, this work, first
published after his death, is nothing but a great treasure. His original
writing style, here also unmistakable, the fullness of the harmony, the
surprising turns of phrase, the skilful diffusion of shadow and light,
and many other excellent characteristics, which make Mozart a
model for our time, make us feel very deeply his loss. This concerto is
in D major and is among the most beautiful and brilliant that we
have from this master, with respect to both the ritornellos and the
solos. The first Allegro takes up the first twelve pages and we miss
nothing in it except the figuring of the basses in the tuttis. The
following Andante in G major is a kind of Romanze in 4/4, very
elegant and moving. The finale is an Allegro di molto in 2/4, which
changes on the penultimate page to 3/8. Unquestionably this movement has the greatest difficulties; but with respect to the modulation
also very excellent beauties. It is only to be regretted that this
masterly concerto, because of its scoring and obbligato writing, is
impractical for smaller musical circles and can only be performed by
large, fully-manned orchestras. The engraving is very clear and correct and does considerable honour to the printing-shop of Herr
Councillor Bossler.

Source *D-Mbs* 4° Mus.th.306, cols.153–4.
Commentary The concerto is K451, published by Bossler at Speyer. The
print was first announced in the *Musikalische Korrespondenz der teutschen*
Filarmonischen Gesellschaft for 28 December 1791, but only became available in
March 1792.
Literature Gertraut Haberkamp, *Die Erstdrucke der Werke von Wolfgang Amadeus*
Mozart (Tutzing, 1986) 218–19.

181 *Musicalien-Catalog der Philharmonischen Gesellschaft in Laibach*
[Ljubljana]. *Zum Gebrauche für auswärtige Herren Mitglieder dieser*
Gesellschaft. Nro. 1. Seit 1. Nov. 1794 bis lezten Juni 1804

Chamber Music N°   b) Ouvertures

Marinelli   15
. . .

Mozart   22

Source   *YU-Lu* 21/58 [unpaginated].
Commentary   The beginning of the incipit of no.15, the overture to Gaetano Martinelli's *Gli accidenti inaspetatti*, is virtually identical (except for the common time signature) to KAnh.C11.07, a symphony attributed to Mozart in Breitkopf & Härtel's early 19th-century *Alter handschriftlicher Catalog von W. A. Mozart's Original Compositionen Abschrift* (*A-Wgm* 4057/38, p.9 no.60):

ultimamente
composta

The brevity of the incipit in the Breitkopf & Härtel catalogue makes it impossible to determine whether the references are to the same work. No.22, K*deest*, may be identical to a Mozart overture in D major listed in an 1898 catalogue of music prints and manuscripts owned by the Philharmonische Gesellschaft; however, the source is no longer extant. Another copy of the work, attributed to Matthias Baumgartner (*c*1736–84), a Viennese church musician, is in *A-Wgm* XIII 1295. Other works by Mozart listed in the Laibach catalogue include the symphonies K319, 320, 250, 425, 551, 550, 543 and 385; the overtures to *Die Zauberflöte* K620, *Le nozze di Figaro* K492, *La clemenza di Tito* K621, *Don Giovanni* K527, *Der Schauspieldirektor* K486 and *Die Entführung aus dem Serail* K384; the Divertimento K334/320*b*; the piano and wind quintet K452 and the piano quartet K478 (listed as a *Quintuor*, instruments unspecified); the wind Serenade K375 (a version for two clarinets, two horns and one bassoon); the duets 'Come ti piace, imponi', 'Deh prendi un dolce amplesso', and 'Ah, perdono al primo affetto' from *La clemenza di Tito* K621; the Requiem K626; the offertory K222/205*a*; and the piano concertos K467, 488 and 466. The Philharmonic Society in Ljubljana (then Laibach) was first founded in 1702; disbanded later in the century, it was reconstituted in 1794. Records of the society before 1794 do not survive.
Literature   Friedrich Keesbacher, *Die philharmonische Gesellschaft in Laibach* (Laibach [Ljubljana], 1862).

French (Paris)

182 Friedrich Melchior Grimm to Caroline of Hessen-Darmstadt, 11 December 1769

The operas which your Highness has done me the honour of requesting are ready and will be sent this week to M. Widemann's address. The music of *Bastien et Bastienne* has never been engraved. Several years ago, Mondonville attempted to set *Thésée* to music; this attempt was very badly received and the music was not engraved. There is only the *Thésée* of Lully, which I do not want to send without explicit letters of instruction. On the other hand, your Highness will find in the package two copies of the *Tableau parlant*, the music of which has turned our heads here. The engraving of Philidor's opera is proceeding very slowly.

Source Jochen Schlobach, ed., *Correspondance inédite de Frédéric Melchior Grimm* (Munich, 1972), 102–3.

Commentary For Grimm and Caroline of Hessen-Darmstadt, *see* Document 27. Schlobach assumes that the *Bastien et Bastienne* mentioned by Grimm is Mozart's, although this is not certain. Possibly the work is Favart's parody *Les amours de Bastien et Bastienne* (1753), which was given not only at Paris but also at Brussels, Vienna and Frankfurt between 1753 and 1764; German-language productions were mounted at Berlin and Vienna in 1763 and 1764, respectively. Grimm's references to Philidor (presumably *L'amant déguisé ou le jardinier supposé*, 1769), Mondonville and Lully suggest that Caroline's interest was in current Paris productions. On the other hand, Grimm might have known that the melodies of Favart's *Bastien* had been published as early as 1763.

183 *Journal de musique, historique, théorique, pratique, sur la musique ancienne et moderne*, Paris 1771

Most remarkable are two children, one of whom, M. Alday, seven or eight years old, plays the mandolin with extraordinary facility and rapidity of execution. The other is M. d'Arcy, nine or ten years old, who plays the harpsichord, the pianoforte and the organ not only with the assurance of the masters, but also with their refinement and taste. To this merit he adds a still greater one: that of composition. His works are enchantingly tasteful, and one cannot marvel enough at discovering so many ideas in such a young head. Nothing so remarkable has been seen since little Mozart.

Source *F-Pn* V.25409, p.218.

Commentary François-Joseph Darcis [d'Arcis, d'Arcy] (1759–c1783) performed a concerto by J. C. Bach at the Concert Spirituel on 5 April 1771.
Grimm took a different view of Darcis, describing his first stage work, *Le bal
masqué* (Versailles, 1772), as '. . . pitiful from beginning to end. Not a shadow of
talent nor the appearance of an idea in the entire piece; still less of science,
harmony and modulation; insipid melodies, written in couplets, taken from here
and there: this is all the merit of the work by this little scamp' (*Correspondance
littéraire*, ix, Paris, 1879, pp.481–2). For the portion of Grimm's review that
refers to Mozart, see *Dokumente* 127, *Documentary Biography* 141.

184 *Les Spectacles de Paris, ou Calendrier Historique & Chronologique des
Théâtres . . . Pour l'Année 1779* (Paris, 1778)

Personnel of the Concert Spirituel for the year 1779. . . . Composers.
MM. Alessandry, Cambiny, Cannabich, Floquet, Gossec, Mozart,
Rigel, Sterkel.

Source *US-Io* Rare PN 2620 A43 v. 28, pp.1–2.

185 *Journal de Paris*, Paris 27 March 1779

Concert Spirituel at the Château des Tuileries, tomorrow 28 March 1779.
   The concert will begin with a symphony by Signor *Amédéo Mozarts*.
– Madame *le Brun* will sing an Italian aria by Signor *Sacchini*. – M.
Vonnderlich will perform a flute concerto. – A *motet à grand chœur*,
composed by M. l'Abbé *Rose*, will be performed in which Mlle.
Duchateau, MM. *Dorsonville*, *Chéron* & *le Gros* will sing. – M. *le Brun*
will perform an oboe concerto of his own composition. – Madame
Todi will sing an Italian aria by Signor *Piccini*. – M. *Pieltain* will
perform a new violin concerto of his own composition. – Madame *le
Brun* will sing a new Italian aria, with oboe accompaniment, composed by Signor *Anfossi*.

Source *US-NYpl* *DM (1779), p.345. Repeated in the *Journal de Paris* for 28
March (p.349), where the motet by Rosé is replaced by an oratorio by Riegel:
'*La Sortie d'Egypte*, a French oratorio by M. *Rigel*, will be performed in which
Mlles *Duchateau*, *Malpied*, MM. *le Gros* & *Moreau* will sing.'

186 *Journal de Paris*, Paris 21 May 1779

Concert Spirituel at the Château des Tuileries, Sunday 23 May.
   The concert will be divided into two parts; the first will begin with
a symphony by Signor *Sterkel*. – Mlle *Giradin* will sing, for the first
time, a motet by M. *Deshaye*. – M. *Bréval* will perform a new violoncello concerto of his own composition. – Madame *le Brun* will sing an

Italian aria composed by Signor *Mortellary*. The second part will begin with a symphony by Signor *Amédéo Mozartz*. – Mlles *Malpied* & *Giradin*, MM. *le Petit* & *Moreau* will sing a new motet for four voices, composed by M. l'Abbé *Buce*, music director at the Church of St. Martin de Tours. – M. *Pieltain* will perform a new violin concerto of his own composition. – Madame *le Brun* will sing an Italian aria, composed by Signor *Anfossi*, with oboe accompaniment performed by M. *le Brun*.

Source   *US-NYpl* *DM (1779), p.566. Repeated without change in the *Journal de Paris* for 23 May, p.575.

187   *Journal de Paris*, Paris 3 June 1779

Today, Concert Spirituel at the Château des Tuileries.
    The concert will begin with a symphony by Signor *Amédio Mozards*. – M. *Wounderlich* will perform a flute concerto. – Madame *le Brun* will sing an Italian aria by Signor *Sacchini*. – M. *le Brun* will perform, for the last time, an oboe concerto of his own composition. A new *motet à grand choeur*, *Te Deum*, by M. *Gossec*, will be performed in which Mlles *Giardin* & *Joinville*, MM. *le Gros* & *Moreau* will sing. – Mlle *Deschamps* will perform for the last time a violin concerto by M. *Jarnovich*.
    Madame *le Brun* will sing, for the last time, an Italian aria with oboe accompaniment, composed by M. *le Brun*.

Source   *US-NYpl* *DM (1779), p.618.

188   *Les Spectacles de Paris, ou Calendrier Historique & Chronologique des Théâtres . . . Pour l'Année 1780* (Paris, 1779)

Personnel of the Concert Spirituel for the year 1780. . . . Composers. MM. Alessandry, Cambiny, Cannabich, Deshayes, Floquet, Gossec, Mozart, Rigel, Sterkel.

Source   *US-Io* Rare PN 2620 A43 v. 29, pp.1–2.

189   *Journal de Paris*, Paris 23 March 1780

Today, Concert Spirituel at the Château des Tuileries.
    The concert will begin with a symphony by Sig. *Amédéo Mozarts*. – M. *Adrien* will sing an Italian aria by *Anfossi*. – M. *Caravoglia* will perform an oboe concerto. – Mme. *Windling* will sing an Italian aria by M. *Bach*. – M. *le Noble* will perform, for the first time, a violin concerto of his own composition. – Mme. *Todi* will sing an Italian aria by *Anfossi*. – M. *Windling* will perform a flute concerto by M. *Stamitz*.

The concert will conclude with the *Stabat Mater* of *Pergoleze*, in which Mme. *Todi* & M. *Nihoul* will sing.

Source *US-NYpl* *DM (1780), p.342; also advertised in the *Annonces, affiches et avis divers* for 23 March ('une Symphonie del Sig. Amedéo Mozarts').

190 *Journal de Paris*, Paris 13 May 1780

Tomorrow, Concert Spirituel at the Château des Thuilleries.
The concert will begin with a symphony by Signor *Amidio Mozarts*. – Mme. *St. Huberti*, Mlle. Gertrude *Giradin*, MM. *le Gros* & *Laïs* will sing a motet by *Jomelli*, *Veni Sancte Spiritus*. – Mlle. *Duverger* will perform a harp concerto by M. *Bach*. – Signor *Rovédini* will sing an Italian aria by Signor *Sacchini*. – M. *Fodor*, will perform a new violin concerto of his own composition. – A *motet à grand choeur, Te Deum*, composed by M. *Gossec*, will be performed in which Mme. *St. Huberti*, Mlle. *Giradin*, MM. *le Gros* & *Laïs* will sing. – M. *Rathé* will perform a new clarinet concerto of his own composition. – Mme. *St. Huberti* will sing an Italian aria composed by M. le Chevalier *Gluck*.

Source *US-NYpl* *DM (1780), p.551; reprinted in the *Journal de Paris* for 14 May and in the *Annonces, affiches et avis divers* for 13 and 14 May.

191 *Journal de Paris*, Paris 8 April 1781

Today, Concert Spirituel at the Château des Tuileries.
The concert will begin with a symphony by Signor *Amédeo Mozarts*. – Mlle *Renaut* will sing an Italian aria. – M. *Sallantin* will perform an oboe concerto composed by Signor Antonio *Rozetti*. – A new oratorio, *Esther*, by M. *Edelmann*, will be performed in which Mlle *St. Huberti* [and] Mrs *Laïs*, *Adrien* & *Cheron* will sing. – M. *Grosse* will perform a new violin concerto of his own composition. – Mlle *St. Huberti* will sing an Italian aria with violin accompaniment, performed by M. *Pérignon*. – M. *Punto* will perform a concerto for horn of his own composition.

Source *US-NYpl* *DM (1781), pp.396–7.

192 *Les Spectacles de Paris, ou Calendrier Historique & Chronologique des Théâtres . . . Pour l'Année 1782* (Paris, 1781)

Personnel of the Concert Spirituel for the year 1782. . . . Composers. MM. Haydn, Gossec, Floquet, Rigel, Méreaux, Cambini, Sterkel, Mozart, Vogel, Bonézi.

Source *US-Io* Rare PN 2620 A43 v. 31, pp.1–2.

193 *Journal de Paris*, Paris 27 March 1782

Today, Concert Spirituel.

The concert will begin with a symphony by Signor *Amedeo Mozart*. – M. *Naudi* will sing, for the first time, a motet for haute-contre of his own composition. – M. *Virbes* will perform on the fortepiano a concerto of his own composition. – Mme *Mara* will sing a new Italian aria. – M. *Eck* will perform a violin concerto. – Mme *Mara* will sing an Italian aria. – M. *Punto* will perform a concerto for horn. – The *Stabat* of *Pergoleze* will be performed, in which Mlle *St. Huberti* & M. *Laïs* will sing.

Source *US-NYpl* *DM (1782), p.343; also advertised in the *Annonces, affiches et avis divers* for 27 March.

194 *Les Spectacles de Paris, ou Calendrier Historique & Chronologique des Théâtres . . . Pour l'Année 1783* (Paris, 1782)

Personnel of the Concert Spirituel for the year 1783. . . . Composers. MM. Haydn, Gossec, Floquet, Rigel, Méreaux, Cambini, Sterkel, Mozart, Vogel, Bonézi.

Source *US-Io* Rare PN 2620 A43 v. 32, pp.1–2.

195 *Journal de Paris*, Paris 17 April 1783

Concert Spirituel. *Today, the 17th, at the Château des Tuileries.*

The concert will begin with a symphony by M. *Amedeo Mozart*. – M. *de Vienne* will perform a flute concerto of his own composition. – The younger Mlle *Buret* will sing an Italian aria. – M. *Solers* will perform a clarinet concerto. – Mme *Todi* will sing a scena by Sig. *Paesiello*. – M. *Viotti* will perform a violin concerto of his own composition. The concert will conclude with the *Stabat* of *Pergolèse*, sung by Mme *Todi* & M. *Murgeon*.

Source *US-NYpl* *DM (1783), p.450; also advertised in the *Annonces, affiches et avis divers* for 17 April.

196 *Journal de Paris*, Paris 22 March 1785

Today, the 22nd, Concert Spirituel at the Château des Tuileries.

The concert will begin with a symphony by M. *Amedeo Mazart*. – M. *Rousseau* will sing a *Hiérodrame*, with words by *Voltaire* and music by M. *Cambini*. – M. *Viom*, of the Académie Royale de Musique, will perform, for the first time, a harpsichord concerto of his own composition. – Mlle *Burdet* the elder will sing an Italian aria. – M. *Hugot* will perform, for the first time, a sacred ode, with words by J. B. *Rousseau* and music by M. l'Abbé *le Sueur*, music director at the Church of SS. Innocens. MM. *Rousseau, Laïs* & *Chéron* will sing. – M. *Guérillot* will perform a violin concerto. – Mlle *Vindling* will sing an Italian aria.

Source *US-NYpl* *DM (1785), p.334; also advertised in the *Annonces, affiches et avis divers* for 22 March ('Symphonie de M. Amédéo Mozart').
Commentary A review of this concert in the *Journal de Paris* for 24 March does not mention the Mozart symphony.

197 *Journal de Paris*, Paris 26 December 1785

Concert. *Today, the 26th, Concert at the Musée de Paris, rue Dauphine,* for the benefit of Mme *Gautherot,* formerly Mlle *Deschamps.*
The concert will begin with a symphony by M. *Haydn.* – Mme *Gautherot* will sing an *ariette* by Signor *Misliweck.* – Mlle *Williaume* will play a fortepiano concerto by *Mozart.* – Mlle *Saint-James* will sing a scena by M. *Piccini.* – Mme *Gautherot* will play a violin concerto by M. *Viotti.* – Mlle *Vaillant* will sing an Italian aria. – M. *Devienne* will play a flute concerto. – Mlle *Saint-James* will sing an aria by *Panurge.* – Mme *Gautherot* & M. *Gervais* will play a *symphonie concertante* by M. *Davaux.*

Source *US-NYpl* *DM (1785), p.1491.
Commentary Little is known of Willeaume, who played three times at the Concert Spirituel between 1785 and 1787. Her performance on 10 April 1786 also included a Mozart concerto (*see* Document 200).
Literature Constant Pierre, *Histoire du Concert Spirituel 1725–90* (Paris, 1975), 216, 329, 331 and 337.

198 *Tablettes de renommée des Musiciens, Auteurs, Compositeurs, Virtuoses, Amateurs et Maîtres de Musique vocale et instrumentale, les plus connus en chaque genre. Avec une Notice des Ouvrages ou autres motifs qui les on rendu recommandables. Pour servir a l'Almanach-Dauphin* (Paris, 1785)

Composers, Virtuosos, Amateurs and Music Masters for string instruments. . . . Some of the best-known are: . . . Mozart, composer for the Concert Spirituel, has written a violin method and several sonatas and clavecin concertos.

Source Facsimile edition, p.25.
Commentary Mozart's works are confused here with those of his father, Leopold, whose *Gründliche Violinschule* of 1756 had been published in a French translation in Paris in about 1770. By 1785, in addition to his juvenile works, many of Mozart's accompanied and solo sonatas, as well as his concertos, had

appeared in French editions, or were available in Paris in editions published elsewhere, including Vienna.

199 *Journal de Paris*, Paris 23 March 1786

Concert. *Saturday the 25th, Concert Spirituel at the Château des Tuileries.*
   The concert will begin with a symphony by M. *Haydn*, after which Mlle *Vaillant* will sing an Italian aria. – M. *Hermann* will perform on the piano forte, for the first time, a concerto of his own composition. – M. *David* will sing an Italian aria composed by Signor *Rusli*. – MM. *Ozi* & *Soler* will perform a new *Symphonie concertante*, for clarinet & bassoon, composed by M. *Ozi*, musician of the King's Chapel. – M. *Chéron* will sing a new *Hyérodrame*, words by M. *Moline*, music by M. *Tomeoni*. – M. *Kreitz*, of the King's music, will perform a violin concerto of his own composition. – M. *David* will sing an Italian aria by Signor *Giordaniello*. – A symphony by M. *Amedeo Mozart* will be performed.

Source   *US-NYpl* *DM (1786), p.331. Also advertised in the *Journal de Paris* for 25 March and in the *Annonces, affiches et avis divers* for 22 and 25 March ('Symphonie del Signor Amédéo').
Commentary   A review of this concert in the *Journal de Paris* for 27 March does not mention the Mozart symphony.

200 *Journal de Paris*, Paris 10 April 1786

Concert. *Today, the 10th, Concert Spirituel at the Château des Tuileries.*
   The concert will begin with a symphony by M. *Mozart*, after which Mme *Toméoni* will sing an Italian aria by M. *Sarti*. – Mlle *Villieaume* will play on the piano forte a Concerto by M. *Mozard*. – M. *Rousseau* will sing, for the second time, a *Hyérodrame*, words by M. *Moline*, music by M. *Berton*, of the Académie Royale de Musique.
   2nd *Part*. A symphony by M. *Haydn* will be performed, after which Mme *Toméoni* will sing an Italian aria by M. *Cimarosa*. – Mme *Gautherot* will perform a violin concerto by M. *Jarnowick*. *Dilexi*, a *motet à grand choeur* composed by M. l'Abbé *le Sueur*, will be performed, in which MM. *Rousseau* & *Chéron* will sing.

Source   *US-NYpl* *DM (1786), p.408. Also advertised in the *Annonces, affiches et avis divers* for 10 April 1786.
Commentary   For Willeaume, *see* Document 197. A review of the previous two weeks' concerts published in the *Mercure de France* for 29 April (p.243) does not mention the Mozart concerto but states that Willeaume and another performer at the Concert Spirituel, Mlle Landrin, 'played the fortepiano with much success'.

201 *Journal de Paris*, 3 April 1789

Concert. *Tomorrow the 3rd, Concert Spirituel at the Château des Tuileries.*
1ˢᵗ *Part.* Symphony by M. Amédée *Mozart*, after which M. *Rovedino*, of the Théâtre de *Monsieur*, will sing, for the first time, an Italian aria. – M. *Caffro* will perform an oboe concerto of his own composition. – M. *Mengozzi* will sing a new Italian aria by M. *Cannetti*, with bassoon accompaniment performed by M. *Perret*.
2ⁿᵈ *Part.* Symphony by M. *Haydn*, after which Mˡˡᵉ *Balletti* will sing an Italian aria. – M. *Aldée* will perform a new violin concerto of his own composition. – Mˡˡᵉ *Balletti*, MM. *Mengozzi* & *Rovedino* will sing a new trio, music by M. *Gonzaniga*.

Source *US-NYpl* *DM (1789), p.418. Also advertised in the *Journal de Paris* and the *Annonces, affiches et avis divers* for 3 April 1789 ('de M. Amédeo Mozart').

202 *Mercure de France*, 27 June 1789

Entertainments. Théâtre de Monsieur.
La villanella rapita, or *La villageoise enlevée*, performed on the 15th of this month, gave great pleasure, as much for the choice of the music as for the merit of the new débutants. This work was written by Signor Francesco Bianchi; it was successful in Italy because its melodies are agreeable and gay, the ensembles make a good effect, and in particular because the poem is more interesting than is usually the case with Italian subjects, although it still lacks that unity of scenes to which the French attach so much merit, but with which the Italians, for good reasons, do not burden themselves. It is doubtful whether the somewhat ordinary music of the original score, if it had been retained, would have pleased ears accustomed to the original and brilliant ideas of Paisiello and Cimarosa. But as it is normal to allow the débutants to choose the pieces in which they wish to be heard, and this choice was well performed, it resulted in a work full of strength and warmth, deserving the success it obtained.
The pieces retained from the original are the introduction and the first finale, and these are the best in the work. The substituted ensembles included a charming terzetto by Signor Mozzart, a duo by the Spanish composer Signor Martini, and two quartets by Signor Guglielmi, one drawn from a serious opera and the other, which served as the second finale, from a comic opera. Both made very good impressions. Almost all of the arias were substituted.

Source *GB-Lbl* 298.a-g. (1789), p.184.
Commentary This performance of *La villanella rapita*, given on 15 June, included music by Paisiello, Bianchi, Guglielmi, Ferrari, Sarti and Martín y Soler in addition to Mozart's 'Mandina amabile' K480. (*See also* Documents 8 and 81.) Mozart composed the trio, as well as the quartet 'Dite almeno, in che

mancai' κ479, for the 1785 Vienna production of Bianchi's opera (*Dokumente* 225, *Documentary Biography* 255–6).

203 *L'année littéraire*, Paris 1789

Entertainments. Théâtre de Monsieur.

In the midst of the decline of almost all theatrical productions, the Théâtre de Monsieur sustains itself with success, and attracts large audiences because it offers patrons excellent music executed with a perfection virtually unknown in France: one has, perhaps, never seen in any theatre in Europe so excellent and rare a company of actors and Italian singers of such superior merit.

The opera buffa *La vilanella ràpita*, or *La villageoise enlevée*, performances of which are always greeted with new enthusiasm, is not the work of a single musician. It is a collection of the most exquisite pieces of several great masters; and these pieces are so well-chosen, so well-adapted to the action, that they form an admirable ensemble. The genius of a single man could never include so many beauties in a single piece, because genius is uneven, and its productions are not always felicitous. In *La villanella rapita*, the new performers with which the administrators have enriched this theatre displayed the most surprising talents, which are rarely found together. To the beauty of the voice, and the perfection of the singing, they add the greatest understanding of the stage and a performance that announces consummate actors. Signor Viganoni, who plays the role of the Count, puts as much warmth and interest into his acting as grace and expression in his singing; his arietta 'Mi perdo, si, mi perdo', etc. produces a fresh sensation every time it is heard: the public, thinking only of its own pleasure, always has him repeat it, without regard to the fatigue that the repetition of such a difficult piece might cause him; but his voice is so reliable and so well trained that the audience never perceives this fatigue, and he always gives more pleasure the second time than the first. The vivacity, brightness and comic strength of Signor Mandini, accompanied by a superb voice and a manner of singing full of taste, interest and precision, wins him complete approval in the role of the villager Philippe. His wife, Signora Mandini, charged with the role of the *villageoise*, is an excellent actress whose performance is at the same time natural and refined, brilliant and true, and graceful but not mannered. Others have more beautiful voices; but it is impossible to sing better, to have a tone more pleasant, more touching, more Italian.

The piece itself is superior to the majority of Italian farces that have no other merit than their music; the subject has some resemblance to *Ninette à la Cour*. The character of the *villageoise* is very dramatic, with a titillating naivety; that of the *villageois* is very comic.

There are several very agreeable and interesting situations; the disguise of the *villageois* as a baron is the only crude buffoonery that disfigures the work.

Source *US-CAw* 37565.51 (1789), pp.115–18.

Commentary A review published in the *Journal de Paris* for 17 June (p.757) stated only that 'the music appears to have been very well chosen; at least seven or eight pieces were of the greatest merit'. No mention is made of Mozart.

204 Arthur Young, *Travels during the Years 1787, 1788, and 1789. Undertaken more particularly with a View of ascertaining the Cultivation, Wealth, Resources, and National Property, of the Kingdom of France* (London, 1792) [refers to June 1789]

[Paris] The 24th [of June 1789]. . . . Such an incessant buzz of politics has been in my ears for some days past, that I went tonight to the Italian opera, for relaxation. Nothing could be better calculated for that effect, than the piece performed, La Villanella Rapita, by Bianchi, a delicious composition. Can it be believed, that this people, who so lately valued nothing at an opera but the dances, and could hear nothing but a squall, – now attend with feeling to Italian melodies, applaud with taste and rapture, and this without the meretricious aid of a single dance! The music of this piece is charming, elegantly playful, airy, and pleasing, with a duet, between Signora Mandini and Vigagnoni, of the first lustre. The former is a most fascinating singer, – her voice nothing, but her grace, expression, soul, all strung to exquisite sensibility.

Source *GB-Lbl* 184.b.9, p.120.

Commentary Arthur Young (1741–1820) was a prominent writer on agriculture. Selections from his travel journal concerned with opera and theatre were reprinted (after the 1793 Berlin edition) in the *Annalen des Theaters*, xiv (Berlin, 1794), 69–81. For *La villanella rapita, see* Document 202.

205 *Inventaire général des effets appartenants au Roi existants dans les magazins des menus de plaisirs de Sa Majesté, tant à Paris, qu'a Versailles Fontainebleau, Choisy, Compeigne et St Hubert; le dit Inventaire fait le Ier Janvier 1780* (Paris, 1780 and later)

1789 . . . 1 Symphony by Mozart

Source Barry S. Brook, *La symphonie française dans la seconde moitié du XVIIIe siècle* (Paris, 1962), i, 493.

Commentary Possibly the symphony is K297/300a or K385 ('Haffner'). Although K297/300a is usually thought to have been published in Paris by Sieber in 1789, Neal Zaslaw points out that it may have appeared as early as 1783; Sieber's edition of K385 appeared in 1789.

Literature Neal Zaslaw, *Mozart's Symphonies: Context, Performance Practice, Reception* (Oxford, 1989), 330–31; Gertraut Haberkamp, *Die Erstdrucke der Werke von Wolfgang Amadeus Mozart* (Tutzing, 1986), i, 124–5.

British (London)

206 *The Morning Herald and Daily Advertiser*, London 16 February 1784

Hanover-Square Grand Concert. The Nobility and Gentry are respectfully informed that the Second will be on Wednesday next. . . .

Act I. Overture, Mogart – Quartetto for two Violins, Tenor and Bass, Haydn – Song, Signor Tasca – Concerto Violin, Mr. Cramer – Song, Signora Dorcetti, being her first performance in this Kingdom – Concerto Grose, for Flute, Hautboy, Violin, and Violoncello, by Mess[rs]. Florio, Ramm, Cramer and Cervetto, composed by Mr. Graff.

Act II. Overture, by particular desire, Mr. Graff – Concerto, for two Bassoons, Mess[rs]. Schwartz – Song, Signor Tasca – Solo Violoncello, Mr. Corvetto – Song, Signora Dorcetti – Sinfoni, double orchestra, Bach.

Doors to be opened at Seven, and begin at Eight o'clock precisely.

Source *GB-Lblc* without shelfmark [unpaginated]. Also announced in *The Morning Post and Daily Advertiser* for 17 February and *The Public Advertiser* ('Overture, Mogert') and *The Morning Chronicle and London Advertiser* ('Overture, Mozach') for 18 February [unpaginated].

Commentary The overture (symphony) by Mozart cannot be identified, although possibly it was one of a number of similar works performed in Paris during the preceding years (*see* Documents 184 ff). Up to this time, perhaps only one of Mozart's symphonies, κ297/300*a*, had been published there (*see* Document 205) and early manuscript copies are rare. After the concerts of 1764–5, this is the earliest recorded performance in London of a Mozart symphony. The Hanover Square Grand Concerts, sponsored by Bertie, Lord Willoughby, 4th Earl of Abingdon (1740–99), were a continuation of the Bach-Abel concerts. According to advertisements in *The Morning Chronicle and London Advertiser* for 28 January and *The Morning Herald and Daily Advertiser* for 31 January, the orchestra was eleven violins, four violas, three cellos, four double basses, two flutes, two oboes, two bassoons and two horns. Wilhelm Cramer was the leader, and Muzio Clementi, although he resigned in mid-series, was the harpsichordist. The 'official' composer was Friedrich Hartmann Graf.

Literature Simon McVeigh, 'The Professional Concert and Rival Subscription Series in London, 1783–1793', *RMA Research Chronicle*, no.22 (1989), 1–135.

207   *The Morning Chronicle and London Advertiser*, London 2 March 1784

Hanover-Square Grand Concert. The Nobility and Gentry are respectfully informed, that the Third will be To-morrow. . . .
   Act I. Overture, Mozard. Quartetto, Mr. Pieltian. Song, Signor Doretti; Sonata Piano Forte, Mr. Clementi; Song, Miss Cantelo; Concerto Grosso for Flute, Tenor, and Violin, by Mess[rs]. De Camp, Blake, and Cramer, composed by Mr. Graff.
   Act II. A new Sinfonie, Haydn. Song, Mr. Harrison; Concerto for Bassoon and Hautboy, by Mess[rs]. Schwartz and Ramm, composed by Stamitz; Duetto, Mr. Harrison and Miss Cantelo; Lesson on the Harp, by Madame Clery. – Full Piece.
   Doors to be opened at Seven, and begin at Eight o'clock precisely.

Source   *GB-Lblc* without shelfmark [unpaginated]. Also announced in *The Morning Post and Daily Advertiser* for 2 March and *The Morning Herald and Daily Advertiser* and *The Public Advertiser* ('Overture, Mogart') for 3 March [unpaginated].
Commentary   Reviews published in *The Public Advertiser* for 5 March and *The Morning Herald and Daily Advertiser* for 6 March do not mention the Mozart overture.

208   *The Public Advertiser*, London 28 April 1784

Hanover Square Grand Concert. The Nobility and Gentry are respectfully informed that the Ninth Night will be This Day.
   Act I. Overture, Mozart; Trio for Violoncello, Tenor and Violin, by Mess[rs]. Cervetto, Blake, and Cramer, composed by Mr. Giardini; Song, Signor Tasca; Sonata Piano Forte, Mr. Dance. Song, Miss Cantelo; Concerto for two French Horns by Mess[rs]. Pajola and Pieltain, composed by Mr. Graff.
   Act II. Sinfonie, Mr. Graff; Song, Mr. Harrison; Concerto Hautboy, Mr. Ramm; Duetto, Mr. Harrison and Miss Cantelo; Sinfonie, Haydn.
   The Doors to be opened at Seven, and the Concerto to begin precisely at Eight.

Source   *GB-Lblc* without shelfmark [unpaginated]. Also advertised in *The Morning Herald and Daily Advertiser* for 28 April.
Commentary   A review of this concert appeared in *The Public Advertiser* for 29 April [unpaginated]: 'Hanover Square Grand Concert. After the first Night of this Entertainment, we asserted its claim to Preeminence. Upon this Ground we still stand, throwing down the Glove to any Music-loving Champion whatsoever. If, daring to take it up, he proves indubitably that other concerts can surpass this, we will retire from the Lists with Shame. Mozart's Overture pleased us by many brilliant Passages, not wandering from the Line of either Taste or Judgment'.

209 *The Public Advertiser*, London 5 May 1784

Hanover Square Grand Concert. The Nobility and Gentry are respectfully informed, that the Tenth Night will be This Day, May 5.

Act I.

Overture for two Orchestras, Bach; Quartetto for two Violins,
Tenor, and Basse, by Mess[rs]. Cramer, Borghi, Black, and
Cervetto, composed by Mr. Abel; Song, Mr. Harrison; Concerto
Harpsichord, Master Cramer; Song, Miss Cantelo; Concertante for
two Hautboys, by Messrs. Suck and Ramm, composed by Mr. Graff.

Act II.

Sinfonie, Mozart; Sonata on the French Harp, Master Mayer; Song,
Signor Tasca; Concertante for two Violins, by Messrs. Borghi and
Cramer, composed by Stamitz; Duetto, Mr. Harrison and Miss
Cantelo; Sinfonie, Haydn.

The Doors to be opened at Seven, and the Performance to begin
precisely at Eight.

Source *GB-Lblc* without shelfmark [unpaginated].

Commentary Reviews published in *The Morning Herald and Daily Advertiser* for
6 May and *The Public Advertiser* for 7 May do not mention the Mozart symphony.

210 Carl Friedrich Cramer, *Magazin der Musik*, Hamburg
December 1783 [*recte* 1784]

**Notice concerning the grand concerts given under the direction
of Lord Abington in London**. . . . **The second concert, on 18
February**, was exceedingly brilliant and numerous. It opened with a
grand symphony by Mozart, beautiful and varied in all its parts.
This was followed by a double bassoon concerto by the two Sch-
wartzs, father and son, the most perfect that has ever been heard
here. It pleased exceedingly. Then Madame d'Orcetti, who has been
heard in many places with great success . . . sang two arias by Majo:
Disperato in van m'affanno &c. and Cedere e forza, o Cara, with
such taste, fire and good execution, that it was universally hoped to
keep this splendid singer longer here in London. . . . **The 9th concert, on 28 April**, began with a very brilliant symphony by Mozart.
Danze's pianoforte sonata garnered much applause. A trio by
Giardini for violin, viola and violoncello was excellently played and
listened to with great attention. A horn concerto and a grand symphony by Graaff had much success . . . and a concluding symphony
by Haydn was performed with much fire.

Source Facsimile edition, cols.226–7 and 231.
Commentary *See* Documents 206 and 208.

211 *The European Magazine and London Review,* London September
1784

Impartial and Critical Review of Musical Publications.
Trois Sonates pour le Clavecin ou le Forte Piano, composees par W.
A. Mozard, Œuvre V. A Mannheim, chez le Sr. Gotz. Marchand et
Editeur de Musique.

Upon a review of these *Sonates*, we find in them a considerable
degree of merit: fancy, taste and judgment unite through the work,
and distinguish Mr. Mozard as a fertile and judicious composer.

The first movement of the first sonata is bold and brilliant; but
though florid, it is no way wild; and though singular, is without
affectation. Many master-strokes discover themselves, and shew us
real Genius led by the hand of Science. The second movement opens
pleasingly, though very oddly, and proceeds with much elegance and
design; while the rondo with which the piece concludes, equally
demands our admiration: its subject strikes us as simple, gay and
pretty; with a great share of ease and familiarity, it is original; and
the whole movement abounds with much spirit of fancy, regular and
connected. Its modulations, though not striking, are well chosen, and
the return of its subject natural.

The second *Sonata,* tho' conceived with much spirit, and executed
with equal judgement, is not, considered on the whole, comparable
to the first: we cannot pronounce it brilliant, though it was evidently
intended to be so; nor are we struck with that novelty of idea which
distinguishes its companion. The first movement is masterly, and not
without strokes of imagination; the second rich, but rather exuber-
ant; and the last, though spirited and tolerably original, not so
happily conceived as the latter movement of the first Sonata.

With the third piece we are highly pleased: it opens with vigour,
and proceeds with much play of fancy: the modulation is easy and
natural, and the melody smooth and connected. The second movement is very agreeable in its subject, and conducted to the end with
great management; but we do not think it quite so free in its stile as
the middle movement of either of the two former Sonatas: somewhat
of a stiffness hangs about it in passages; yet it is by no means sterile
of elegance, nor, indeed, without a considerable share of ease. The
rondo which forms the latter movement possesses a variety of merit:
its air is exceedingly pleasing, a glow of imagination runs through it,
the construction of its harmony is good, and the stile uniform.

Source *GB-Lbl* P.P.5459.z (1784), pp.225–6.

Commentary The sonatas are k309/284*b*, 310/300*d* and 311/284*c*, composed in Paris in 1778 and first published by Heina in 1782. The date of Götz's edition is uncertain.

212 *The Daily Universal Register*, London 24 September 1785

New Music. Just imported from Vienna, and to be had at the Print Warehouse, No. 28, the Top of the Haymarket,
Haydn Gran Simphonia, Opera 39, Price 3s.
Ditto 12 Minuetti, 2s.6d.
Fialia 3 Quartetti, Op.3. 6s.
Kozeluch Gran Concerto, per im Cimbalo, Op.9, 6s.
Morat ditto,   ditto,   Op.1, 6s.
Ditto,   ditto,   2, 6s.
Ditto,   ditto,   3, 6s.

Source *GB-Lblc* without shelfmark [unpaginated].
Commentary With the exception of the Haydn symphony, all of the works advertised here were published in Vienna by Artaria between January and April 1785. They include Joseph Haydn's Menuets H IX:8, Joseph Fiala's string quartets op.3, Leopold Kozeluch's Concerto op.9 and Mozart's Concertos k413/387*a*, 414/385*p* and 415/387*b*. Haydn's symphony, H I:73 ('La Chasse'), was first published by Torricella in 1782. According to Hoboken, Artaria's edition, taken over from Torricella, did not appear until 1786.

213 *The Morning Post and Daily Advertiser*, London 17 January 1786

New Music. This Day is published, by W. Napier, Music-Seller to their Majesties, No.474, Strand,
   A Grand Concerto for the Harpsichord, with accompaniments for two Violins, two Oboes or German Flutes, a Tenor and Bass, ad libitum, composed by A. Mozart, op.4th, price 4s. The Harpsichord part may be had separately at Half-a-Crown:
   Where also may be had, lately published, A Concerto for the Harpsichord, with Accompaniments, by J. F. Kloffler, price 4s. without the Accompaniments, 2s.6d.
   These are the two Concertos which have been repeatedly performed by Mr. Cramer, junr. at the Anacreontic Society.

Source *GB-Lblc* without shelfmark [unpaginated].
Commentary The concertos are k414/385*p* and a D major keyboard concerto by Johann Friedrich Klöffler (1725–90). 'Mr. Cramer, junr.' is Johann Baptist Cramer (1771–1858), who performed k414/385*p* again at a Hanover Square concert on 13 February 1786. *See* Documents 212 and 214.

214 *The Daily Universal Register*, London 11 February 1786

Hanover Square Grand Professional Concert. The Second Concert at this Place, will be on Monday, the 13th of February.

Act the First

Overture, Haydn. Trio for Tenor, Violoncello, and Violin, by Messrs. Blake, Cervetto, and Cramer – Gardini. Song, Signor Tenducci. Concerto Flute, Florio. Song, Miss Madden, being her first appearance in Public. The Eleventh Grand Concerto – Handel.

Act the Second

Overture, Mr. Abel. Song, Signor Tenducci. Concerto Piano Forte, Mr. Cramer, Jun. Duetto, Signor Tenducci and Miss Madden. Overture, double Orchestra – Bach.

To begin at Eight o'Clock precisely.

Subscriptions are received, and Tickets delivered by Messrs. Ransom, Morland, and Hammersley, No.57, Pall-mall.

Tickets transferable as usual: Ladies to Ladies, and Gentlemen to Gentlemen.

Source *GB-Lblc* without shelfmark [unpaginated]. Also advertised in *The Gazetteer* and *The Public Advertiser* for 11 February, and *The Morning Chronicle and London Advertiser*, *The Morning Herald and Daily Advertiser*, and *The Morning Post and Daily Advertiser* for 13 February.

Commentary For Johann Baptist Cramer, *see* Document 213. The concerto performed by him at the Hanover Square Grand Professional Concert, and previously at meetings of the Anacreontic Society, was K414/385*p*. *See* Documents 212 and 213. A review of this concert appeared in *The Morning Herald and Daily Advertiser* for 15 February:

Grand Professional Concert. The second night of this fashionable concert introduced a novelty in Miss *Madden*, sister to Mrs. Cramer, who sung in the first act, *Paisiollo's* air, the recitative of which begins 'Sembran sogni, &c.' with taste that reflected credit on Mr. Tenducci, by whom she was taught, and with whom she sung a duet, by the same composer, in the second act; in which she gave an earnest of her being hereafter a capital singer.

Haydn's overture, with which the concert opened, is a beautiful composition; its effect was charming. The trio of *Giardini's*, which followed, never was played with more elegance than last night by Messrs *Blake, Cervetto, Cramer*. Tenducci acquitted himself with credit in 'Ah! se il Parde, &c.' but in *Sarti's* incomparable Rondeau 'Oh generosa! Oh grande!' he evinced considerable superiority over the stile in which it was sung during the late season at the Opera. *Florio* played a delightful flute concerto, with great expression; and young Cramer, in a fine concerto by Mozart, shewed a skill on the *piano forte* which lifts him above parallel.

The new overture by Abel, proves his science by the transition in the middle movement: it was delightfully played: as was the double orchestra overture by *Bach*; the effect did credit to this distinguished band. A very fashionable audience attended, and testified the highest approbation of the selection and performance.

Other reviews, published in *The Daily Universal Register* for 14 and 16 February, do not mention Cramer or the Mozart concerto.

215 *The Morning Post and Daily Advertiser*, London 14 February 1786

New Music. This Day is published, by W. Napier, Music Seller to their Majesties, No.474, Strand, A Grand Concerto for the Piano Forte and Harpsichord, with Accompaniments by Mozart, as performed by Mr. Cramer, junior, at the Hanover Square Concert and at the Anacreontic Society, price 4s.

The charming Concerto by Mozart, as performed last night at the Hanover-Square Concert, was no less admired as a fine composition, than for the exquisite performance of young Cramer.

Source *GB-Lblc* without shelfmark [unpaginated].
Commentary The concerto is k414/385*p*. *See* Documents 212–14.

216 *The Daily Universal Register*, London 17 October 1786

New Music and Musical Instruments, *Just Published.* . . . Three Sonatas for the Harpsichord or Piano Forte, with an Accompaniment for the violin, composed by W. H. Mozart, Op.7, price 7s. 6d. . . . printed and published for Longman and Broderip, No.26 Cheapside, and No.13, Haymarket.

Source *GB-Lblc* without shelfmark [unpaginated].
Commentary The sonatas k333/315*c*, 284/205*b* and 454, first published by Torricella in Vienna in 1784, were entered by Longman & Broderip at Stationers' Hall on 25 September 1786. The date 'um 1790' given in Köchel (6/1964) and *NMA* VIII:23/i–ii (critical report) should be revised accordingly. Longman & Broderip's edition was also recorded in the *Calendrier Musical Universel . . . pour l'année 1788* (Paris, 1787), 203.

217 *The Public Advertiser*, London 22 February 1787

Madame Mara's Third Concert. Hanover Square. The third Performance will be This Day, the 22d of February.

Act I. Overture Mozart; Song, Signor Balelli; Quintetto, Playel; Song, Madame Mara; Concerto Clarinet, Mahon.

Act II. New Symphony, Clementi; Song, Mr. Stuart; Concerto Violoncello, Mara; Song, Madame Mara; Symphony, Haydn.

To begin at Eight o'Clock.

Source *GB-Lblc* without shelfmark [unpaginated]. Also advertised in *The Morning Herald and Daily Advertiser* for 22 February.

218 *The Morning Herald and Daily Advertiser*, London 14 March 1787

Hanover-Square. For the Benefit of Miss Abrams. To-morrow, the 15th inst. will be a Grand Concert of Vocal and Instrumental Music.

Act I. New Overture, Pleyel. Song, Miss T. Abrams, Mortellari. Concerto Piano Forte, Mr. Cramer Jun. Song, Miss Abrams, Sacchini. Concerto Violin, Mr. Salomon.

Act II. Overture, Mozart. Song, Mr. Harrison; Concerto German Flute, Mr. Graeff. Duetto, the Miss Abrams, Allessandri. Concerto Oboe, Mr. Parke. Quartetto Messrs. Harrison, Webb, and Miss Abrams, Sacchini. Symphony Haydn.

Tickets 10s. 6d. each, to be had of Miss Abrams, No.7, North-street, next Tottenham-street, Rathbone-place.

The Concert to begin precisely at Eight o'Clock.

Source *GB-Lblc* without shelfmark [unpaginated].

219 *The World*, London 21 May 1787

Mrs. Billington's Concert. . . . Young Cramer and Parke played delightfully. Mozart was the writer of the Concerto for the former.

Source *GB-Lblc* without shelfmark [unpaginated].
Commentary Elizabeth Billington (1765–1818), a famous coloratura singer, keyboard player and composer, made her début at Covent Garden in 1786. In 1806 she sang Vitellia in *La clemenza di Tito*, the first complete Mozart opera given in London. For Cramer, *see* Document 213. Parke was an oboist.
Literature Roger Fiske, *English Theatre Music in the Eighteenth Century* (Oxford and New York, 2/1986), 619–20.

220 *The Daily Universal Register*, London 9 November 1787

Further Account of the Anacreontic Third Meeting. Wednesday 7th inst. The Concert opened with a new symphony by Mozart, which was well received, and had great merit. . . . The Concert finished with a Symphony by Mozart, very inferior to the first.

Source *GB-Lblc* without shelfmark [unpaginated].
Commentary A sonata by Kozeluch, an aria by Paisiello, a symphony by Clementi, an unidentified duet, and a concerto by Geminiani were also performed on this occasion. The Mozart symphonies may have been K385 ('Haffner') and K319, published by Artaria in Vienna in 1785 and sold in London by mid-December 1787. *See* Document 224.

221 *The World Fashionable Advertiser*, London 21 November 1787

The *Professional* people, have not yet settled on their *Composer*. It is determined not to be *Graaffe*. *Mozart*, and *Paesiello*, should both be employed.

Source *GB-Lblc* without shelfmark [unpaginated].

Commentary   A notice published in *The World* for 5 December is apparently a direct response to the suggestion that Mozart or Paisiello be engaged for the Professional Concerts: 'The preparations for the Professional Concert are on the best scale. But why travel for composers to Paris and Vienna, when there is such a man as Baumgarten at home?' Mozart had planned to visit in England the year before (*see* Document 75) and his reputation there was furthered by his pupils and colleagues Thomas Attwood, Michael Kelly, and Stephen and Ann Storace, who had returned from Vienna to London in the spring of 1787.

222   *The Daily Universal Register*, London 14 December 1787

Anacreontic Society. *Seventh Night.*

This truly convivial Society, in the conduct of which good sense is mingled with wit, mirth, and harmony, was on Wednesday evening attended by, at least, three hundred Gentlemen. The band was, as usual, led by Mr. Cramer. It is needless to say more. An overture of Mozart was first introduced, the effort of which was sensibly felt. Mr. Cramer, jun. again distinguished himself upon the harpsichord, which did honour to Mozart the composer; we know not on which to bestow the greatest praise.

Mr. Jones introduced that ancient English instrument the harp, upon which he gave an excellent lesson, with variations, that were at the same time scientific and beautiful. – The two young *Leanders*, in a concerto for horns, distinguished themselves to great advantage; but we would advise them to attend to their subject with *strictness*, and not let exertion overpower reason and judgement. A quartetto of Pleyell's, by Cramer, Dance, Napier, and Smith, was exquisite. – Haydn's favourite overture, the second movement of which is obligated for the horns, completed the concert. The two *Leanders*, in the obligata horn part, were beyond our praise. After supper, which, as usual, was excellent, and what is better divided into separate parties, Mr. Sedgwick sung the Anacreontic song. Mr. Bellamy sung the 'Festive Board was met', in a most capital style. Several catches and glees were sung in the course of the evening, and the company returned at one o'clock.

Source   *GB-Lblc* without shelfmark [unpaginated].

Commentary   The Anacreontic Society held its seventh meeting on Wednesday 12 December. For Cramer, *see* Document 213. The symphony may have been K385 or K319; *see* Document 224.

223   *The Daily Universal Register*, London 21 December 1787

The sons of Anacreon met in full glee, on Wednesday evening, to the number of two hundred and fifty, and before supper there were near three hundred. . . . Mr. Cramer was the leader of the band. The concert opened with a grand overture of Koselucks, in which Mr. Cramer sustained his part with great ability, particularly in the adagio part of the second movement, and the allegro part of the third. A quartetto of Pleyel's, by Cramer, Dance, Smith, and a Gentleman, whose name we do not recollect, gave the young *Leanders* another opportunity of exerting themselves with wonderful effect, in the obligato part for the horn.

Mr. Cramer, junior, likewise distinguished himself in an harpsichord lesson of Mozart's. His execution and taste are both of a very superior kind; but we beg to be indulged with a gentle and well-intended hint; and we trust his good nature will forgive us. – The frequent introduction of rapid passages, which are extraneous to the subject, and oftentimes intrude upon it. Mr. Cramer needs not this assistance, brilliant as it is, to establish his character as a masterly performer of the first rank.

At ten, the company retired to supper in the great room, which as usual, consisted of a cold collation. The wines were excellent. . . . When the Gentlemen returned to the Concertroom, Non nobis Domine, was sung in a good style by Mr. Sedgwick – he then sung the Anacreontic Song with its usual effect.

Source *GB-Lblc* without shelfmark [unpaginated].
Commentary For Cramer, *see* Document 213.

224 *The Times*, London 1 January 1788

New Music. This day is published, by Longman and Broderip, Music Sellers. . . . Mozart, Two Symphonies for Grand Orchestra, Op.8 and 9. . . . Ditto, Six Quartets, dedicated to Mr. Haydn, Op.10. . . . Ditto, Quartett for the Harpsichord.

Source *GB-Lblc* without shelfmark [unpaginated].
Commentary The symphonies were K385 ('Haffner') and K319, published in Vienna in 1785 by Artaria, who in the same year also published the six quartets dedicated to Haydn. Because Longman & Broderip had already advertised the piano quartet K478 on 1 December 1787, it may be that the quartet advertised here was K493, also published by Artaria in 1787. Birchall & Andrews's almost contemporary edition of the work apparently derives from an independent source, possibly one taken to London by Mozart's English friends. Longman & Broderip's advertisement for K385 and K319 first appeared in *The World* for 21 December and *The Daily Universal Register* for 22 December 1787, shortly after performances of unidentified Mozart symphonies at a meeting of the Anacreontic Society on 9 November (*see* Document 220). The advertisement of 1 January 1788 was known to C. F. Pohl (*Mozart in London*, Vienna, 1867, p.142) but misunderstood by Deutsch, who stated that two symphonies, a piano quartet and the six quartets dedicated to Haydn were *performed* in London in 1788 (*Dokumente* 290, *Documentary Biography* 331).

225   *The Morning Post and Daily Advertiser*, London 7 January 1788

For the Benefit of Mr. Cramer. By permission of the Worshipful the Haberdashers Company, sanctioned by the Gentlemen of the City Assembly, and at the particular desire of his Musical Friends and Patrons in the City.

At Haberdashers Hall, Maiden-lane, Wood-street, on Wednesday the 9th of January, will be performed, A Grand Miscellaneous Vocal and Instrumental Concert.

First Act. Overture – Mozart. Concerto Bassoon – Mr. J. Parkinson. Song – Mr. Sedgwick. Concerto, Piano Forte – Mr. Cramer, Jun. Song – Mrs. Billington. Concerto Violin – Mr. Cramer.

Second Act. Grand Overture Double Orchestra, M.S. – Bach. Quartetto for two Violins, Tenor, and Violoncello, by Messrs. Cramer, Borghi, Blacke, and Smith – Pleyel. Song – Mr. Harrison. Concerto, Hautboy – Mr. Parke. Song – Mrs. Billington. Symphony – Haydn.

The Concert to begin precisely at Eight o'Clock.

Source   *GB-Lblc* without shelfmark [unpaginated]. Also announced in *The Morning Post and Daily Advertiser* and *The Times* for 9 January 1788.
Commentary   Possibly the Mozart symphony was K319 or 385, advertised by Longman & Broderip in *The World* and in *The Daily Universal Register* (*see* Document 224). The violinist Wilhelm Cramer (1746–99) was leader of the orchestra at the Antient and Professional Concerts and of the opera orchestra at the Pantheon. He also led the orchestra at the Concerts of the Nobility in 1784 when two unidentified Mozart symphonies were performed; *see* Document 206.

226   *The Public Advertiser*, London 11 February 1788

Professional Concert, Hanover-Square. The First Concert will be This Evening, Monday the 11th instant.

Act I. New Overture, Mozart; Quartetto for two Violins, Tenor, and Violoncello, by Messrs. Cramer, Borghi, Blake, and Cervetto – Pleyel; Song, Mr. Harrison; Sonata Piano Forte, Mr. Clementi; Song, Mrs. Billington; Concerto Violin, Mr. Cramer.

Act II. New Concertante, for Violin, Tenor, Violoncello, and Hautboy, by Mess[rs]. Cramer, Blake, Cervetto, and Parke – Pleyel; Song, Mr. Harrison; Concerto Hautboy, Mr. Parke; Song, Mrs. Billington; New Symphony, Haydn.

Source   *GB-Lblc* without shelfmark [unpaginated]. Also announced in *The Morning Post and Daily Advertiser*, *The Morning Chronicle and London Advertiser*, *The Gazetteer*, *The Morning Herald and Daily Advertiser*, *The Times* and *The World* for 11 February.
Commentary   The symphony may have been K319 or 385, both of which were available in London in December 1787. A review of this concert in *The Times* for 13 February noted only that 'the selections were ... particularly happy and

marked by the best judgment'. According to a notice published in *The Times* for 31 January, the orchestra at the Professional Concerts was six first violins, six second violins, four violas, three cellos, three double basses, two flutes, two oboes, two horns, two bassoons and fortepiano.

227 *The Morning Post and Daily Advertiser*, London 25 February 1788

Professional Concert, Hanover Square. The Third Performance will be This present Evening, February the 25th.

Part I. New Overture – M.S. – Pleyel. Quartetto for Two Violins, Tenor and Violoncello – By Messrs. Cramer, Borghi, Blake, and Cervetto – Haydn. Song – Mr. Harrison. Sonata Piano Forte – Mr. Cramer, Jun. Song – Mrs. Billington. Concerto for a Clarinet and Bassoon – By Mess[rs]. Mahon and Parkinson.

Part II. Overture, Double Orchestra – M.S. – Bach. Song – Mr. Harrison. Concerto Hautboy – Mr. W. Parke. Song – Mrs. Billington. New Symphony – Mozart.

The Doors will be opened at Seven o'clock, and begin precisely at Eight.

Source *GB-Lblc* without shelfmark [unpaginated]. Also advertised in *The Gazetteer*, *The Morning Herald and Daily Advertiser*, *The Morning Post and Daily Advertiser* and *The World* for 18 February.

228 *The Times*, London 25 February 1788

New Music. This Day is published, by J. Bland, No.45, Holborn . . . A Duett for the Harpsichord, by Mosart, 2s.

Source *GB-Lblc* without shelfmark [unpaginated].
Commentary The 'Duett' published by Bland was K501. The date 'um 1790' in Köchel (6/1964) should be revised accordingly.

229 *The Times*, London 11 March 1788

Hanover-Square. For the Benefit of Mr. Salomon, This Evening, March the 11th, will be performed, A Concert of Vocal and Instrumental Music.

Act I. Overture – Mozart; Quartetto – Pleyel; Song – Mr. Harrison; Concerto Flute – Mr. Graeff; Duetto – Miss Abrams; Concerto Violin – Mr. Salomon.

Act II. Overture – Clementi; Concerto Piano Forte – Mad. Guedon; Song – Mr. Harrison; Concerto Oboe – Sig. Caffaro (from Napolis); Song – Mrs. Billington; Symphony – Haydn.

Hanover-Square. For the Benefit of *Miss Abrams*, on Thursday the 13th instant, Will be a Concert of Vocal and Instrumental Music.

Act I. Overture – Clementi; Quartetto – Pleyel; Song – Miss T. Abrams – Cimarosa; Concerto Oboe – Mr. Park; Duetto – Miss Abrams – Alessandri; Concerto Forte Piano – Miss Eliza Abrams, Klofflen.

Act II. Overture – Haydn; Quartetto – Miss Abrams – Mr. Harrison, and Mr. Knyvett – Sacchini; Song – Mr. Harrison; Concerto – Mr. Salomon; Song – Miss Abrams – Misliwick; Symphonie – Mozart.

To begin at Eight o'Clock.

Source *GB-Lblc* without shelfmark [unpaginated].
Commentary Harriet Abrams (1760–?1825) had studied with Thomas Augustine Arne and was a singer and composer of popular songs. Uncharacteristically, the advertisement was not repeated on the day of the performance; there is no record that her concert took place.

---

230 *The Morning Post and Daily Advertiser*, London 24 March 1788

Professional Concert. Hanover-square. The Sixth Performance will be This present Evening, the 24th Instant.

Part I. Overture, Mozart. – Quartetto for two violins, tenor, and violoncello, by Messrs. Cramer, Borghi, Blake and Cervetto, Pleyel. – Song, Mr. Harrison. – Concerto violin, Mr. Pieltain. – Song, Mrs. Pieltain. – Overture, double orchestra, M. S. Bach.

Part II. Symphony, Pleyel. – Song, Mrs. Pieltain. – Concerto Clarinet, Mr. Mahon. – Song, Mr. Harrison. – Symphony la Chasse, Haydn.

The doors will be opened at Seven o'clock, and the Concert commence precisely at Eight.

Source *GB-Lblc* without shelfmark [unpaginated]. Also advertised in *The Gazetteer, The Morning Herald and Daily Advertiser, The Morning Post and Daily Advertiser* and *The World* for 24 March.

---

231 *The Morning Post and Daily Advertiser*, London 31 March 1788

Professional Concert. Hanover-Square.
The Seventh Performance will be this present Evening, the 31st instant.

Part I. Overture, Mozart. – Quartetto for two violins, tenor and violoncello, by Messrs. Cramer, Borghi, Blake, and Cervetto, Giardini. – Song, Mr. Harrison. – Concerto hautboy, Mr. Parke. – Song, Mrs. Pieltain. – Concerto violin, Mr. Cramer.

Part II. Overture double orchestra, M. S. Bach. – Song, Mrs. Pieltain. – Sonata piano forte, Mr. Clementi. – Song, Mr. Harrison. – Symphony, Winter.

The Doors will be opened at Seven o'clock, and the Concert commence precisely at Eight.

Source *GB-Lblc* without shelfmark [unpaginated]. Also advertised in *The Morning Herald* and *The World* for 31 March.

Commentary A review of this concert appeared in *The Morning Post and Daily Advertiser* for 1 April 1788 [unpaginated]: 'The Professional Concert, undiminished in its musical brilliancy, was also equally splendid in its visitations last night, boasting some of the first in fashion as well as elegance. Parke, Cramer, and Clementi, afforded the instrumental excellence, and it was as good as the best talents could supply. Harrison was, as usual, elegant and affecting. Mrs. Pieltain still appears as the substitute for Mrs. Billington, and with increased success. The compositions discovered no very prominent merit as to themselves, but the correct and animated powers of the Orchestra left criticism without a wish.'

232 *The Morning Post and Daily Advertiser*, London 14 April 1788

Professional Concert, Hanover-Square. The Ninth Performance will be This Evening, the 14th instant.

Part I. Overture – Mozart. Quartetto for two Violins, Tenor, and Violoncello, by Mess[rs]. Cramer, Borghi, Blake and Cervetto. – Haydn. Song, Mr. Harrison. Concerto Piano Forte, Mr. Cramer, jun. Scena, Mrs. Billington. Concerto Hautboy, Mr. W. Parke.

Part II. Concertante for a Violin, Tenor, Violoncello, and Hautboy, by Mess[rs]. Cramer, Blake, Cervetto, and Parke. M. S. Pleyel. Scena, Signor Marchesi. Duetto for the Piano Forte and French Harp, by Mr. Cramer jun. and Madame Krumpholtz. Song, Mrs. Billington. Symphony – Pfeiffer.

The door will be opened at Seven o'clock, and the Concert commence precisely at Eight.

Source *GB-Lblc* without shelfmark [unpaginated]. Also advertised in *The Morning Herald and Daily Advertiser* and *The World* for 14 April.

233 *The World*, London 2 February 1789

Professional Concert. Hanover Square. The First Performance will be This present Evening.

Part I. Overture, Mozart. New Quartetto, M.S. for two Violins, Tenor and Violoncello, by Messrs. Cramer, Blake, Shield, and Cervetto – Haydn. Song, Miss Cantelo. Sonata, Piano Forte, Mr. Dance. Scena, Signor Marchesi. Concerto Violin, Mr. Cramer.

Part II. New Overture, M.S. – Haydn. Song, Miss Cantelo. Solo violoncello, Mr. Cervetto. Scena, Signor Marchesi. Symphony – Rosetti.

Source *GB-Lblc* without shelfmark [unpaginated]. Also advertised in *The Gazetteer, The Morning Chronicle and London Advertiser, The Morning Herald and Daily Advertiser, The Morning Post, The Public Advertiser* and *The Times* for 2 February.

Commentary   According to *The Morning Post* for 6 January, the orchestra at these concerts included five first violins, six second violins, four violas, three cellos, three double basses and two each of oboes, flutes, horns and bassoons. Dance played the fortepiano; the leader was Cramer.

234   *The Morning Post*, London 11 May 1789

The Opera. Haymarket.

The attraction of a New Opera, and a new performer, drew a very large audience to this place on Saturday.

La Vendemia, (the Vineyard), so far as the music is concerned, is the production of Signor Gazzaniga. It has the merit of being light and pleasing, and is also very correct; but there is very little to excite any high idea of the Composer. Besides the music of Gazzaniga, a song by Paesiello, another by Tarchi, another by Pozzi, and a duet by Mozart, are introduced in this opera. . . .

Benucci had two encores, and Sestini sung a very pretty air, by Pozzi, with so much spirit, that the audience very properly made her repeat it. Mozart's delicious duet was encored also, and Benucci and Storace sung it very well.

Source   *GB-Lblc* without shelfmark [unpaginated].
Commentary   Giuseppe Gazzaniga's *La vendemmia* was first given in London at the King's Theatre, Haymarket, on 9 May 1789. For Ann Storace, *see* Document 64. Francesco Benucci (*c*1745–1824), who sang at the King's Theatre from 9 May to 11 July, had played Figaro in Vienna in 1786 and Guglielmo in *Così fan tutte* in Vienna in 1790. In *La vendemmia*, Benucci and Storace sang the duet 'Crudel! perché finora' from *Figaro*. A review of a performance on 16 May was published in *The Morning Post* for 18 May: 'La Vendemia drew but a very indifferent audience to this house on Saturday. The pit was scantily supplied. . . . The charming duet of Mozart was encored.'

235   *The World*, London 20 February 1790

The Two Oratorios. . . . Both full, and both deserving to be so, is the short account of last night – and the Messiah, in all its successes since 1741, never before filled *two Houses on one night*. By the bye, at first, to the disgrace of the popular taste, this work, sublime as it is, had no success at all!

The chief novelty was little Bridgetower, the African; he performed with much excellence, and he promises more, and so he ranks with the premature wonders, more frequent in music than in any other art – the Thomasino, Mozart, &c. &c.

Source   *GB-Lblc* without shelfmark [unpaginated].
Commentary   The child prodigy violinist George Polgreen Bridgetower (?1779–1860) made his début at the age of nine in Paris at the Concert Spirituel

on 13 April 1789. His performance of a solo as an entr'acte at the Drury Lane performance of *Messiah* on 19 February 1790 was his first great English success. Beethoven's 'Kreutzer' sonata was originally written for Bridgetower, who, together with the composer, gave the first performance of the work on 24 May 1803. The 'Thomasino' is Thomas Linley (1756–78), the child prodigy violinist who performed with Mozart in Florence in 1770.

Literature Gwilym Beechey, 'Thomas Linley, junior, 1756–1778', *The Musical Quarterly*, liv (1968), 74–82.

236 *The Times*, London 1 March 1790

. . . a third comic opera . . . was produced on Saturday, called *La Villanella Repita*, which, excepting the title, had not anything very ravishing to recommend it. The music of Bianchi and Mozart, with the assistance of Signora Storace, could not command but two encores, her song in the first act, and the duet with Borselli in the second – these, with the finale of the first, and quintetto in the second, were the only White Boars of the evening worth notice.

Source *GB-Lblc* without shelfmark [unpaginated]. Edition: Frederick C. Petty, *Italian Opera in London 1760–1800* (Ann Arbor, Michigan, 1980), 274.

Commentary The pasticcio *La villanella rapita* was given at the King's Theatre, Haymarket, on 27 February 1790. The production included music by Bianchi, Martín y Soler and Paisiello, as well as Mozart's 'Dite almeno in che mancai' K479 and 'Mandina amabile' K480, composed for a performance of Bianchi's *La villanella rapita* in Vienna in 1785. Additionally, Ann Storace sang 'Deh vieni non tardar' from *Figaro* and 'Batti, Batti' from *Don Giovanni*. Fausto Borselli (birth and death dates unknown) sang at the King's Theatre, Haymarket, in 1789 as *primo buffo* and in 1790 as *secondo buffo*. Another review of *La villanella rapita* was published in *The Morning Herald* for 1 March [unpaginated]:

> All the music of the opera deserving celebrity is by Mozart – and it is to the praise of Storace that so many of these have been introduced. To the merit of this favourite singer, all the success the Opera experienced is also to be attributed. The air, by Mozart, 'Bella rosa porporina' and the trio by the same master, in which Storace and Mussini took a pre-eminent lead, with another air, may be adduced in proof. In the second act, Mozart's music equally challenged approbation, particularly the quintette, 'Dite almeno in che maniera.' This was a beautiful composition, and Storace's superiority in it very conspicuous. Another noticeable performance was 'Ochietto forbetto'; but this we have heard, in Allegranti's time, executed much better. The composer of this popular duet is the present Martini, who produced the duet sung by Kelly and Mrs. Crouch in Comus. The finales are pretty, but very short of Paisiello; that in the last act was best, but is like the Opera, a *Pasticcio*, and contains the music of three or four masters, oddly combined.

The attribution of the aria 'Bella rosa porporina' to Mozart may be a mistake; no such text setting by him is known. A third review appeared in *The Gazetteer and New Daily Advertiser* for 2 March [unpaginated]: 'A new Opera, entitled, La Villanella Rapita, was performed with success. It has much good music, particularly the airs by Mozart.'

237   *The Gazetteer and New Daily Advertiser*, London 1 January 1791

The Siege of Belgrade. . . . The Music composed principally by Mr. Storace, With a few Pieces selected from Martini, Salieri, and Paesiello.

Source   *GB-Lblc* without shelfmark [unpaginated].
Commentary   Stephen Storace's *The Siege of Belgrade* was given its première at Drury Lane on 1 January 1791. The opening chorus of the Turkish soldiers was based on the 'Ronda alla turca' of K331/300i. [*See Plates 8–9*].

238   *The Diary or Woodfall's Register*, London 3 January 1791

The Theatre. Drury-Lane. . . . This opera [*The Siege of Belgrade*], although it is by no means so replete with whimsicality of situation as the Strangers at Home, or the Haunted Tower, yet has it very strong claims up on the town. The musick, which is Storaces, is excellent; those Airs allotted to his sister, Mrs. Crouch, Mrs. Bland, and Mr. Kelly, are particularly pleasing. The Choruses of Turks and Austrians were also well managed. . . . The following are the most approved Airs in the above Opera.
Chorus. of Turkish soldiers.

Source   *GB-Lblc* without shelfmark [unpaginated].
Commentary   *See* Document 237. Anna Maria Crouch (1763–1805) and Maria Theresa Bland (1769–1838) were both popular singers in the late 1780s and early 1790s. Crouch appeared frequently in Storace's operas; Bland was best known for singing ballads.

239   *The Times*, London 18 March 1791

Hanover Square. Mr. Salomon's Concert. The Subscribers are respectfully acquainted, that the Second Performance Will be This Evening, the 18th Inst.

Part I.
Overture, Mozart.
Aria, Signor Tajana.
Concerto German Flute, Mr. Graeff.
Aria, Signora Storace.
New Quartetto for two Violins, Tenors, and Violoncello by Messrs. Salomon, Damen, Hindmarsh, and Menel – Haydn.

Part II.
By particular desire, the New Symphony of Haydn will be repeated, as performed on the first night.
Scena Recitativo and Aria, Signor David.

Concerto Bassoon, Mr.Kuchler, (Being his first appearance in
England.)
Duetto, Signor David and Signora Storace – Paeseillo.
Full Piece, Pleyel.

Mr. Haydn will be at the Harpsichord
Leader of the Band, Mr. Salomon

Door to be opened at Seven, and to begin at Eight o'Clock.
Subscriptions at Five Guineas, for the Twelve Concerts, are
received an Tickets delivered at Messrs. Lockharts, No.36, Pall
Mall.
Tickets transferable, as usual, Ladies to Ladies, and Gentlemen to
Gentlemen.
The Subscribers are intreated to give particular orders to their
Coachmen to set down and take up at the Side Door in the
Street, with the Horses Heads towards the Square.
The Door in the Square for Chairs only.

Source *GB-Lblc* without shelfmark [unpaginated]. Also advertised in *The
Public Advertiser* for 18 March ('Overture, Mazant'). Editions: H. C. Robbins
Landon, *Haydn: Chronicle and Works*, iii: *Haydn in England, 1791–1795* (Bloomington, 1976), 60.
Commentary According to Landon, the symphony by Haydn was probably
no.92, and the new quartet one of op.64. The symphony ('overture') by Mozart
cannot be identified.

240 *The Monthly Review*, London October 1791

Art. XVIII. Observations on the present State of Music in London.
By William Jackson, of Exeter. . . . Harrison and Co. 1791
The remarks of able professors of any art or science come with
weight; and from the reputation and productions of the author of this
pamphlet, we expected information and ingenuity. Many of his sentiments, however, militate so violently against the general opinion of
the lovers and judges of music throughout Europe, and are so decisi-
vely delivered, that it seems incumbent on us to examine the prin-
ciples on which they are founded. . . .
'The old Concerto (says he) is now lost, and modern full-pieces are
either in the form of Overtures or Symphonies. The overture of the
Italian opera never pretends to much; that of the English opera
always endeavours to have an air somewhere, and the endeavour
alone makes it acceptable.' – Civil again! Richter's eternal repetitions, and Abel's timidity, are praised, for they are no more: – 'but
later composers, to be grand and original, have poured in such floods
of nonsense, under the sublime idea of being inspired, that the
present Symphony bears the same relation to good music as the
ravings of a bedlamite do to sober sense.

Now, might not the ingenious writer as well have said, at once, that the authors of these floods of nonsense are Haydn, Vanhall, Pleyel, and Mozart, and the admirers of them tasteless idiots, as leave us to guess who he means?

Source Kerry S. Grant, *Dr Burney as Critic and Historian of Music* (Ann Arbor, 1983), 215.

Commentary William Jackson (1730–1803) was organist at Exeter Cathedral from 1777. He apparently met Mozart in London in 1764 or 1765 (not in *Dokumente, Documentary Biography* 571). The author of this review was Charles Burney.

241 *The Times*, London 24 December 1791

Died. On the 5th inst. at Vienna, Wolfgang Mozart, the celebrated German composer.

Source *GB-Lblc* without shelfmark [unpaginated].

Appendix

Addenda and Corrigenda
to Joseph Heinz Eibl, Mozart:
Chronik eines Lebens

1765

19 July (Document 9) Leopold Mozart presented the British Library with copies of Mozart's sonatas K10–15 and, probably, the motet *God is our Refuge* K20.

18 September (Document 11) Mozart performed before Prince William V of Orange at The Hague. Between about 10 and 18 September he also performed twice for Princess Caroline of Nassau-Weilburg, sister of William V.

1 October (Document 13) Mozart probably performed at the house of Joseph Yorke, British Minister at The Hague.

1766

26 May (Document 19) The Mozarts were visited by Karl Wilhelm Ferdinand, Hereditary Duke of Brunswick, on 26 May (not mid-June).

between 20 August and c10 September (Document 23) The Mozarts gave two public concerts in Geneva at the town hall.

15 and 18 September (Documents 24 and 25) The Mozarts gave public concerts at Lausanne. The visit there probably lasted from 14 or 15 September to 18 or 19 September (not 11 to about 16 September).

1772

?late December (Document 39) About the time of the première of *Lucio Silla*, Mozart may have performed in an organ contest in Milan.

1774

between 13 and 21 August (Document 41) Mozart and his father performed at celebrations for the 100th anniversary of the pilgrimage church Maria Plain. Mozart played 'an organ and a violin concerto'; the Mass K194/186*h* may also have been given at this time.

1778

21 April (Document 43) An Italian aria by Mozart may have been given at the Concert Spirituel.

1785

Summer (Document 62) Mozart met the English music publishing agent John Pettinger in Vienna. According to Pettinger, Mozart at the time was 'hard at work on some compositions for string quartet'.

12 August (Document 63)   Two Masonic songs by Mozart (now lost) were performed at the lodge 'Zur Eintracht'.

1786

late November–early December (Document 74)   Mozart met Christoph Gottlob Breitkopf.

1787

23 February (Document 64)   Mozart probably performed the scena and rondo 'Ch'io mi scordi ti te . . . Non temer, amato bene' K505 and the concerto K466 at Ann Storace's farewell benefit concert at the Kärntnertortheater.

1789

May (Document 95)   During his visit to Potsdam, Mozart may have visited Berlin and stayed at the inn *Zur Stadt Paris*.

1791

26 January (Document 105)   Mozart probably placed an advertisement in the *Wiener Zeitung*, offering to sell an organ.

17 November (Document 112)   The Viennese Lodge 'New-Crowned Hope' was inaugurated with a cantata by Mozart, *Laut verkünde unsre Freude*, K623 (not 18 November).

3 or 4 December (Document 113)   Mozart may have been visited by Salieri.

Sources Consulted

1. Manuscript sources

AUSTRIA

Salzburg, Museum Carolino Augusteum (A-Sca)
Hs. 739 germ. Anton Korbinian Raudenbichler, [*Tagebuch* 1780–87]
Hs. 829 germ. *Bruderschaftsbuch . . . hl. Dreifaltigkeit*, 1699–*c*1770

Vienna, Haus- Hof- und Staatsarchiv (A-Whhst)
Archiv der Generalintendanz der Hoftheater. D. Sonderreihe 19   Hoftheater receipts

GERMANY

Koblenz, Landeshauptarchiv (D-KBa)
Hs. 710 Memoirs of Franz Georg Freiherrn Boos von Waldeck, Musikintendant at the Kurtrierische court, or possibly Ludwig Joseph Wilhelm Graf Boos von Waldeck, Kurtrierische Hofmarschall [includes entries for 1763]

Regensburg, Fürst Thurn und Taxis Hofbibliothek (D-Rtt)
FZA HFS A.2443/1–2 (Hoftheater)
FZA HFS A.2442 (Hoftheater. Italienische Oper)
FZA HFS A.2428 (Hofmusik)

GREAT BRITAIN

Hertford, Hertfordshire Record Office (GB)
D/EP AF 4   George Nassau Clavering, Earl Cowper, *Livre de dépance* for April 1767 to April 1770
D/EP AF 5   George Nassau Clavering, Earl Cowper, *Livre de dépance* for April 1770 to April 1774
D/EP AF 127   Steward's miscellaneous bills and vouchers of George Nassau Clavering, Earl Cowper, 1770

Kew, Public Record Office (GB-Kpro)
T 56/20, T 60/22, LC 5/162, LC 9/310 and 311, AO 1/420/201   Payments in the Royal Household 1764–5

London, British Library (GB-Lbl)
Add.19211   *Journal &c. Began July 4th 1764 By* G[ervase]: L[eveland]
Add.40663   Correspondence of Mrs Elisabeth Montague (1720–1800), socialite
Add.23646   *Journal of H. Royal Highness The Duke of Gloucester's Journey to Italy in* [1772 and to Denmark and Germany 1769–70]
Add.33067 and 33068   Private correspondence of the Duke of Newcastle, 1756–65
Add.33091   Correspondence of Thomas Pelham, 1st Earl of Chichester, 1754–72
Add.35350   Letters to the 2nd and 3rd Earls of Hardwicke, mainly from artists and men of letters, 1742–1829

Add.35358   Correspondence of Philip Yorke, 1st Earl of Hardwicke, and his son, Sir Joseph Yorke, English ambassador at The Hague, 1760–64

Add.35359   Correspondence of Philip Yorke, 1st Earl of Hardwicke, 1760–64

Add.35361   Correspondence of Philip Yorke, 2nd Earl of Hardwicke, with his brother, Charles Yorke, 1761–6

Add.35367 and 35368   Letters of Sir Joseph Yorke, English ambassador at The Hague, to his brother Philip Yorke, 2nd Earl of Hardwicke, 1764–5

Add.35373   Letters of Daniel Laval, secretary to Sir Joseph Yorke, English ambassador at The Hague, 1757–72

Add.35376   Miscellaneous family correspondence of the Earls of Hardwicke, 1748–89

Add.35378   Letters of Sir Philip Yorke, 2nd Earl of Hardwicke, written during a tour of the Continent, 1777–8

Add.35401   Letters of Daniel Wray, trustee of the British Museum, to Philip Yorke, 2nd Earl of Hardwicke, 1740–67

Add.35538   Letters of Sir Robert Murray Keith, English ambassador at Vienna

Add.35607   General correspondence of Philip Yorke, 2nd Earl of Hardwicke, 1762–6

Add.35623   Correspondence of Lord Hardwicke, 1 September 1784 to 30 June 1785

Add.36258 and 36259   Journal of a tour by Philip Yorke, 2nd Earl of Hardwicke, to Germany, Austria, Switzerland and Italy, 1778–9

Add.38774   Letters of Sir Robert Murray Keith, English ambassador at Vienna, to Lord Bute, 1780–82

Add.40759, ff.1–32   Sir Philip Frances, journal of a tour in Italy, July to November 1772

Add.40714   Miscellaneous letters, bills and accounts of Sir William Hamilton, English ambassador at Naples, 1764–89

Add.51315   Correspondence of Sir William Hamilton, English ambassador at Naples, 1766–1800

Add.51386   Private correspondence of John Montagu, 4th Earl of Sandwich, 1748–66

Add.57806   Letters from Lady Temple to Lord Temple, 1738–77

Eg.2157   Letters of Sir Joseph Yorke, English ambassador at The Hague, to Sir James Porter, 1758–76

Eg.2641   Correspondence of Sir Horace Mann, British Envoy at Florence

Eg.3501   Private correspondence of the 5th Duke of Leeds, including letters from Sir Robert Murray Keith, English ambassador at Vienna, 1784–90

London, Public Record Office (GB-Lpro)
L.C.9/310 and 311   Accounts of the Lord Chamberlain, Great Wardrobe Bills, 1763–5

2. Printed sources

Allergnädigst privilegirte Anzeigen (Vienna, 1771–6) [*GB-Lbl* P.P.4695.C]

Allgemeine Bibliothek für Schauspieler und Schauspielliebhaber, ed. Christian August Bertram (Leipzig and Frankfurt, 1776) [*D-Mbs* Z 81.820]

Allgemeine deutsche Bibliothek (Berlin, 1766–96) [*US-CAw* BP 361.1]

Allgemeine Literatur-Zeitung (Jena, 1785–1800) [*US-CAw* BP 361.2]

Allgemeiner Theater Almanach von Jahr 1782. (Vienna, 1781) [*D-Mth* Per. 221]

Allgemeines Intelligenzblatt von und für Deutschland welches Abhandlungen über Polizei-Kameral und Justizwesen, desgleichen Nachrichten und Anzeigen, die Gelehrsamkeit, Künste, Handlung und Gewerb betreffend, nebst vermischten Anzeigen zum gemeinen Besten enthält (Stuttgart, 1789) [*A-Su* 162.904 I]

Allgemeines Magazin der Natur, Kunst und Wissenschaften (Leipzig, 1753–67) [*US-CAw* KE 25092]

Allgemeine Uebersicht der Wissenschaften und Künste in den k. k. Staaten (Vienna, 1789) [*A-Wsl* A 14438]

Allmanach der kais. könig. National-Schaubühne in Wien (Vienna, 1787–8) [*A-Wsl* G 14747]

Allmanach für Theaterfreunde auf das Jahr 1791 (Vienna, 1790) [*A-Wsl* G 83479]

Almanach d'Alsace (Strasbourg, 1782–9) [*US-CAw* Fr 7086.81.115]

Almanach de Strasbourg, ed. J. J. Oberlin (Strasbourg, 1780–81) [*US-CAw* Fr 7086.81.115]

Amsterdam. Avec privilege de nos seigneurs les états de Holland et de West-Frise (Amsterdam, 1765–6) [*F-Pa* 4o8929]

Anhang zum Verzeichniss von Musikalien welche bey Johann Christoph Westphal & Comp. auf den grossen Bleichen in Hamburg zu haben sind. Anno 1785 (Hamburg, 1785) [*B-Br* Fetis 5205/MN Mus. 103]

Annalen des Theaters [continuation of *Ephemeriden der Litteratur und des Theaters*] (Berlin, 1788–97) [*D-B* Yp 1953]

Année Littéraire, L' (Paris, 1754–90) [*US-CAw* 37565.51]

Annonces, affiches et avis divers de Poitou (Poitou, 1773–9) [*US-CAw* KF 23536]

Anzeiger des Teutschen Merkur (Weimar, 1783–9) [*D-Mbs* 8. Per. 138]

[Arnold, Friedrich Ernst] *Beobachtungen in und über Prag, von einem reisenden Ausländer* (Prague, 1787) [*US-CAw* Slav 7437.87]

Auberlen, Samuel Gottlob *Leben, Meinungnen und Schiksale von ihm selbst beschrieben* (Ulm, 1824) [*US-CA* 1356.14]

Aufrichtige Postkläppererboth, Der [from 22 January 1784 *Post von Wien*] (Vienna, 1783–4) [*A-Wsl* A 11676]

Augsburger musikalischer Merkur (Augsburg, 1795) [*D-Mbs* 8. Mus. Th. 2283]

Augsburgische Kunstzeitung [from 1772 *Augsburgisches monatliches Kunstblatt*] (Augsburg, 1770–72) [*D-Mbs* Rar. 1354]

Augspurgische Ordinari Postzeitung (Augsburg, 1762–6, 1770–73, 1775, 1777 and 1795) [*D-Mbs* 4. Eph. Pol. 53 (1762–6, 1770, 1775, 1777 and 1795); *D-As* without shelfmark (1771–3)]

Avvisi di Mantova (Mantua, 1770–71) [*GB-Lblc* F.795]

Baader, Clemens Alois *Lexikon verstorbener baierischer Schriftsteller des achtzehnten und neunzehnten Jahrhunderts* (Augsburg and Leipzig, 1824–5) [*US-CAw* 46522.22]

Baierisch-historischer Calender, oder Jahrbuch der merckwürdigsten baierischen Begebenheiten alt- und neuer-Zeiten, ed. Lorenz von Westenrieder (Munich, 1787–8) [*US-CAw* Ger 9820.5]

Barbé-Marbois, François *Voyage d'un Français aux Salines de Bavière et de Salzbourg en 1776* (Paris, 1797) [*D-Mbs* Bavar. 2772]

Barbieri, C. F. *A New Treatise on the Theori-Practical, Fundamental & Thorough Bass, also on Composition. Respectfully Dedicated to Mrs Geo^e Clerk Craigie of Dumbarnie, By C. F. Baribieri . . . Second edition greatly augmented & Improved . . . Edinburgh Printed for the Author, & Sold by Robt Purdie 70. Princes St J.* [word or words obliterated] *and all the Principal Music Sellers in London* (Edinburgh, n.d.) [*US-NYp* Drexel 3015]

Bayer, Leonhard   *Kurzgefasste geschichte von Augsburg* (Augsburg, 1785) [*US-CAw* Ger 10021.2.20]

Behrisch, Heinrich Wolfgang von   *Die Wiener Autoren, ein Beytrag zum gelehrten Deutschland* (n.p., 1784) [*D-Mbs* Var. 594/3]

Berlinische Monatsschrift, ed. F. Gedicke and J. E. Biester (Berlin, 1783–96) [*US-CAw* PGer 128.1]

Berlinische Nachrichten von Staats- und gelehrten Sachen (Berlin, 1789) [*D-AN* If 26]

Beschreibung der k. k. Haupt und Residenzstade Wien (Vienna, 1770) [*US-CAw* Aus 28277.70]

Beyträge zur vaterländischen Historie, Geographie, Statistik und Landwirthschaft, samt einer Uebersicht der schönen Litteratur, ed. Lorenz von Westenrieder (Munich, 1788–1817) [*D-Mbs* Hbl 300 E 1010]

Bibliotheca Bavarica oder Sammlung verschiedener kleine Schriften, Abhandlungen, und Nachrichten aus aller Theilen der Baierischen Geschichte, ed. P. P. Finauer (Munich, 1767) [*US-CAw* Ger 9240.12]

Bibliothek der schönen Wissenschaften und freyen Künste (Leipzig, 1757–65) [*GB-Lbl* P.P.4647]

Bibliothèque des Sciences et des Beaux Arts (The Hague, 1765–6) [*GB-Lbl* P.P.4261.f]

Biographische Skizze von Michael Haydn (Salzburg, 1808) [*US-AA* Rare ML 410 H43 S34]

Blatt ohne Titel, Das (Vienna, 1782) [*A-Wsl* A 15417]

Böcklin, Franz Friedrich Sigmund August von   *Beiträge zur Geschichte der Musik, besonders in Deutschland* (Freiburg im Breisgau, 1790) [*GB-Lbl* Hirsch I.637]

[Brandes, Georg F.]   *Bemerkungen über das Londoner, Pariser und Wiener Theater* (Göttingen, 1786) [*US-CAw* Thr 275.5*]

Briefe eines Biedermannes an einen Biedermann über die Freymaeurer in Wien (Munich, 1786) [*A-Wsl* A 24222]

Briefe einiger Frauenzimmer aus Wien, an ihrer Freundinnen in Berlin über verschiedene Gegenstände (Frankfurt and Leipzig, 1789) [*A-Wn* 54.615-A]

Briefe von und an Gottfried August Bürger: ein Beitrag zur Literaturgeschichte seiner Zeit, ed. Adolf Strodtmann (Berlin, 1874) [*C-Tul* Old Class LG B9288b]

Brieftasche, Die: eine lokale Tagschrift für Wien (Vienna, 1783–4) [*A-Wsl* A 11715]

Briefwechsel meist historischen und politischen Inhalts, ed. August Ludwig Schlözer (Göttingen, 1782–91) [*US-CAw* HP 322.1]

Brünner Zeitung (Brünn [Brno], 1785) [*A-Wsl* A 92302]

Buchhandlerzeitung (Hamburg, 1778–85) [*US-CAw* B 2167.7]

[Christmann, Johann Friederich]   *Elementarbuch der Tonkunst zum Unterricht beim Klavier für lehrende und lernende mit praktischen Beispiele: eine musikalische Monatsschrift* (Speyer, 1782–3) [*GB-Lbl* P.P.1945.ao]

Churbaierischer Intelligenzblatt (Munich, December 1774 to April 1775, and 1777) [*D-Mbs* 4. Bavar. 3021]

Courier de l'Europe (London, 1778–9) [*US-CAw* HP 330.1]

Courier lyrique et amusant (Paris, 1785–7) [*US-CAw* PFr 141.8]

Court Miscellany or Ladies New Magazine, The (London, 1765) [*GB-Lbl* P.P.5457]

Critical Review, The (London, 1756–1800) [*GB-Lbl* 261.g.1–264.g.1]

Daily Universal Register, The (London, 1785–7) [*GB-Lblc* without shelfmark]

Dalberg, F. von   *Vom Erfinden und Bilden* (Frankfurt, 1791) [*A-Wu* I 55721]

Deutsche Chronik, ed. Christian Friedrich Daniel Schubart (Augsburg, 1774–6) [*US-CAw* HP 333.2*]

Deutsche Zuschauer, Der, ed. Peter Adolf Winkopp (n.p., 1785) [*US-CAw* Ger 4.8*]

Diario Ordinario (Rome, 1770–73) [*US-PRu* 0925.3]

Directorium Benedictinum pro Dioecesi Salisburgensi, juxta Ritum Breviarii ordinis SS. P. Benedicti, Adjunctis Festis proprii Salisburgensis (Salzburg, 1767–78) [*A-Ssp* 50632, many with manuscript annotations]

Ditters, Carl, Edler von Dittersdorf *Ueber das deutsche Singspiel den Apotheker* (Vienna, 1787) [*A-Wsl* A 12718]

Dramaturgisches Wochenblatt für Berlin und Deutschland, ed. Johann Gottfried Hagmeister (Berlin, 1792) [*D-Mth* Per. 224]

Dressler, Ernst Christoph *Fragmente einiger Gedanken des musikalischen Zuschauers die bessere Aufnahme der Musik in Deutschland betreffend* (Gotha, 1767) [*US-Wc* Music 5000 Item D-049]

Dutens, Louis *Memoirs of a Traveller now in Retirement* (London, 1806) [*US-NYpl* AN (Dutens)]

Eberl, Ferdinand *Antwort auf die unverschämte Kritik über die Leopoldstädter Cosa Rara* (Vienna, 1787) [*A-Wsl* A 139084]

Ephemeriden der Litteratur und des Theaters [continued as *Annalen des Theaters*], ed. Christian August von Bertram (Berlin, 1785–7) [*GB-Lbl* P.P.4753.be.]

Ephemeriden über Aufklärung, Litteratur und Kunst (Marburg, 1785) [*US-CAw* PGerm 172.2*]

Erinnerer, Der: eine moralische Wochenschrift, ed. Johann Kaspar Lavater and Johann Heinrich Füßli (Zürich, 1765-7) [*CH-Zz* Z VII 172–173]

Eschstruth, Hans Adolf, Freiherr von *Musicalische Bibliotek für Künstler und Libhaber* (Marburg, 1784–5) [*D-Mbs* Mus. Th. 980]

État actuel de la musique du roi et des trois spectacles de Paris (Paris, 1766) [*US-CAw* TS C88]

Etwas für alle über die Aufführung des Baums der Diana in dem marinellischen Schauspielhause in der Leopoldstadt (Vienna, 1788) [*A-Wsl*, A 142129]

European Magazine and London Review, The (London, 1784–9) [*GB-Lbl* P.P.5459.z]

Eymar, A. M. d' *Anecdotes sur Viotti, précédés de quelques Réflexions sur l'expression en music* (Geneva, 1800) [*GB-Lbl* Hirsch 4871]

Finauer, Peter Paul *Historisch-literarisches Magazin für Pfalz-Baiern und angränzende gegenden* (Munich, 1782) [*US-CAw* Ger 42.1]

Forkel, Johann Nikolaus *Musikalischer Almanach für Deutschland* (Leipzig, 1782–4 and 1789) [*US-NYp* Drexel 622–625]

Forster, Georg *Ansichten vom Niederrhein, von Brabant, Flandern, Holland, England und Frankreich im April, Mai und Junius 1790* (Berlin, 1791)

Franckfurter Kayserliche Reichs-Ober-Post-Amtszeitung (Frankfurt, 1763 and 1790–91) [*F-Pn* M. 10857 (1763); *D-Rtt* Publ. 820/33–34 (1790–91)]

Fränkischen Archivs, Das (Schwabach, 1790–91) [*D-AN* XI a 49]

Freymüthige, Der (Ulm, 1787) [*US-CAw* CP 50.24]

[Friedel, Johann] *Anekdoten und Bemerkungen über Wien* (Vienna, 1787) [*A-Wsl* A 11396]

    Briefe aus Wien verschiedenen Inhalts an einen Freund in Berlin (Leipzig and Berlin, 1783) [*D-Mth* 1143]

    Galanterien Wiens, auf einer Reise gesammelt, und in Briefe geschildert von einem Berliner (Vienna, 1784)

Garden, Francis, Lord Gardenstone *Travelling Memorandums made in a Tour upon the Continent in the Years 1786, 1787 & 1788* (Edinburgh, 1802) [*US-Io* D 917 G21 1802]

Gazette de Berne (Berne, 1766) [*CH-BEsu* Rc 321]

Gazette de Cologne (Cologne, 1763) [*F-Pn* 8° G. 15989]

Gazette de Leyde: Nouvelles extraordinaires de divers (Leiden, 1765–6) [*CH-Zz* Z Rh 165]

Gazette de Vienne (Vienna, 1762) [*A-Wsl* 24188 A]

Gazette d'Utrecht (Utrecht, 1763–6) [*F-Pa* 4° H. 8931]

Gazetteer and New Daily Advertiser, The (London, 1790) [*GB-Lblc* without shelfmark]

Gazette littéraire et universelle de l'Europe (Lausanne, 1768) [*A-Su* 160.931 I]

Gazzetta Toscana (Florence, 1770–73) [*US-NYpl* BWQ]

Geisler, Adam Friedrich, d.j. *Reise von Wien über Prag, Dresden, und durch einem Theil der Lausitz nach Berlin und Potsdam* (Leipzig, 1787) [*GB-Lbl* 10230. a.2(1.)]

Gemeinnütziges Wochenblatt (Augsburg, 1790) [*D-Mbs* 8. I. Per 199y]

Gerbert, Martin *Iter alemannicum, accedit italicum et gallicum* (St Blasien, 2/1773) [*US-NYpl* BTXA]

  De cantu et musica sacra a prima ecclesiae aetate usque ad praesens tempus (St Blasien, 1774) [*US-NYp* Mus. Res. *MFG]

Gercken, Philipp Wilhelm *Reisen durch Schwaben, Baiern, die angränzende Schweiz, Franken, die Rheinische Provinzen und an der Mosel &c. in den Jahren 1779–1783* (Stendal, 1783–6 and Worms, 1788) [*GB-Lbl* 1428.g.5–6.]

Giornale delle arti e del commercio (Macerata, 1780–81) [*US-CAw* Sci 95.12]

Giornale di Firenze: Opera periodica che ha per oggetto la conservazione del corpo umano, e tutto ciò che può essergli utile (Florence, 1769–70) [*I-Mcom* J Per. 225]

Giornale d'Italia spettante alla scienza naturale, e principalmente all'agricoltura, alle arti, ed al commercio (Venice, 1769–73) [*I-Mcom* O Per. 934]

Gnädigst privilegirtes Leipziger Intelligenzblatt (Leipzig, 1787–91) [*US-PRu* 0902.395]

Göttingische Anzeigen von gelehrten Sachen (Göttingen, 1753–1801) [*D-Gs* 8. E. Lit. 160/5]

Göttingisches historisches Magazin, ed. C. Meiners and L. T. Spittler (Hanover, 1787–91) [*US-CAw* BP 367.1]

Gray, Robert *Letters during the course of a tour through Germany, Switzerland and Italy, in the years MDCCXCI and MDCCXCII, With reflections on the manners, literature and religion of those countries* (London, 1794) [*US-Io* ar W 16582]

Gräzer Magazin über verschieden Gegenstände der Literatur und Oekonomie (Graz, 1787) [*US-CAw* Aus 30031.3]

[Greene, William] 'Diary of William Greene, [Paris] 1778', *Proceedings of the Massachusetts Historical Society*, liv (1920–21), 84–138

Gruber, Johann Sigmund *Biographien einiger Tonkünstler: ein Beitrag zur musikalischen Gelehrtengeschichte* (Frankfurt and Leipzig, 1786) [*D-Mbs* Mus. Th. 2/1414; another copy *GB-Lbl* 1203.b.23]

[Hamberger, Julius Wilhelm] *Merkwürdigkeiten bey der römischen Königswahl und Kaiserkrönung* (Gotha, 1791) [*US-CAw* Ger 121.27]

Hamburgisches Wochenblatt (Hamburg, 1768) [*US-Io* Rare AP 30 H19]

[Haug, B.] *Zustand der Wissenschaften und Künste in Schwaben* (Augsburg, 1781–2) [*D-Mbs* H. lit. P. 412]

Hautinger, Johann Nepomuk *Reise durch Schwaben und Bayern im Jahre 1784* (n.p., n.d.) [*US-CAw* Ger 3435.264.45]

Hermann, Benedikt Franz *Reisen durch Österreich, Steyermark, Kärnten, Krain, Italien, Tyrol, Salzburg, und Baiern, im Jahre 1780* (Vienna, 1781–3) [*GB-Lbl* 979.f.21]

Historischer Calender, ed. Lorenz von Westenrieder (Munich, 1790–1815) [*US-*

CAw Ger 9820.5]

Historisch-litterarisch-bibliographisches Magazin, ed. Johann Georg Meusel (Zürich, 1788–91) [*US-CAw* PGerm 209.3]

Hommel, Rudolph   *Briefe über die Kaiserwahl* (Leipzig, 1791) [*US-NYpl* BE]

Hunter, William   *Travels in 1792 through France, Turkey and Hungary to Vienna, Concluding with an Account of that City* (London, 1796) [*GB-Lbl* 1560/4604]

Jackson, William   *Thirty Letters on Various Subjects* (London, 1783) [*US-CAw* EC75 J1398 783t]

  Observations on the Present State of Music in London (London, 1791) [*GB-Lbl* 557*.c.19.(9.)]

Jahrbuch der Menschengeschichte in Bayern, ed. Lorenz von Westenrieder (Munich, 1782–3) [*D-Mbs* 8. Bav. 2927]

[Joseph II, Emperor]   *Voyage en France de Monsieur le comte de Falkenstein* (Paris, 1778) [*US-Io* Rare DC 25 G27]

Journal aller Journale oder Geist der vaterländischen und fremden Zeitschriften (Hamburg, 1786–7) [*US-CAw* PGerm 247.3]

Journal de Bruxelles ou le Penseur (Brussels, 1766) [*F-Pa* 8° H. 26646]

Journal de musique, historique, théorique, pratique, sur la musique ancienne et moderne [from 1773 *Journal de musique par une Société d'amateurs*] (Paris, 1770–77; facs. edn, Geneva, 1972) [*F-Pn* V.25409 and V.25404/408]

Journal de Paris (Paris, 1778–91) [*US-NYpl* *DM]

Journal des Luxus und der Moden (Weimar, 1789–90) [*F-Pn* M.22274/300 (*Journal des Luxus und der Moden*) and M.22273/87 (*Intelligenz-Blatt des Journals des Luxus und der Moden*)]

Journal de Vienne dedié aux amateurs de la littérature (Vienna, 1784-5) [*A-Wsl* A 14881]

Journal für Freimaurer (Vienna, 1784–7) [*US-CAw* Soc 6510.2]

Journal zur Kunstgeschichte und zur allgemeinen Litteratur, ed. Christoph Gottlieb Murr (Nuremberg, 1775–89) [*US-CAw* PGerm 247.1]

Junker, Carl Ludwig   *Zwanzig Komponisten: eine Skizze* (Berne, 1776) [*US-NYp* Drexel 1221]

Kratter, Franz   *Briefe über den gegenwärtigen Zustand der Litteratur und des Buchhandels in Oesterreich* (n.p., 1788) [*US-CAw* B 6743.7]

Kritisches Theater-Journal von Wien: eine Wochenschrift (Vienna, 1788–9) [*A-Wn* 6.080-A]

Kurfürstl. gnädigst privilegiertes Münchner Wochen- oder Anzeigsblatt (Munich, 1790) [*D-Mbs* Bavar. 4646y]

[Lang, Joseph Gregor]   *Reise auf dem Rhein 1789* (Koblenz, n.d.) [*D-Mbs* It. Sing. 539y1]

Litterarische Chronik (Berne, 1785–8) [*US-CAw* PGer 267.13]

Litterarisches Magazin von Böhmen und Mähren (Prague, 1786–7) [*A-Wn* BE.9.J.33]

Litteratur- und Theater-Zeitung, ed. Christian August von Bertram (Berlin, 1778–94) [*GB-Lbl* P.P.4753.bd.]

Litteratur und Volkerkunde (Dessau, 1782–91) [*US-CAw* PGerm 267.1]

Lloyd's Evening Post (London, December 1764 to May 1765) [*GB-Lblc* without shelfmark]

London Chronicle (London, 1764 and 1779) [*GB-Lblc* without shelfmark]

London Evening Post, The (London, 1764–5) [*GB-Lblc* without shelfmark]

Lounger (London, 1785–7) [*US-CAw* P 51.860]

Lyric Muse Revived in Europe or a Critical Display of the Opera in all its Revolutions, The (London, 1768) [*US-CA* 100.44.5]

Magazin der Musik [from 1789 *Musik*], ed. Carl Friedrich Cramer (Hamburg, 1783–6, and Copenhagen, 1789; facs. edn, Hildesheim, 1971)

Magazin der Sächsischen Geschichte (Dresden, 1784–91) [*US-CAw* Ger 45.3.3]

Magazin des Buch- und Kunsthandels (Leipzig, 1780–82) [*D-Mbs* 8.N.Libr.200m]

Magazin für Böhmen und Mähren, ed. Joseph Dobrowsky (Prague, 1786–7) [*A-Wn* BE. 9. F33]

Magazin für das Nützliche (Munich, 1775) [*D-Mbs* 4.Bav.3004/17]

Magazin für die neue Historie und Geographie, ed. Anton Friedrich Busching (Hamburg, 1767–88) [*US-CAw* Ger 28.76]

Magazin für die neueste Litteratur, Kenntniss baierischer Schriftsteller (Munich, 1775) [*US-CAw* Ger 28.76]

Maier, C. *Ueber das Nationaltheater in Wien* (Vienna, 1782) [*A-Wsl* A 10562]

Meiners, C. *Kleiner Länder- und Reisebeschreibungen* [vol.1: Vienna and Salzburg] (Berlin, 1791) [*D-Mbs* 8. Geo. U. 234]

Mercure de France (Paris, 1764 and 1778–91) [*GB-Lbl* 298.a-g.]

Mercurio Poetico, Il (Milan, 1771) [*I-Mcom* G Per. 154]

Merkur für Wien (Vienna, 1785) [*A-Wu* I 90095]

Meusel, Johann Georg *Teutsches Künstlerlexikon oder Verzeichnis der jetztlebenden teutschen Künstler* (Lemgo, 1778–89) [*C-Tul* (reference)]

[Miller, Lady Anne] *Letters from Italy Describing the Manners, Customs, Antiquities, Paintings, &c. of that Country, In the Years MDCCLXX and MDCCLXXI to a Friend residing in France* (London, 1776) [*GB-Lbl* 175.e.8–10]

[Moll, Karl Ehrenberts von] 'Des Herrn Karl Ehrenberts von Moll, Ritter und Oesterreichischen Landmanns, Briefe an den Herrn Professor Heinrich Sander in Karlsruhe über eine Reise von Kremsmünster nach Moßheim im Salzburgischen. Im Herbste 1780. (Aus der Handschrift)', in Johann Bernoulli, *Sammlung kurzer Reisebeschreibungen und anderer zur Erweiterung der Länder- und Menschenkenntniß dienender Nachrichten* (Berlin and Leipzig, 1783), xi, 283–358 and xii, 185–236 [*US-NYpl* KBC]

Monatliche Nachrichten einicher Merkwürdigkeiten, in Zürich gesammelt (Zürich, 1766) [*CH-Zz* Z R 600–612]

Monatsschrift von und für Mecklenburg, ed. W. Barensprung, H. F. Becker and A. C. Siemssen (Schwerin, 1788–91) [*US-CAw* Ger 39.5.3]

Monthly Review, The (London, 1764–91) [*GB-Lbl* 267.d.6]

Morning Post and Daily Adveriser, The (London, 1789) [*GB-Lblc* without shelfmark]

Müller, Johann Heinrich Friedrich *Theatral-Neuigkeiten, Nebst einem Lustspiele und der dazu gehörigen Musik* (Vienna, 1773) [*D-Mth* R 599]

Geschichte und Tagebuch der Wiener Schaubühne (Vienna, 1776) [*D-Mth* R 592]

Abschied von der k. k. Hof- und National-Schaubühne (Vienna, 1802) [*US-CAw* *GC7 M8877 802a]

Münchener Intelligenzblatt (Munich, 1790) [*D-Mbs* 4. Bavar. 3253s]

Musikalische Korrespondenz der teutschen Filarmonischen Gesellschaft (Speyer, 1790–92) [*D-Mbs* 4° Mus. th. 306]

Musikalische Realzeitung (Speyer, 1788–90; facs. edn, New York, 1971)

Nederlandse jaarboeken (n.p., 1760–65) [*US-CAw* KE 979 and 980]

Neefe, Christian Gottlob *Dilettanterien* (n.p., 1785) [*A-Wgm* 2989/4]

Neu-ausgefertigter Land- Haus- und Würthschafts-Calender welches ein gemeines Jahr von 365. Tägen ist, Nach der Gnadenreichen Geburt unsers Erlösers und Seligmachers JESU Christi M.DCC.LII [-M.DCC.LXXIX] (Salzburg, 1751[–78]) [*A-Ssp* 50581, many with hand-written annotations]

Neue allgemeine deutsche Bibliothek (Berlin, 1793–1806) [*F-Pn* Z.40034/139 and Z.40140/49 (Anhang)]

Neue Bibliothek der schönen Wissenschaften und freyen Künste (Leipzig, 1765–1806) [*US-CAw* 49553.6]

Neue Monatsschrift für Mecklenburg (n.p., 1788–1801) [*US-CAw* Ger 39.5.3]

Neuer Schreib-Kalender, Auf das Jahr nach der gnadenreichen Geburt unsers Herrn und Seligmachers Iesu Christi M.DCC.LXVI [*-M.DCC.LXXIX*] (Salzburg, 1765[–78]) [*A-Ssp* 50580, many with manuscript annotations]

Neueste aus der anmüthigen Gelehrsamkeit, Das (Leipzig, 1751–62) [*US-CAw* GP 7 N3947]

Neues Westphälisches Magazin (Dresden and Leipzig, 1789) [*A-Wn* B.1789]

New Spectator (London, 1784–6) [*US-CAw* P 59.881]

Nicolai, Friedrich *Beschreibung einer Reise durch Deutschland und die Schweiz im Jahre 1781, Nebst Bemerkungen über Gelehrsamkeit, Industrie, Religion und Sitten* (Berlin and Stettin [Szczecin], 1783–4) [*US-NYpl* EAW]

Notizie del Mondo (Florence, 1770–73) [*US-NYpl* BAA]

Nouvelliste suisse, historique, politique, littéraire et amusant, Le (Neuchâtel, 1748–69) [*CH-Zz* Z WB 2841-2884]

Nuovo almanacco di Venezia (Venice, 1771) [*D-Mbs* 8.Chronolg.130]

Nuovo giornale de' letterati d'Italia (Modena, 1773–4) [*US-CAw* PItal 287.5]

Nützlicher Zeitvertreib für oesterreichischer Bürger (Vienna, 1786-7) [*A-Wn* 180.609 A]

Oberdeutsche allgemeine Literaturzeitung, ed. Lorenz Hübner (Salzburg, 1788–95) [*D-Mbs* 4. Eph. Lit. 27a]

Oberdeutsche Freund der Wahrheit und Sittlichkeit, Der: eine periodische Schrift, ed. Franz Xaver Huber (Salzburg, 1787–8) [*A-Su* 2.376 I]

Ordentlich-wöchentliche Münchner Frag- und Anzeigs-Nachrichten (Munich, 1763)

Ordinari Münchner Zeitung (Munich, 1762–3) [*D-Mbs* 4. Eph. pol. 68]

Owen, John *Travels into different parts of Europe in the years 1791 and 1792, With familiar remarks on Places-Men-and Manners* (London, 1796) [*US-CAw* KF 1531]

Parisische Briefe (Berlin, 1766) [*SF-Hy* 359. VIII. 11]

[Peiba, Abraham] *Gallerie von teutschen Schauspielern und Schauspielerinnen der älteren und neueren Zeit* (Vienna, 1783) [*A-Wsl* A 139093]

[Perinet, Joachim] *XXIX Geheime Korrespondenzen: erste und lezte Sammlung* (Vienna, 1787) [*US-CAw* *GC8 P4184 787n]

[Pezzl, Johann] *Skizze von Wien* (Vienna and Leipzig, 1787–90)

Pezzl, Johann *Charakteristik Joseph II* (Vienna, 1790) [*US-CAw* Aus 2340.2]

Pfalzbaierischer litterarischer Almanach (Munich, 1780–81) [*D-Mbs* 8.Bav.68]

Pfalzbaierisches Museum (Mannheim, 1785–6) [*D-Mbs* Per. 164m]

Pfälzisches Museum (Mannheim, 1783–9) [*D-Mbs* Per. 164m]

Pilati, Carlo Antonio *Voyages en differens pays de l'Europe en 1774, 1775 & 1776 ou Lettres écrits de l'Allemagne, de la Suise, de l'Italie, de Sicile, et de Paris* (The Hague, 1777) [*US-BEb* D 917 P48]

Pillwein, Benedikt *Biographische Schilderungen oder Lexikon salzburgischer, theils verstorbener, theils lebender Künstler, auch solcher, welch Kunstwerke für Salzburg lieferten* (Salzburg, 1821) [*A-Smi* 701 A1 Pil 80 (photocopy)]

Piozzi, Hester Lynch (Mrs Thrale) *Observations and Reflections Made in the Course of a Journey Through France, Italy and Germany* (London, 1789; ed. Herbert Barrows, Ann Arbor, 1967)

Portmann, Johann Gottlieb *Leichtes Lehrbuch der Harmonie, Composition und des Generalbasses, zum Gebrauch für Liebhaber der Musik, angehende und fortschreitende Musici und Componisten* (Darmstadt, 1789) [*D-Mbs* 4° Mus. th. 1246]

Post von Wien, Die (Vienna, 1784) [*A-Wsl* 11676 A]

Pressburger Zeitung (Pressburg, 1763–6, 1770 and 1791) [*H-Bn* H.694/1238]

Provinzialnachrichten aus den kaiserl. königl. Staaten und Erbländern (Vienna, 1782–3) [*D-Mbs* 8.Aus.3767]

Ragguagli di varj paesi (Milan, 1767) [*I-Mb* Giorn. R. 117]

Rapport von Wien (Vienna, 1788–9) [*A-Wsl* A 11677]

Rautenstrauch, Johann *Österreichische Biedermanns-Chronik: ein Gegenstück zum Fantasten- und Prediger-Almanach* (Freiheitsburg [Vienna], 1784) [*US-CAw* Aus 2348.93.5]

Realzeitung (Nuremberg, 1773) [*D-Mbs* 8. Eph. pol. 64m]

Realzeitung (Vienna, 1784) [*D-Mbs* 8.Per.172]

Rechnenschaft, dem Wiener Publikum abgelegt über die Direkzion des kais. königl. National-Hoftheaters im verflossenen Theatral-Jahre 1789 (Vienna, 1790) [*A-Wgm* 2825/8]

Reck, Johann Jakob Christian von *Ueber den gegenwärtigen Zustand des deutschen Theaters den Einfluß der reisenden Theatergesellschaften nebst der Untersuchung was das Theater seyn sollte und wie es seiner Bestimmung näher gebracht werden konnte* (Erlangen, 1787) [*A-Wgm* 922/22]

Reichard, Heinrich August Ottakar *Taschenbuch für die Schaubühne auf das Jahr 1787* (Gotha, 1786) [*D-Mth* Per. 31; another copy *GB-Lbl* P.P.4739.cd.]

[Reichardt, Johann Friedrich] *Bemerkungen eines Reisenden über die zu Berlin vom September 1787 bis Ende Januar 1788 gegebene öffentliche Musiken, Kirchenmusik, Oper, Concerte, und Königliche Kammermusik betreffend* (Halle, 1788) [*GB-Lbl* 7898.aaaa.3.]

Reise von Wien nach Paris, In einem Briefen an einem Freund (Vienna, 1781) [*GB-Lbl* 10239.a.2(2.)]

Rellstab, Johann Carl Friedrich *Über die Bemerkungen eines Reisenden die Berlinischen Kirchenmusik, Concert, Oper, und königliche Kammermusik betreffend* (Berlin, n.d.) [*A-Wgm* 476/8]

Rhapsodist (Amsterdam, 1771–83) [*US-CAw* PNEth 332.3]

Rheinischer Zuschauer (Mannheim, 1778) [*US-CAw* PGer 332.8]

[Richter, Joseph] *Briefe eines Eipeldauers an seinen Herrn Vetter in Kakran über d'Wienstadt* (Vienna, 1785) [*A-Wsl* A 24222]

[Riegger, Joseph Anton Stephan [Josef Antonín Štěpán], Ritter von] *Materialien zu alter und neue Statistik von Böhmen* (Leipzig, 1787–93) [*US-CAw* Slav 7270.30]

Riegger, Joseph Anton Stephan [Josef Antonín Štěpán], Ritter von *Archiv der Geschichte und Statistik, insbesondere von Böhmen* (Dresden, 1792–5) [*US-CAw* Slav 7272.32]

Sacchi, Giovenale *Vita del Cavaliere Don Carlo Broschi* (Milan, 1784) [*US-Wc* ML 420.B8S14 Case]

Salzburger Intelligenzblatt, oder wöchentliche Nachrichten zum allgemeinen Nutzen und zur Erbauung, ed. Lorenz Hübner (Salzburg, 1784–92) [*D-Mbs* 4. Per. 10]

Salzburger monatliche Beyträge zur Litteratur Oberdeutschlands, ed. Lorenz Hübner (Salzburg, 1784-9) [*A-Sca* 8759]

Sammler, Der (Chur, 1779–84) [*US-CAw* Swi 33.5]

Sander, Heinrich *Beschreibung seiner Reisen durch Frankreich, die Niederlände, Holland, Deutschland und Italien* (Leipzig, 1781) [*US-NYpl* BTXA]

Schauplatz der Natur und Künste in vier Sprachen, deutsch, lateinisch, französisch, und italiänisch (Vienna, 1782–3) [*A-Wsl* A 73463]

Schink, Johann Friedrich *Dramatische und andere Skizzen nebst Briefen über das*

Theaterwesen zu Wien (Vienna, 1783) [*D-Mth* R59]

Schizzi, Folchino *Elogio Storico di Wolfgango Amedeo Mozart* (Cremona, 1817) [*US-NYp* *MEC (Mozart)]

Schlesische Provinzialblätter (Breslau [Wroclaw], 1785–91) [*US-CAw* PGerm 340.1]

Schletter, Salomon Friedrich *Beiträge zur deutschen Schaubühne* (Brünn [Brno], 1791) [*A-Wsl* A 90201]

Schubart, Christian Friedrich Daniel *Vaterlandschronik* [from 1790 *Chronik*] (Stuttgart, 1787–90) [*D-Mbs* 8.Per. 27d]

    Leben und Gesinnungen, von ihn selbst im Kerker aufgesetzt (Stuttgart, 1791) [*US-CAw* 48565.10.14]

    Ideen zu einer Ästhetik der Tonkunst (Vienna, 1806) [*GB-Lbl* Hirsch 5463]

[Schulz, Friedrich] *Reise eines Liefländers von Riga nach Warschau, durch Südpreussen, über Breslau, Dresden, Karlsbad, Bayreuth, Nürnberg, Regensburg, München, Salzburg, Linz, Wien und Klagenfurt, nach Botzen in Tyrol* (Berlin, 1795–6) [*US-NYpl* GLX]

Schwäbisches Museum, ed. J. Michael Armbruster (Kempten, 1785–6) [*D-Mbs* 8. Per. 165]

Schweizerische Monaths-Chronik (Zürich, 1766–7) [*US-CAw* Swi 19.7]

[Smith, Amand Wilhelm] *Philosophische Fragmente über die praktische Musik* (Vienna, 1787) [*A-Wgm* 991/7]

Spectacles de Paris, Les, ou Calendrier Historique & Chronologique des Théâtres . . . Pour l'Année 1779[–86] (Paris, 1778[–85]) [*US-Io* Rare PN 2620 A43 v.28–35]

Spion in Wien, Der (Vienna, 1784) [*A-Wsl* 11611 A]

Staats- und gelehrte Zeitung des hamburgischen unpartheyischen Correspondenten (Hamburg, 1762–91) [*US-PRu* 0902.873]

Stetten, Paul von *Kunst-, Gewerb- und Handwerks Geschichte der Reichs-Stadt Augsburg* (Augsburg, 1779–88) [*US-CAw* Ger 10021.6]

Sulzer, Johann Georg *Beobachtungen und Anmerkungen auf einer im Jahre 1775 und 76 gethanen Reise aus Deutschland nach der Schweiz und Oberitalien und ueber den St. Gotthard zurück nach Deutschland* (Berne and Winterthur, 1780) [*GB-Lbl* 1049.d.2]

Tablettes de renommée des Musiciens, Auteurs, Compositeurs, Virtuoses, Amateurs et Maîtres de Musique vocale et instrumentale, les plus connus en chaque genre. Avec une Notice des Ouvrages ou autres motifs qui les on rendu recommandables, Pour servir a l'Almanach-Dauphin (Paris, 1785; facs. edn, Geneva, 1971)

Tagebuch der Mainzer Schaubühne (n.p., 1788) [*A-Wn* 4.059-B]

Tagebuch der Mannheimer Schaubühne (Mannheim, 1786–7) [*D-Mth* Per. 00009]

Taschenbuch des Wiener Theaters (Vienna, 1777) [*US-CAw* TS 383 45]

Theater-Journal für Deutschland (Gotha, 1777–84) [*US-CAw* TS 45 15]

Theater-Zeitung für Deutschland, ed. Johann Friedrich Unger (Berlin, 1789) [*D-Mth* Per. 229]

Times, The (London, 1788–91) [*GB-Lblc* without shelfmark]

Türk, Daniel Gottlob *Clavierschule, oder Anweisung zum Clavierspielen für Lehrer und Lernende, mit kritischen Anmerkungen* (Leipzig and Halle, 1789) [*D-Mbs* 4° Mus.Th.1575]

Uiber das deutsche Singspiel den Apotheker des Hrn. v. Dittersdorf (Vienna, 1786) [*A-Wsl* 12718 A]

Ungrisches Magazin, oder Beyträge zur ungrischen Geschichte, Geographie, Naturwissenschaft und der dahin einschlagenden Litterature, ed. C. G. von Windisch (Pressburg, 1781–7) [*US-CAw* Aus 80045.4]

Unterhaltungen (Hamburg, 1766–8) [*S-Uu* Tidskrifter/Tyska]

Variétés sérieuses et amusantes (Amsterdam, 1765) [*A-Wn* 26.T.27]

Verzeichnis der Brüder und Mitglieder der gerechten und volkomenen St. Johannes □ *zur gekrönten Hoffnung im Orient zu Wien* (Vienna, 1788) [*US-Cn* Case HS 602.V54 1788]

Verzeichniss derer Musicalien, welche in der Niederlage auf den grossen Bleichen bey Johann Christoph Westphal und Comp. in Hamburg in Commission zu haben sind (Hamburg, 1782) [*A-Wgm* 205/3]

Verzeichniss einiger neuen Werke welche in der musicalischen Niederlage bey Johann Christoph Westphal & Comp. in Hamburg angekommen sind (Hamburg, July 1786) [*A-Wgm* 205/3]

Vollständiges Diarium der römisch-königlichen Wahl und kaiserlichen Kronung . . . Leopold des Zweiten (Frankfurt, 1791) [*US-CAw* Aus 2297.5]

Voyage de deux Français en Allemagne, Danemarck, Suede, Russie et Pologne, fait en 1790–1792 (Paris, 1796) [*US-Io* Rare D 965 F74 1796]

Wahrheiten in Ernst und Scherze (Vienna and Berlin, 1787) [*A-Wn* 44.386 A]

Wahrheit von dem Nationaltheater, Eine, Wien den 8ten May (n.p., 1790) [*A-Wn* 54.406 A]

Welt, Die: eine Wochenschrift (Vienna, 1762–3) [*A-Wu* I 90939]

Weltmann, Der: eine Wochenschrift (Vienna, 1780–82) [*H-Bn* H. 23. 633]

Wienerblättchen, Das (Vienna, 1783 and 1785) [*A-Wsl* 9316 A]

Wienerbothe, Der: eine Tageschrift (Vienna, 1789 [March, June–July, October–December] to 1790 [June]) [*A-Wsl* 40848 A]

Wiener Ephemeriden, ed. Otto Heinrich, Freiherr von Gemmingen (Vienna, 1786) [*D-Mbs* 8. Per. 36; another copy *A-Wsl* 11877 A]

Wiener Früh- und Abendblatt (Vienna, 1787) [*A-Wsl* 93513 A]

Wienerische Theaterkritik (Vienna, 1794) [*A-Wn* 624.755 A.Th]

Wienerische Zuschauer, Der (Vienna, 1785–6) [*A-Wsl* 11250 A]

Wiener Kronik (Vienna, 1784–5) [*A-Wsl* 11066 A]

Wiener Mannigfaltigkeiten: ein wöchentliches Leseblatt für Gelehrte und Ungelehrte zur Unterhaltung und Verbreitung nützlicher Kenntnisse (Vienna, 1785–6) [*A-Wsl* 11786 A]

Wiener Musik- und Theateralmanach auf das Jahr 1785 (Vienna, 1784) [*A-Wsl* G 87.278]

Wiener Plunder (Vienna, 1784) [*A-Wsl* 11486 A]

Wiener Tagebuch (Vienna, 1789 [April]) [*A-Wsl* 83006 A]

Wiener Theaterkalender auf das Jahr 1787 (Vienna, 1786) [*A-Wsl* 14640 A]

Wiener Wochenschrift (Vienna, 1781) [*D-Mbs* 8. Per. 202; another copy *A-Wsl* 11971 A]

Wochenblatt für die innerösterreichischen Staaten, Die (n.p., 1775) [*US-CAw* PGerm 418.2]

Wöchentliche Anzeigen zum Vortheil der Liebhaber der Wissenschaften und Künste (Zürich, 1766 [August–December]) [*CH-Zz* Z WB 2132–2134]

Wöchentliche Unterhaltungen für und über die Herren in Wien (Vienna and Prague, 1783) [*A-Wn* 43.701 A]

Young, Arthur *Travels during the Years 1787, 1788, and 1789, Undertaken more particularly with a View of ascertaining the Cultivation, Wealth, Resources, and National Property, of the Kingdom of France* (London, 1792) [*GB-Lbl* 184.b.9.]

Zehn Briefe aus Oesterreich an den Verfasser der Briefe aus Berlin (Vienna, 1784) [*US-CAw* Aus 2348.83.2; another copy *A-Wu* I 271 184]

Index

Index of Works by Mozart

Numbers refer to document numbers, not pages.
Documents 1–121: W. A. Mozart; Documents 122–3: Apocrypha;
Documents 124–81: Reception, German; Documents 182–205:
Reception, French; Documents 206–41: Reception, English

I. By Köchel numbers: K^1(1862)/K^6(1964) or −/K^3(1937)/K^6

175

General Index

Numbers refer to document numbers, not pages.
Documents 1–121: W. A. Mozart; Documents 122–3: Apocrypha;
Documents 124–81: Reception, German; Documents 182–205:
Reception, French; Documents 206–41: Reception, English